A
NAME
IN
HEAVEN

By Rickie Bartlett

Table of Contents

INTRODUCTION

There is a land of many wise honorable ladies and gentlemen known as Hero's. Within this land are many cities, green fields, purple mountains, rivers and oceans. Here in this beautiful land gallantry takes another stand. In this majestic place is the endless notion of romance and true love, not only between men and women, but also between men and men, and women and women.

True authentic love has never been easy to attain in this majestic land. Many who have dared to possess it have suffered horrendous opposition, oppression and even death.

A day is soon coming in this land when ignorance, misunderstanding, judgment, and hatred will only be found in books of days past and nightmares remembered. The lost and deceived that litter this civilization will soon be transformed by the utterance of God's loving Word with a new understanding. While those who refuse to rid their hearts of hatred and judgment will perish from this majestic land for eternity.

Since the beginning of time most of mankind has lived in small remote villages and communities. For many generations most of the population could not read. As a result only a select few were capable of reading the Bible. As generations passed even fewer were able to read the original Hebrew, Aramaic, and Greek manuscripts. This was the situation for many generations. Thus leaving most of the population dependent on Bible teachers and their own limited understanding of the Bible.

If you were to add up each person who has been born and died since the beginning of man to 1950 it does not equal the number of people alive today. There are more people living on the earth today than ever before. The world's population today is the most educated and sophisticated generations that has ever walked the earth.

The scriptures tell us in the last days man will have an abundance of Bible understanding like no other generations before them. The scriptures also tell us more knowledge will be revealed to today's generations. Again, the scriptures have been proved to be accurate.

The state of the world today is both disturbing and encouraging. With the misrepresentation of God's Word to promote man made religious ideas and church dogma we now find ourselves in religious and spiritual anarchy world wide.

The world has changed dramatically in this generation. We are now a global society financially, culturally, and socially. It is now more vital than ever that all mankind find tolerance, acceptance, and love for one another if we are ever going to find peace together as a global society.

People today have come to realize they have been deceived about many Biblical teachings. Fortunately we are not ignorant and living in small remote villages anymore and knowledge is abundant. People today have been enlightened in regard to many false teachings. Unfortunately most false teachings have come through the worlds largest churches. Surprisingly today's culture has become very tolerant of Biblical deception.

A Name In Heaven introduces a new and earthshaking Bible revelation that will shock the entire world. This information became lost in interpretation long ago. A Name In Heaven also provides immense clarity to many false teachings about the Bible.

An angel from our Heavenly Father came to me and spent five hours guiding me through this revelation. After the angel left I spent eight months researching the Bible and historical documentation to further prove its accuracy to myself. This angel taught me that we all have a moral obligation to be tolerant, accepting, kind, and loving to each other regardless of our differences. This angel also revealed Bible knowledge that will shock the entire world.

A Name In Heaven reveals an immense open Lgbt community, culture, and society that existed in Biblical times. This revelation clearly identifies Lgbt people and the historical Biblical events they took part in. A Name In Heaven uses Bible scripture to prove and support gays, lesbians, and transgender people held high ranking positions, and royal positions and were highly respected and loved by ancient Israel as well as the surrounding nations in Biblical times.

I have used the original 1611 English translation of the King James Bible as a reference in this revelation. Today's modern Bibles are cluttered with profitable opinions and church dogma, due to man's efforts to promote their own church beliefs, and keep certain classes of society oppressed. I find this original 1611 translation into English to be more pure. I also recommend using,

A Name in Heaven Bible

or A Name In Heaven Bible Revised,

for a more pure reading of God's true original Words and understanding.

I am the first person to write a book with such Biblical revelation and clarity since the days the Bible writers walked the earth. I am the first and only individual person to independently revise a Bible in history. All other Bibles have been revised by large groups of Scholars appointed by King's, large religious organizations, and major publishing houses for mass appeal and financial gain.

This Bible revelation is a spiritually liberating experience for all people of every nation whether heterosexual, straight, gay, lesbian or transgender.

This angelic visit changed my perspective and view of the world population and my life forever. My hope is that this revelation will bring you and your loved ones Biblical clarity. As well as bringing your hearts peace and joy for the rest of your lives in the loving embrace of our Heavenly Father's Word.

Fasten your seat belts: every topic in this revelation is taboo in today's world. Your in for an eye opening, heart lifting, roller coaster ride that will change your life forever.

The Angel's Arrival

Revelation 1:3
Blessed is he that readeth, and they that hear the words this prophecy, and keep those things which are written therein: for the time is at hand.

Matthew 10:26-27
Fear them not therefore: for there is nothing covered, that shall not be revealed; and hid, that shall not be known. What I tell you in darkness, that speak ye in light: and what ye hear in the ear, that preach ye upon the housetops.

2Timothy 3:16+17
All scripture is given by inspiration of God, and is profitable for doctrine, for reproof, for correction, for instruction in righteous: That the man of God may be perfect, thoroughly furnished unto all good works.

I am putting this revelation from our Heavenly Father into book form now because I have been very ill for the last ten years and believe my life is coming to a close. I do not want to leave this life without sharing my angelic experience with mankind before I die. This revelation from our Heavenly Father will save the lives and souls of millions world wide. I am so grateful our Heavenly Father has given me this opportunity to share my experience with all of you.

Be advised I am not a corporate preacher. I am just a regular Christian guy. A guy who was living his life doing his job driving a delivery van, raising two children, and enjoying all of God's blessings and minding my own business.

On October 30, 1996 I had what I believe to be a direct spiritual experience with one of God's angels. After this five hour revelation I knew I had been chosen to share my experience with the rest of the world. Two days prior to this I was at work delivering packages all over town. I always had my radio on. Sometimes I listened to music or talk radio but normally I listened to Christian sermons.

On October 28, 1996 I listened to a preacher give a sermon representing one of Americas largest churches. His sermon was on "Homosexuals" and how he believed God felt about them. I don't remember all that he said now thirteen years later but he went on and on about how gays were destroying American families, American children, and America as a whole. Saying things such as, "If they don't give up their homosexuality and turn heterosexual God is going to put them in a burning hell for eternity." He preached for an hour using scripture he believed validated God's hatred for gays and encouraged all Christians to hate in the same fashion.

I have been a Christian all of my life. At the time of this sermon I was 39 years old and had by then attained what I considered to be a lot of Bible knowledge, through participation in many congregations, sermons, conventions, and personal study. With all of that Bible knowledge under my belt that radio broadcast brought me to spiritual ruin. I was heartbroken over all the hurtful things he said. That preacher left me believing God hated me and others. I just sobbed for the rest of the day. I was not only heartbroken that God didn't love me but angry as well. I thought it was so unfair that God would hate me for something I did not choose and could not change.

By the end of my work day after hours of crying and anguish I said out loud, "Father I can't take this anymore! I can't bear the thought of you hating me anymore! I'm through with you! I'm not studying your Word or going to church anymore! I'll make my own rules for my life from now on!"

For two days I lived without God in my life. I was determined to hold a grudge against Him forever. I felt like an empty shell and at the same time missed my Heavenly Father tremendously. After much longing and regret I knelt in my living room and said out loud,

"I'm sorry Father, for getting so mad at you. I love you Father, and I don't want to live without loving you **even if you don't love me back.** I know you are a loving, wise, and righteous God. I feel as if you don't include me in your purpose. I know your Word inside and out more than most. I have never read one word of kindness you have spoken towards people like me. All I've ever heard or read are statements saying people like me are detestable, people like me are going to be put to death and will never make it to Heaven. Well Father, if that's the way you feel about me I have no other choice but to accept my fate as you have destined for me. I will continue to love you and serve you as I always have to the best of my ability till the day I die of sickness, old age, or by your hand on judgment day. I love you Father, please forgive me for my angry heart the last few days."

I got up off my knees and went into the bathroom absolutely exhausted from all the emotion. I blew my nose cleaned off my face and returned to the living room and plopped into a chair feeling like I had just been through hell and back.

As I sat there I decided I would just have to learn to live with the fact that I would continue to love God, continue to be as obedient as I could as always and be put to death on judgment day for having a "same gender attraction" and have peace about it. I promised myself I would not live one more moment of my life in heartache or anguish over my plight in life or death over something I never chose and couldn't change. I decided in my spare time I would read every Bible and every Bible text in my house which are many word for word. I wanted to see if I could find one word or sentence of hope showing that God might possibly love me or have said a kind word about someone like me. I also wanted to continue to obtain more Bible knowledge which I have always had a strong hunger for.

I started with my Bible Aid text page one. While reading in the "A's" word by word, a voice in my head kept saying, "Go to the word eunuch." I just kept ignoring the voice. Before I knew it I was having an argument with the voice. We were going back and forth. The voice kept saying, "Go to the word eunuch." I kept saying, "No!" (not out loud, this was going on in my head). I said: "No! If I start skipping around from this word to that word I might miss something important." This went on for about twenty minutes while I was trying to read. Finally, I gave in to the voice.

The voice in my head sounded like my own. I felt like I was arguing with myself. A sort of thinking to yourself kind of experience that people do all the time. Nothing at that time seemed unusual or abnormal to me. I thought perhaps I was just rattled and stressed from the emotional experience I had just had. Perhaps it was the stress of the last few days and I was just having trouble concentrating. I went to the word eunuch and started to read.

Suddenly, I felt a tremendous spiritual force enter the room. His presence was so strong I knew exactly where he was standing. I could not see him but somehow I knew exactly where he was in the room. I felt the angel moving towards me suddenly standing next to me. He felt so close I thought if I moved suddenly one half inch I would bump into him. I was so terrified. I felt as if I was frozen stiff. I started to look around to see if anything was moving in the room. I have seen in scary movies where a demon comes into a house and things started moving around the room with objects flying up against walls and what not. I was afraid the spirit in the room might start doing things like that. I was so terrified and overwhelmed. I was on the verge of crying. Just as I had the thought that the spirit person might be harmful I felt the angel embrace me.

Suddenly, I felt a very warm and loving spirit cover and enter my entire body. The angel felt as if he was about a foot taller than me. I could not see him but his presence felt about a foot taller. This warm loving and forgiving spirit covered me so completely that he felt like he went from my head to my toes and throughout all my internal organs and tissues. I felt a feeling of tremendous love and forgiveness and total safety. At that moment I realized he was a loving angel from God on a mission. The tremendously powerful and overwhelming intensity of love and forgiveness engulfed every fiber of my body. The angel radiated with tremendous love and forgiveness like I had never felt before. The powerful feelings of love and forgiveness that radiated from this angel all throughout my body made me believe he had forgiven me for every sin, every mistake, and every deliberate wrong I had ever committed throughout my entire life. I just wanted to curl up in a ball and cry like a small child.

Suddenly, with that embrace we became of one mind, one person together, in mind and flesh. He was aware that I was becoming afraid and he wanted to comfort me as if I was a small child just about to cry out of fear. The reason I know this is because at the instant he embraced me I knew what the angel was thinking. I knew all that he knew. With that embrace I suddenly had all his knowledge and wisdom. His thoughts were so clear to me. It was as if his thoughts were my thoughts. I felt like I had all the knowledge he had all the wisdom and experience of the entire universe and life. As if I had been a part of the universe for thousands of years. It felt so natural as if everything was the way it was meant to be. My feet didn't feel like they were touching the floor, as if my feet were about an inch off the floor When I looked down to see if my feet were on the floor they were. I felt so light as if the angel had me on his lap like a toddler rocking me as if to comfort me and he was so overwhelmingly loving and comforting.

The tremendous overpowering feeling of love and forgiveness made me realize how tremendously powerful God's love and forgiveness for mankind must be. It is so powerfully strong and overwhelming. I wish every person on the planet could experience that level and intensity of love. One thing I knew without any doubt there was a loving angel in my house all around me where ever I walked. I walked and moved with extreme caution in fear I might move to fast and bump into him. I did not see anything unusual, no unusual light, no shadows, nothing started moving, no sound, no breathing. There weren't any spoken words between us after the argument over the word eunuch. There was no need for words because I knew his thoughts. All he had to do was think it and I knew what he was thinking and I did what he said.

The presence of this angel was so dominate and overpowering. The tremendous powerful force of love and forgiveness was so strong I wanted to cry. Because he felt so loving and so comforting and I felt so unworthy and so undeserving. It was a sense of complete unconditional love and compassion like I had never experienced before.

The first thing I learned from this angel was that God's tremendous and intense love for mankind is powerful enough to heal any physical deformity, ailment, hang up, emotional problem, mental illness, and all imperfections that plague mankind just through God's tremendous ability to love us. Until that angel's embrace I did not realize the power of God's love alone was strong enough to do such tremendous things. It makes me wonder if we as humans could heal each other through the power of love. Maybe if mankind went throughout every day feeling and displaying this tremendous love for ourselves and others perhaps we wouldn't have all the imperfections we are plagued with.

One thing I can tell you when there is an angel in your presence the presence is so strong and so absolute you will not question who or what is there. You will know without question that you are in the presence of an angel. I knew the angel and I were going on a journey. I knew he was there to teach and show me something tremendous, something loving and forgiving, and something earthshaking that would change lives forever.

I will show you where that loving and forgiving angel lead me for five hours. I was led from scripture to scripture. I was trying to write down all I was learning all the scriptures and information that were presented to me. This was all happening at great speed. My brain and my hands could not keep up. A flood of information was coming at me so fast. All I did for 5 hours was read scripture as the angel revealed their meanings to me as I wrote down the abbreviations. There wasn't any time to write down words or sentences everything was going so fast. The angel presented 2200 scriptures and there meanings in the same order I will give them to you now. I didn't need to write down any words just the Bible abbreviations.

The meanings of these scriptures will remain in my brain forever. Even now I am so sick and exhausted that I can barely balance my check book. Yet that angel experience and the meanings of these scriptures are so clear to me. It is as if I had the angel visit yesterday.

The angel was revealing the meanings of these scriptures as I read them. As I read the scriptures I was getting a visual scene as if watching television. The Bible characters where coming to life before my eyes so real and vivid. I felt like I could feel the texture of their hair and smell their faint body odor. I could feel the breeze blowing. I could see trees in the back ground swaying, buildings and movement of people in backgrounds, as if I was there myself with these Bible characters just observing. All the while the angel was revealing a myriad of Bible secrets and a revelation in perfect order before my very eyes.

After all that I have said I still feel that I cannot find the words to adequately describe the magnitude of that experience. I will never forget that five hour angelic visit as long as I live. It changed my life forever and I know it will change the lives of millions just like it did for me. After this experience on October 30, 1996 I knew I had a responsibility to share this Bible revelation with the entire world. For 13 years I waited impatiently for our Heavenly Father to give me an opportunity to put this revelation in writing. I never, ever, planned to tell anyone I received this Bible revelation from an angel. Because I feared people would think I was crazy, ultimately throwing my credibility to the wind.

In the days and months that followed October 30, 1996 I shared just a little of this revelation with a few people who are close in my life, as well as 25 of the largest church leaders in the Twin Cities. I deliberately avoided mentioning the presence of the angel. I told it in a way that gave the impression I stumbled across this revelation due to my great ability to understand the Bible. I didn't feel comfortable lying but I just couldn't bring myself to say an angel came to me and revealed this information. I was afraid the church leaders would think I was loosing my mind or loosing touch with reality. I felt the 25 church leaders wouldn't think I was credible if I told them an angel came into my house and took control of my mind and hand for 5 hours.

I shared this revelation with them in part to see if they could find something inaccurate about it. I wrote each of them a brief two page letter with a few basics and told them I would give them two weeks to muse on it and then give them a call which I did. They all politely said they could not dispute any of it and they had never made that connection before. They said they were surprised they never noticed the connection with all of their years of education and personal Bible study. I wasn't sure if they were just trying to be polite or whether they really understood it. I did later come to realize at least one preacher did not understand it. I don't know if he was trying to be polite or what exactly. He stated on the phone that he did see the connection and invited my family and I to attend his church which we did. Two months later he brought two visiting preachers to the church to give an eight hour seminar. A seminar for eight hours teaching how much God hated gay people. Teaching how football would turn gay boys heterosexual and how baking in the kitchen would turn lesbian girls heterosexual. I kid you not.

It has always been my opinion when a person says God came to them, or God told them to do something, or they saw a spirit or angel, etc., it is best to keep a mental note and red flag in regard to that person. Many people have a hard time keeping God and reality in perspective. To often when people think of God they envision clouds and naked babies with harps. When it comes to Satan they envision fire and red flaming men with pitch forks. I never once questioned the decision to keep my angelic experience to myself for my entire life. I never intended to tell that to anyone. For the past 13 years I kept the angel out of discussions. As I sit here to write this book, to put the entire experience on paper, all the truth just as it really happened, I now realize I cannot lie to the world about this angel experience.

When I got out the paper and pen and sat down at the dinning room table I prayed to God to guide me and to help me write everything accurately. All I have before me are the abbreviated scriptures on paper. The meanings of these scriptures I will never forget. They are etched in my memory forever. I need to fill in the meanings the angel showed me in order to teach this revelation to others. After about one minute of struggling back and forth over my reputation, I realize I must write the total truth just as all of it really happened. I will just have to risk people thinking I'm crazy and out of touch with reality. Those with the gift of understanding will get it and after all that's who I'm writing to. If anyone thinks I am crazy-so be it.

An angel came to me on October 30, 1996 and revealed these Bible secrets in the same order as I will reveal them to you now. I spent eight months researching these scriptures and historical documentation trying to prove it wrong. I couldn't believe it was true. With all of today's highly educated Bible teachers I felt someone should have known this information or should I say interpretation if it were true. After my research it was confirmed this revelation was the truth from God.

I shared parts of this with my wonderful young children who at that time were 10 and 12 years old. I told them how important this was to mankind and how I needed to write this book. I asked them to take on more chores around the house to give me more time to devote to the writing. God bless them they were happy to help. But after about two weeks I realized that even with their help it wasn't going to be possible. I didn't have the time or energy that was needed. I was falling behind on things that needed to be done. My children were over loaded and without my attention considering I was a single parent. I worked 7 days a week and was broke and exhausted all the years that I raised them. I decided I would just have to wait until they were grown and gone to write this book.

By the time my children were grown I had been ill for years. I didn't know what was wrong with me. I didn't have health insurance and I couldn't afford to go to a doctor. For years I thought I was slowly dying. In the last few years that I was raising my children I had been a Metro Mobility Bus Driver. I regularly started to fall asleep while I was driving. I went into my boss's office and explained what was happening. They were convinced after speaking with me that I had sleep apnea. They insisted that I go straight to a doctor and they put me on a medical leave.

I found a doctor and he put me into a sleep hospital. Within the first four hours that I was there my oxygen levels went down to 62 percent and my organs began to shut down. They had to revive me five times in that four hour period. Needless to say I had a very severe case of sleep apnea. The doctor sent me home and began treating my sleep apnea. I am still in recovery it is a very slow process. By that time I was in such bad shape I didn't think I was going to make it. I was on a medical leave for 12 weeks. I returned to work and six weeks later I fell asleep driving the bus again. I came back to my boss's office and told him it happened again. I told him I didn't feel it was safe for me, my customers, or the general public that I remain a professional driver and I quit. I went on unemployment at the worst time in American history along with 30 million other Americans and realized the Lord had finally provided an opportunity for me to write this book. This was all in God's timing.

Brothers and sisters fasten your seat belts. Your life is about to change forever. In the upcoming pages I will share with you as best I can the nature of this revelation I received. Please know that I write from a place of the following beliefs:

There is ONE God, and He has different names around the world. This is the God of Abraham, of Moses, and of David and so on.

God put mankind on this planet with a plan and purpose. He did not put mankind here to wander aimlessly blind and confused without purpose or direction or instruction. Our Heavenly Father intended for mankind to see Him through nature and His glorious creations as well as in the inspired writings of His Word in the ancient manuscripts. The Bible is a testament of mankind's history and future and for our instruction, safety and protection. God expects His children to have a good understanding of His Word and to embrace His intense love and compassion for us. So we can embrace the blessings and joys He created for us and all of mankind. His purpose was for mankind to have that same intense love and compassion for each other. While living in peace, joy, harmony, and obedience.

God created mankind thousands of years ago and to date not one man has experienced God's original plan and purpose. Satan has prevented God's children from this plan and purpose from the beginning with his lies and manipulations and deceptions. You cannot believe there is a God and believe there is not a Satan. It is after all God through the ancient manuscripts who teaches us about Satan and his practices.

You cannot take bits and pieces of the Bible and pick and choose to believe one thing because it suits you and not believe another because it doesn't suit you. If you do this you are creating your own God in your own head. This God does not exist. Not outside of your own individual mind anyway. You must believe ALL of the scriptures are from God for mankind's benefit not just bits and pieces of it.

Be advised scripture normally refers to people in the male form yet it is speaking to all men, women and children. I shall use the male form as well for convenience. For example, one scripture states; "No man has ever seen God," well, what that means is: no man, woman or child has ever seen God. I wanted you to be aware of this. I didn't want you to think I was leaving out women and children as I cover the scriptural information. When the Bible was written it was a mans world. It is to difficult to translate that every time we are going to come across that type of reference. Keep in mind when the scriptures or I use the male form we are referring to all men, women and children.

I have never liked putting labels on people. People are far to flexible and complex to fit into a box or label. I also feel labels stunt the growth of individuals therefore ultimately causing harm. However, the Bible does use labels and for good reason. For that reason I will label people for teaching and clarity purposes. I will use the term "gay" when I am referring to gay, lesbian, or transgender people, male or female, anyone who has a same gender attraction to keep sentences from getting to wordy.

WHO WERE THE LGBT PEOPLE OF BIBLICAL TIMES?

2Timothy 3:16+17
All scripture is given by inspiration of God, and is profitable for doctrine, for reproof, for correction, for instruction in righteousness: (17) That the man of God may be perfect, thoroughly furnished unto all good works.

In the original Hebrew manuscripts the term "eunuch" was introduced at Genesis 37:36 the term was never used before that to my knowledge. The word "eunuch" is the English translation that was derived from the Hebrew word "saris," and the Greek word "eunoukhos." Eunuchs were appointed in royal courts as attendants or caretakers of the queen and the harem. Due to their closeness to the king's household eunuchs of ability often rose to high rank. Positions such as chamberlains, stewards and cupbearers were exclusively given to eunuchs due to the nature of trust required. Some high ranking military officers are identified as eunuchs as well.

Various eunuchs were mentioned all throughout the scriptures. Once the figure of the eunuch began to appear in the Holy scriptures that figure clearly played an important even revered role among God's people.

I would like to explain what a eunuch was back in Biblical times and explain modern man's misconceptions of these people. Today's Bible teachers and dictionaries define a eunuch as a man who loved God so much he would castrate himself so he could serve God better without the distractions of marriage or sex.

Deuteronomy 23:1, He that is wounded in the stones, or hath his privy member cut off shall not enter into the congregation of the LORD.

This scripture is found in an area where the Bible is talking about sex crimes according to the law covenant of the old testament. Forsaking this law on castration would have been punishable by death for the one castrated as well as anyone aiding in a castration. They would have been stoned to death.

The point is; the literal castration of men was not happening among God's people. However it was happening among the surrounding Heathen nations. There were tens of thousands, perhaps millions, of people on the earth at that time who were labeled as eunuchs. There were eunuchs among God's people as well as eunuchs of other nations on the earth at that time. It is not logical to believe there were tens of thousands of men on the earth running around castrating themselves for God or for any other reason. No more logical than millions of men running around today doing it.

This was the first thing the angel revealed to me on our Biblical journey. It is important that you keep this scripture in the forefront of your mind all throughout this Bible revelation. This scripture is the foundation of all clarity from this point forward.

The label "eunuch" was therefore symbolic representing generations of people from all nations in Biblical times. These generations of people were labeled as eunuchs, yet most of them were not castrated, which meant they did have all of their sexual organs. Therefore, they would have been perfectly normal and sexually functional people. Now we must ask ourselves why were all of them labeled as castrated or eunuch? If the majority had all of their sexual organs they would have been sexually active people. This would have been natural considering God created all of mankind to be sexual for the purpose of pleasure and procreation. One of our Heavenly Father's first commandments to mankind was to populate the earth. Again, proof that mankind was created to be sexual.

Genesis 1:28
And God blessed them, and God said unto them, Be fruitful, and multiply, and replenish the earth, and subdue it: and have dominion over the fish of the sea, and over the fowl of the air, and over every living thing that moved upon the earth.

In today's modern world many people are not sexually active for many reasons. That is perfectly normal. Whether a person is sexually active or not they are still sexual beings. In Biblical times in the nation of Israel and surrounding nations whom didn't know God eunuchs were everywhere. These eunuchs held positions in royal courts such as court officials and judges. Eunuchs were fathers and mothers as well as high ranking military officers. The scriptures describe houses of beauty where royal and common women were bathed, massaged with hot oils, and were given beauty treatments by eunuchs.

Eunuchs are described as caretakers and attendants of the king's wives and daughters. The scriptures point out it was eunuchs who worked in and managed these places for women. Historical documents and scriptures point out every wife and daughter of every king among God's people at that time in Israel and elsewhere had a eunuch sleeping in their bed chamber each and every night for protection. Back then many kings had a hundred or more wives and a hundred or more daughters. It would have taken a lot of eunuchs to fill all of those positions. From the description of these eunuchs they were obviously highly respected and trusted in the nation of Israel.

Now what was a eunuch? Why were these generations of people given a social label? There must have been some reason they were identified as different. These people were going through life carrying a label that indicated they were castrated and yet the majority did have all of their sexual organs. A deeper look into the scriptures reveals who these eunuchs really were.

Esther 2:3

2:3 *"And let the king appoint officers in all the provinces of his kingdom, that they may gather together all the fair young virgins unto Shushan the palace, to the house of the women, unto the custody of* **Hege the king's chamberlain, keeper of the women; and let their things for purification be given them:"**

The word "chamberlain" was a job title held exclusively for eunuchs. Esther 2:3 points out that Hege was the Kings eunuch in charge of the house of the women he was their guardian. Massages and other personal services were performed there by eunuchs.

Esther 2:14

2:14 *"In the evening she went, and on the morrow she returned into the second **house of the women, to the custody of Shaashgaz, the king's chamberlain, which kept the concubines:** she came in unto the king no more, except the king delighted in her, and that she were called by name."*

Again the word "chamberlain" was a job title held exclusively for eunuchs. Esther 2:14 points out that Shaashgaz was the kings eunuch in charge of the second house of the women and was their guardian. There would have been tens of thousands of eunuchs in the nation of Israel in Biblical times.

1 Kings 22:9

22:9 *Then the king of Israel called **a eunuch officer**, and said, Hasten hither Micaiah the son of Imlah.*

Notice in 1 Kings 22:9 the king of Israel called a eunuch officer to summon Micaiah the prophet. This scripture identifies an officer as a eunuch in Israels armed forces.

Eunuchs are mentioned all throughout the Bible. I could go on and on showing one scripture after another proving the same point over and over. But, I'm afraid I will cause you to become sidetracked and you will lose the revelation I'm trying to teach. For the remainder of this book I'm going to give you just a couple of scriptures in detail, word for word, to prove my point. I will list some additional scriptures that prove my point at the end of each subject. This allows you to go to your Bible's for further proof and documentation.

The following scriptures identify and mention various eunuchs, who they were, and how they lived, and various things they did and what they were a part of in Bible references and Biblical events.

Additional Reference:
(Ge37:36, 39:1, 40:1-11, 41:9-13)(Ex18:21)(1Ch28:1-6, 2Ch9:4) (2Ki 25:19)(Jer38:7-13) (Isa22:15,56:4+5)(Da1:3-11)(Matt19:12, 20:8)(Ac8:26-39, 12:20)(Lu16:1-4)(1Co4:1+2) (Ti1:7-9)

Historical documents state that many people believed eunuchs had the spirit of both a man and a woman. They were so loved and respected in ancient times they were given children to raise as their own. I recommend the reading of "Spirit and the Flesh" by Walter Williams. "Spirit and the Flesh" gives a very eye opening documentation of eunuchs in the not so distant past. For example: "Spirit and the Flesh" historically documents that in 1542 Spanish explorers recorded that they saw men marrying men in Native American societies. An ethnologist documented in the 1880's Native American men were taking other men as their husbands. A massive survey of northern California in the 1930's documents American Indian men were marrying men. This is just a taste of the wealth of documented history that proves eunuchs were people with a same gender attraction. There are many other historical records as well to numerous to mention in this book. I will leave that research up to you.

The scriptures point out that these eunuchs were given children and raised children as their own. Let's take a look at the scriptural reference of Mordecai;

Esther 2:7
2:7 "And he brought up Hadassah, that is, Esther, his uncle's daughter: for she had neither Father nor mother, and the maid was fair and beautiful; **whom Mordecai, when her Father and mother were dead, took for his own daughter."**

In Biblical times the head of the household was the oldest living Father. Mordecai's Father felt it was best to give Esther to Mordecai to raise as his own child. "Spirit and the Flesh" as well as other historical documents prove in ancient times feminine men were given children to raise as their own children. It was considered a blessing to have one of your children raised by a feminine eunuch because they were believed to possess the spirit of a man and of a woman. Due to the belief that eunuchs had both spirits they were often spiritual leaders as well.

Esther10:3
10:3 **"For Mordecai the Jew was next unto king Ahasuerus,** *and great among the Jews, and accepted of the multitude of his brethren, seeking the wealth of his people, and speaking peace to all his seed."*

Now that we know the back grounds and privileges eunuchs had in Biblical times it is logical and obvious to believe Mordecai was a eunuch. As history proves eunuchs were so highly revered people gave them their children to raise. Let's face it, it's only logical that Mordecai's Father would have had plenty of females in his family to whom he could have given Esther to for raising not to mention she was a young female. The head of the household gave her to Mordecai to raise. Giving children to feminine eunuchs was a common practice and considered a privilege and blessing back in Biblical times.

Mordecai also wrote the book of Esther. A book that reveals more about eunuchs and their lives than any other book in the Bible. Many Bible translations did not identify people as eunuchs if the translator felt there was some reason it didn't seem logical to them. For example; if the original manuscripts said a eunuch had a wife the translator would not have identified him as a eunuch in spite of the fact that the original manuscripts said he was a eunuch. This happened because modern man has not known the definition of a eunuch not prior to the publication of this revelation anyway. Yet the original Hebrew, Greek and Aramaic manuscripts clearly identified them as eunuchs. Keep in mind these Bible translations were translated by imperfect man. The only manuscripts I totally trust are the original Hebrew, Aramaic and Greek and those I must have translated into English.

Now let's run down the list of what I have taught you and proved with Bible scripture and historical records so far:

- God's scriptures are for setting things straight.
- The vast majority of eunuchs were not literally castrated but some were.
- Castration was a sin punishable by death among God's people.
- The term "eunuch" was a social label, a slang term.
- The vast majority of eunuchs did have all their sexual organs and were logically sexual.
- Eunuchs were abundant among God's people.
- There must have been tens of thousands or perhaps millions of them.

- Eunuchs were in every part of society including the military, second to the kings, royal court's, court's of law as judges, as caretakers and attendants of royal women, and as managers and workers in what is described similar to salons and spa's.
- Eunuchs were so trusted by the kings that they slept in the same bed chamber and guarded the bed chambers and houses of royal women each and every night.
- Eunuchs were parents of children who had been given to them.
- Mordecai was given Esther to raise as his own daughter by his father.
- Mordecai was highly respected as were many eunuchs.

Do you have an ear, are you listening?

Matthew 13:9-20
*13:9 **"Who hath ears to hear, let him hear."***

*13:10 And the disciples came, and said unto him, **Why speakest thou unto them in parables?***

*13:11 He answered and said unto them, **Because it is given unto you to know the mysteries of the kingdom of Heaven,** but to them it is not given.*

*13:12 For **whosoever hath,** to him **shall be given, and he shall have more abundance**: but whosoever hath not, from him shall be taken away even that he hath.*

*13:13 **Therefore speak I to them in parables**: because they seeing see not; and hearing they hear not, neither do they understand.*

13:14 And in them is fulfilled the prophecy of Esaias, which saith,

*By **hearing ye shall hear, and shall not understand;** and seeing ye shall see, and shall not perceive:*

*13:15 For this people's heart is waxed gross, and their ears are dull of hearing, and their eyes they have closed; lest at any time they should **see with their eyes and hear with their ears, and should understand with their heart, and should be converted, and I should heal them.***

*13:16 **But blessed are your eyes, for they see: and your ears, for they hear.***

*13:17 **For verily I say unto you, That many prophets and righteous men have desired to see those things which ye see, and have not seen them; and to hear those things which ye hear, and have not heard them.***

*13:18 **Hear ye therefore the parable of the sower.***

13:19 When any one heareth the word of the kingdom, and understandeth it not, then cometh the wicked one, and catcheth away that which was sown in his heart. This is he which received seed by the way side.

*13:20 But **he that received the seed** into stony places, the same is **he that heareth the word, and anon with joy receiveth it;***

**Brothers and sisters,
Do you have an ear, are you listening?**

**EUNUCH'S WERE MEN AND WOMAN.
THE LABEL "EUNUCH" IDENTIFIES GAY, LESBIAN, AND TRANSGENDER TYPE PEOPLE!
A PEOPLE WHO ARE NOW IDENTIFIED AS THE LGBT COMMUNITY.**

These men and women had perfectly normal sexual organs and therefore would have been sexual people. The male eunuchs slept in the same bedroom and guarded the most beautiful women on the planet each and every night, day after day, year after year. In the morning the male eunuchs bathed the women and rubbed their naked bodies with hot oils and attended to their hair and makeup. The kings trusted them to do all of this and to keep their penises in their pants. Failure to do so would have meant death for the eunuch as well as a ruined lifetime for a woman or girl in those days.

Let's be realistic here: these men were not heterosexual men who loved God a lot. These were gay men. What kind of a King would put a heterosexual man with or without a penis in this position with his most cherished possessions?

THESE MEN WERE GAY!

These men held some of the most prestigious positions in ancient society and were highly respected by the kings and common people alike. Let's look further into these generations of eunuchs or to use the modern term; the ancient Lgbt community.

Deuteronomy 23:1 states that no castrated man was allowed to come into the house or congregation of God. This is because a literally castrated man would have been viewed as unclean according to the law covenant of the old testament because of his physical defect. The only men around at that time who would have been literally castrated would have come from surrounding pagan nations. Eunuch's who were rescued as children from pagan nations and brought to Israel to live and grow up. Eunuch men who at some point in their lives decided to worship the God of the Jews and moved to Israel. Many of these literally castrated eunuchs were young male children taken from surrounding pagan nations when those nations were destroyed and or disbursed by Israel's military.

Remember, Deuteronomy 23:1 points out that any kind of castration by any of God's people would have been punishable by death. However, castration was not uncommon for people of other nations. Pagan's and others often converted to the God of the Jews. Some relocated to Israel while some stayed where they were.

Many young boys were castrated in pagan nations for prostitution. This was a common practice and custom in ancient times. After a pagan nation defeated a nation of their enemies the custom was to take the young sons of the defeated King and other royals and castrate them for prostitution in their churches. They made them live as male prostitutes as a form of humiliation before the survivors of the defeated nation. This also prevented these royal children from growing up and procreating thus rebelling against a nation that defeated their fathers and forefathers.

These young boys were sexual slaves at the temple, the house of worship, it was part of pagan religion to have sex with young boys. The Bible refers to these young boys as Sodomites. These poor unfortunate young boys were treated like dirt and severely abused sexually. Sadly, many would have died of sexual disease in a very short period of time. This is why God hated these nations so much. This is why God sent His armies out to other nations to destroy them again and again throughout Biblical history. When Israel destroyed and or disbursed these nations they brought the literally castrated temple prostitute boys back to Israel with them. They brought them back to Israel for protection and for a normal life that did not include abuse or prostitution. The Israelite' s knew how God felt about child prostitution and they felt great empathy, love, and compassion for these children. So much so that they risked their lives to save them. This explains why our Heavenly Father loves Israel so deeply.

This is another reason why only a very few literally castrated people would have been around especially in the nation of Israel. The reason "eunuch" was a slang term for gay people is because their sexual behavior was the same as the young male temple prostitutes, male with male, female with female. Let me make it very clear these Sodomites were not prostitutes after arriving in Israel after their rescue. The majority of people who were labeled eunuchs were never castrated or prostitutes. It was a symbolic label because of the same gender sexual activity.

1 Kings 14:24
14:24 *"And there were also sodomites in the land: and they did according to all the abominations of the nations **which the LORD cast out before the children of Israel."***

Deuteronomy 23:17+18

*23:17 There shall be no whore of the daughters of Israel, **nor a sodomite of the sons of Israel.***

*23:18 **Thou shalt not bring the hire of a whore,** or the price of a dog, into the house of the LORD thy God for any vow: for even both these are abomination unto the LORD thy God.*

1 Kings 15:12

*15:12 And **he took away the sodomites out of the land,** and removed all the idols that his Fathers had made.*

2 Kings 23:7

*23:7 And **he brake down the houses of the sodomites,** that were by the house of the LORD, where the women wove hangings for the grove.*

The term "Sodomite" was used in the English translation to describe the male temple child prostitutes. The term "Sodomite" is never used to describe any other type of person other than a eunuch child prostitute. Now these male temple prostitutes were **not servicing women**. Keep in mind they had been literally castrated in pagan nations at a young age solely for the purpose of prostitution in the church. What unjust nations! This is why our Heavenly Father despised these nations so much. Keep in mind these male temple child prostitutes would have had the same kind of customers as a male prostitute today. Men are the same today as they were thousands of years ago people have not changed. To quote King Solomon "There is nothing new under the sun."

I realize this was a heart breaking and difficult subject. Unfortunately these two different types of eunuchs needed to be defined. I needed to show you the difference between a literally castrated person and a symbolically castrated person. Both of whom went by the same label. Both had sex with their same gender and yet came from very different lives, backgrounds and social status. God bless the nation of Israel for rescuing those (Sodomites) male temple child prostitutes, for treating them with love, dignity and respect, and for providing them with a safe, nurturing and prosperous life. God bless all mankind for such a loving and righteous God.

Do you have an ear, are you listening?

The Bible writers deliberately singled out these eunuchs and labeled them for a reason. For example, you will notice that the label "eunuch" is frequently mentioned by the Bible writer Mordecai, who wrote the book of Esther, a book titled after his daughter. I could not help but notice the first Bible writer who was a eunuch himself, made a special point to identify those who were eunuch in his writings, every little detail. The Bible writers did this on purpose; this was not a mistake. The Bible writers were inspired by our Heavenly Father and directed personally by angels who obviously felt this was needed and important for future generations.

Notice;
Mordecai brings eunuchs to the forefront
right away at Esther 2:3.

Esther 2:3

2:3 *"And let the king appoint officers in all the provinces of his kingdom, that they may gather together all the fair young virgins unto Shushan the palace, to the house of the women, unto the custody of* **Hege the king's chamberlain, the kings eunuch**, *keeper of the women; and let their things for purification be given them:"*

Again, Mordecai mentions another eunuch named Hege, and makes a special point to identify and label Hege as a eunuch. In Esther 2:3, the mention of Hege as a eunuch is not necessary. Mordecai could have made his point quite clearly without identifying and labeling Hege as a eunuch. As a matter of fact including that label in that scripture sounds rather odd. Let's read the scripture leaving that out and you will see how much better the sentence sounds.

Esther 2:3

2:3 *And let the king appoint officers in all the provinces of his kingdom, that they may gather together all the fair young virgins unto Shushan the palace, to the house of the women, unto the custody of Hege,*
***keeper of the women;........ and let their things for purification be given them:*

Notice how unnecessary it seems that Mordecai needed to identify him by any label. You will find this over and over throughout the Bible scriptures. You will notice in reading the book of Esther the entire book is about eunuchs. They are described in detail. Mordecai used feminine and masculine eunuchs to clearly show readers the type of men they were. If he had only used the masculine eunuchs no one would have understood it.

Mordecai was inspired by an angel to write the book of Esther as he did. To benefit mankind thousands of years later. So they would notice the resemblance in the type of people the scriptures are referring to. Mordecai wrote the book of Esther for mankind in Biblical times and for mankind today. I wonder if Mordecai had any idea what would become of his eunuch brothers and sisters thousands of years down the road. It is not likely he could have ever imagined considering how well loved and respected he knew eunuchs to be in his generation and the generations before him. I'm sure Mordecai had no idea a brother eunuch named Rickie Bartlett thousands of years in the future would be visited by that same angel to interpret what he and his generation took for granted.
As you can see Mordecai had a plan and purpose here to clearly identify his fellow eunuchs. Mordecai labels people as eunuchs all throughout the book of Esther as did Bible writers after him all the way through to the end of the New Testament. These eunuchs were labeled and identified for a reason. They were identified by the Bible writers for gay people today and for all of mankind reading this Bible revelation.

God bless all of mankind for God's great ability to love. Our Heavenly Father clearly shows all of mankind that nothing is impossible when it comes to His beloved children and His plans and desires for them.

**I recommend the reading
of the entire book of ESTHER at this time.**

- The book of Esther was written by Mordecai. He gives great detail regarding how and why he was given Esther as a daughter.
- A love affair between Esther and King Ahasuerus. The King was so in love with Esther he offered her half his riches and half his Kingdom and looked after her with great affection.
- Mordecai overheard a conversation among eunuchs against King Ahasuerus.
- Mordecai and Esther intervened in a plot to assassinate King Ahasuerus.
- Mordecai and Esther intervened when Haman tried to wipe out the Jews as a race.
- Mordecai and Esther exposes the eunuchs who plotted against the King and the eunuchs who were involved in saving the Kings life.
- The book of Esther reveals Esther's horrifying rage and wrath against Haman for trying to murder her Father Mordecai.
- Esther took Haman's jealousy and hatred for her Father and turned it against Haman.
- Esther went on to become the most beloved Queen in ancient history.

It is very important that you read every word of Mordecai's book about his daughter. There is a wealth of revealing information about the ancient Lgbt community here.

BOOK OF ESTHER

Esther 1:1 *Now it came to pass in the days of Ahasuerus, this is Ahasuerus which reigned, from India even unto Ethiopia, over an hundred and seven and twenty provinces:*

1:2 That in those days, when the king Ahasuerus sat on the throne of his kingdom, which was in Shushan the palace,

1:3 In the third year of his reign, he made a feast unto all his princes and his servants; the power of Persia and Media, the nobles and princes of the provinces, being before him:

1:4 When he shewed the riches of his glorious kingdom and the honour of his excellent majesty many days, even an hundred and fourscore days.

1:5 And when these days were expired, the king made a feast unto all the people that were present in Shushan the palace, both unto great and small, seven days, in the court of the garden of the king's palace;

1:6 Where were white, green, and blue, hangings, fastened with cords of fine linen and purple to silver rings and pillars of marble: the beds were of gold and silver, upon a pavement of red, and blue, and white, and black, marble.

1:7 And they gave them drink in vessels of gold, (the vessels being diverse one from another,) and royal wine in abundance, according to the state of the king.

1:8 And the drinking was according to the law; none did compel:

for so the king had appointed to all the officers of his house, that they should do according to every man's pleasure.

1:9 *Also Vashti the queen made a feast for the women in the royal house which belonged to king Ahasuerus.*

1:10 *On the seventh day, when the heart of the king was merry with wine, he commanded Mehuman, Biztha, Harbona, Bigtha, and Abagtha, Zethar, and Carcas, the seven chamberlains that served in the presence of Ahasuerus the king,*

1:11 *To bring Vashti the queen before the king with the crown royal, to shew the people and the princes her beauty: for she was fair to look on.*

1:12 *But the queen Vashti refused to come at the king's commandment by his chamberlains: therefore was the king very wroth, and his anger burned in him.*

1:13 *Then the king said to the wise men, which knew the times, for so was the king's manner toward all that knew law and judgment:*

1:14 *And the next unto him was Carshena, Shethar, Admatha, Tarshish, Meres, Marsena, and Memucan, the seven princes of Persia and Media, which saw the king's face, and which sat the first in the kingdom;*

1:15 *What shall we do unto the queen Vashti according to law, because she hath not performed the commandment of the king Ahasuerus by the chamberlains?*

1:16 *And Memucan answered before the king and the princes, Vashti the queen hath not done wrong to the king only, but also to all the princes, and to all the people that are in all the provinces of the king Ahasuerus.*

1:17 *For this deed of the queen shall come abroad unto all women,* so that they shall despise their husbands in their eyes, when it shall be reported, The king Ahasuerus commanded Vashti the queen to be brought in before him, but she came not.

1:18 Likewise shall the ladies of Persia and Media say this day unto all the king's princes, which have heard of the deed of the queen. Thus shall there arise too much contempt and wrath.

1:19 If it please the king, let there go a royal commandment from him, and let it be written among the laws of the Persians and the Medes, that it be not altered, That Vashti come no more before king Ahasuerus; and let the king give her royal estate unto another that is better than she.

1:20 And when the king's decree which he shall make shall be published throughout all his empire, (for it is great,) all the wives shall give to their husbands honour, both to great and small.

1:21 And the saying pleased the king and the princes; and the king did according to the word of Memucan:

1:22 For he sent letters into all the king's provinces, into every province according to the writing thereof, and to every people after their language, that every man should bear rule in his own house, and that it should be published according to the language of every people.

2:1 After these things, when the wrath of king Ahasuerus was appeased, he remembered Vashti, and what she had done, and what was decreed against her.

2:2 Then said the king's servants that ministered unto him, Let there be fair young virgins sought for the king:

2:3 And let the king appoint officers in all the provinces of his kingdom, that they may gather together all the fair young virgins unto Shushan the palace, to the house of the women, *unto the custody of Hege the king's chamberlain, keeper of the women; and let their things for purification be given them:*

2:4 *And let the maiden which pleaseth the king be queen instead of Vashti. And the thing pleased the king; and he did so.*

2:5 *Now in Shushan the palace there was a certain Jew, whose name was Mordecai, the son of Jair, the son of Shimei, the son of Kish, a Benjamite;*

2:6 *Who had been carried away from Jerusalem with the captivity which had been carried away with Jeconiah king of Judah, whom Nebuchadnezzar the king of Babylon had carried away.*

2:7 *And he brought up Hadassah, that is, Esther, his uncle's daughter: for she had neither Father nor mother, and the maid was fair and beautiful; whom Mordecai, when her Father and mother were dead, took for his own daughter.*

2:8 *So it came to pass, when the king's commandment and his decree was heard, and when many maidens were gathered together unto Shushan the palace, to the custody of Hegai, that Esther was brought also unto the king's house, to the custody of Hegai, keeper of the women.*

2:9 *And the maiden pleased him, and she obtained kindness of him; and he speedily gave her her things for purification, with such things as belonged to her, and seven maidens, which were meet to be given her, out of the king's house: and he preferred her and her maids unto the best place of the house of the women.*

2:10 *Esther had not shewed her people nor her kindred: for Mordecai had charged her that she should not shew it.*

2:11 *And Mordecai walked every day before the court of the women's house, to know how Esther did, and what should become of her.*

2:12 Now when every maid's turn was come to go in to king Ahasuerus, after that she had been twelve months, according to the manner of the women, for so were the days of their purifications accomplished, to wit, six months with oil of myrrh, and six months with sweet odours, and with other things for the purifying of the women;

2:13 Then thus came every maiden unto the king; whatsoever she desired was given her to go with her out of the house of the women unto the king's house.

2:14 In the evening she went, and on the morrow she returned into the second house of the women, to the custody of Shaashgaz, the king's chamberlain, which kept the concubines: she came in unto the king no more, except the king delighted in her, and that she were called by name.

2:15 Now when the turn of Esther, the daughter of Abihail the uncle of Mordecai, who had taken her for his daughter, was come to go in unto the king, she required nothing but what Hegai the king's chamberlain, the keeper of the women, appointed. And Esther obtained favour in the sight of all them that looked upon her.

2:16 So Esther was taken unto king Ahasuerus into his house royal in the tenth month, which is the month Tebeth, in the seventh year of his reign.

2:17 And the king loved Esther above all the women, and she obtained grace and favour in his sight more than all the virgins; so that he set the royal crown upon her head, and made her queen instead of Vashti.

2:18 Then the king made a great feast unto all his princes and his servants, even Esther's feast; and he made a release to the provinces, and gave gifts, according to the state of the king.

*2:19 And when the virgins were gathered together the second time,
then Mordecai sat in the king's gate.*

*2:20 Esther had not yet shewed her kindred nor her people; as
Mordecai had charged her: for Esther did the commandment of
Mordecai, like as when she was brought up with him.*

*2:21 In those days, while Mordecai sat in the king's gate, two of the
king's chamberlains, Bigthan and Teresh, of those which kept
the door, were wroth, and sought to lay hands on the king
Ahasuerus.*

*2:22 And the thing was known to Mordecai, who told it unto Esther
the queen; and Esther certified the king thereof in Mordecai's
name.*

*2:23 And when inquisition was made of the matter, it was found out;
therefore they were both hanged on a tree: and it was written in
the book of the chronicles before the king.*

*3:1 After these things did king Ahasuerus promote Haman the son
of Hammedatha the Agagite, and advanced him, and set his seat
above all the princes that were with him.*

*3:2 And all the king's servants, that were in the king's gate, bowed,
and reverenced Haman: for the king had so commanded
concerning him. But Mordecai bowed not, nor did him
reverence.*

*3:3 Then the king's servants, which were in the king's gate, said
unto Mordecai, Why transgressest thou the king's
commandment?*

*3:4 Now it came to pass, when they spake daily unto him, and he
hearkened not unto them, that they told Haman, to see whether
Mordecai's matters would stand: for he had told them that he
was a Jew.*

3:5 And when Haman saw that Mordecai bowed not, nor did him reverence, then was Haman full of wrath.

3:6 And he thought scorn to lay hands on Mordecai alone; for they had shewed him the people of Mordecai: wherefore Haman sought to destroy all the Jews that were throughout the whole kingdom of Ahasuerus, even the people of Mordecai.

3:7 In the first month, that is, the month Nisan, in the twelfth year of king Ahasuerus, they cast Pur, that is, the lot, before Haman from day to day, and from month to month, to the twelfth month, that is, the month Adar.

3:8 And Haman said unto king Ahasuerus, There is a certain people scattered abroad and dispersed among the people in all the provinces of thy kingdom; and their laws are diverse from all people; neither keep they the king's laws: therefore it is not for the king's profit to suffer them.

3:9 If it please the king, let it be written that they may be destroyed: and I will pay ten thousand talents of silver to the hands of those that have the charge of the business, to bring it into the king's treasuries.

3:10 And the king took his ring from his hand, and gave it unto Haman the son of Hammedatha the Agagite, the Jews' enemy.

3:11 And the king said unto Haman, The silver is given to thee, the people also, to do with them as it seemeth good to thee.

3:12 Then were the king's scribes called on the thirteenth day of the first month, and there was written according to all that Haman had commanded unto the king's lieutenants, and to the governors that were over every province, and to the rulers of every people of every province according to the writing thereof, and to every people after their language; in the name of king Ahasuerus was it written, and sealed with the king's ring.

3:13 And the letters were sent by posts into all the king's provinces, to destroy, to kill, and to cause to perish, all Jews, both young and old, little children and women, in one day, even upon the thirteenth day of the twelfth month, which is the month Adar, and to take the spoil of them for a prey.

3:14 The copy of the writing for a commandment to be given in every province was published unto all people, that they should be ready against that day.

3:15 The posts went out, being hastened by the king's commandment, and the decree was given in Shushan the palace. And the king and Haman sat down to drink; but the city Shushan was perplexed.

4.1 When Mordecai perceived all that was done, Mordecai rent his clothes, and put on sackcloth with ashes, and went out into the midst of the city, and cried with a loud and a bitter cry;

4:2 And came even before the king's gate: for none might enter into the king's gate clothed with sackcloth.

4:3 And in every province, whithersoever the king's commandment and his decree came, there was great mourning among the Jews, and fasting, and weeping, and wailing; and many lay in sackcloth and ashes.

4:4 So Esther's maids and her chamberlains came and told it her. Then was the queen exceedingly grieved; and she sent raiment to clothe Mordecai, and to take away his sackcloth from him: but he received it not.

4:5 Then called Esther for Hatach, one of the king's chamberlains, whom he had appointed to attend upon her, and gave him a commandment to Mordecai, to know what it was, and why it was.

4:6 So Hatach went forth to Mordecai unto the street of the city, which was before the king's gate.

4:7 And Mordecai told him of all that had happened unto him, and of the sum of the money that Haman had promised to pay to the king's treasuries for the Jews, to destroy them.

4:8 Also he gave him the copy of the writing of the decree that was given at Shushan to destroy them, to shew it unto Esther, and to declare it unto her, and to charge her that she should go in unto the king, to make supplication unto him, and to make request before him for her people.

4:9 And Hatach came and told Esther the words of Mordecai.

4:10 Again Esther spake unto Hatach, and gave him commandment unto Mordecai;

4:11 All the king's servants, and the people of the king's provinces, do know, that whosoever, whether man or women, shall come unto the king into the inner court, who is not called, there is one law of his to put him to death, except such to whom the king shall hold out the golden sceptre, that he may live: but I have not been called to come in unto the king these thirty days.

4:12 And they told to Mordecai Esther's words.

4:13 Then Mordecai commanded to answer Esther, Think not with thyself that thou shalt escape in the king's house, more than all the Jews.

4:14 For if thou altogether holdest thy peace at this time, then shall there enlargement and deliverance arise to the Jews from another place; but thou and thy Father's house shall be destroyed: and who knoweth whether thou art come to the kingdom for such a time as this?

4:15 Then Esther bade them return Mordecai this answer,

4:16 Go, gather together all the Jews that are present in Shushan, and fast ye for me, and neither eat nor drink three days, night or day: I also and my maidens will fast likewise; and so will I go in unto the king, which is not according to the law: and if I perish, I perish.

4:17 So Mordecai went his way, and did according to all that Esther had commanded him.

5:1 Now it came to pass on the third day, that Esther put on her royal apparel, and stood in the inner court of the king's house, over against the king's house: and the king sat upon his royal throne in the royal house, over against the gate of the house.

5:2 And it was so, when the king saw Esther the queen standing in the court, that she obtained favour in his sight: and the king held out to Esther the golden sceptre that was in his hand. So Esther drew near, and touched the top of the sceptre.

5:3 Then said the king unto her, What wilt thou, queen Esther? And what is thy request? it shall be even given thee to the half of the kingdom.

5:4 And Esther answered, If it seem good unto the king, let the king and Haman come this day unto the banquet that I have prepared for him.

5:5 Then the king said, Cause Haman to make haste, that he may do as Esther hath said. So the king and Haman came to the banquet that Esther had prepared.

5:6 And the king said unto Esther at the banquet of wine, What is thy petition? and it shall be granted thee: and what is thy request? even to the half of the kingdom it shall be performed.

5:7   Then answered Esther, and said, My petition and my request is;

5:8   If I have found favour in the sight of the king, and if it please the king to grant my petition, and to perform my request, let the king and Haman come to the banquet that I shall prepare for them, and I will do to morrow as the king hath said.

5:9   Then went Haman forth that day joyful and with a glad heart: but when Haman saw Mordecai in the king's gate, that he stood not up, nor moved for him, he was full of indignation against Mordecai.

5:10 Nevertheless Haman refrained himself: and when he came home, he sent and called for his friends, and Zeresh his wife.

5:11 And Haman told them of the glory of his riches, and the multitude of his children, and all the things wherein the king had promoted him, and how he had advanced him above the princes and servants of the king.

5:12 Haman said moreover, Yea, Esther the queen did let no man come in with the king unto the banquet that she had prepared but myself; and to morrow am I invited unto her also with the king.

5:13 Yet all this availeth me nothing, so long as I see Mordecai the Jew sitting at the king's gate.

5:14 Then said Zeresh his wife and all his friends unto him, Let a gallows be made of fifty cubits high, and to morrow speak thou unto the king that Mordecai may be hanged thereon: then go thou in merrily with the king unto the banquet. And the thing pleased Haman; and he caused the gallows to be made.

6:1   On that night could not the king sleep, and he commanded to bring the book of records of the chronicles; and they were read before the king.

6:2 And it was found written, that Mordecai had told of Bigthana and Teresh, two of the king's chamberlains, the keepers of the door, who sought to lay hand on the king Ahasuerus.

6:3 And the king said, What honour and dignity hath been done to Mordecai for this? Then said the king's servants that ministered unto him, There is nothing done for him.

6:4 And the king said, Who is in the court? Now Haman was come into the outward court of the king's house, to speak unto the king to hang Mordecai on the gallows that he had prepared for him.

6:5 And the king's servants said unto him, Behold, Haman standeth in the court. And the king said, Let him come in.

6:6 So Haman came in. And the king said unto him, What shall be done unto the man whom the king delighteth to honour? Now Haman thought in his heart, To whom would the king delight to do honour more than to myself?

6:7 And Haman answered the king, For the man whom the king delighteth to honour,

6:8 Let the royal apparel be brought which the king useth to wear, and the horse that the king rideth upon, and the crown royal which is set upon his head:

6:9 And let this apparel and horse be delivered to the hand of one of the king's most noble princes, that they may array the man withal whom the king delighteth to honour, and bring him on horseback through the street of the city, and proclaim before him, Thus shall it be done to the man whom the king delighteth to honour.

6:10 Then the king said to Haman, Make haste, and take the apparel and the horse, as thou hast said, and do even so to Mordecai the Jew, that sitteth at the king's gate: let nothing fail of all that thou hast spoken.

6:11 Then took Haman the apparel and the horse, and arrayed Mordecai, and brought him on horseback through the street of the city, and proclaimed before him, Thus shall it be done unto the man whom the king delighteth to honour.

6:12 And Mordecai came again to the king's gate. But Haman hasted to his house mourning, and having his head covered.

6:13 And Haman told Zeresh his wife and all his friends every thing that had befallen him. Then said his wise men and Zeresh his wife unto him, If Mordecai be of the seed of the Jews, before whom thou hast begun to fall, thou shalt not prevail against him, but shalt surely fall before him.

6:14 And while they were yet talking with him, came the king's chamberlains, and hasted to bring Haman unto the banquet that Esther had prepared.

7:1 So the king and Haman came to banquet with Esther the queen.

7:2 And the king said again unto Esther on the second day at the banquet of wine, What is thy petition, queen Esther? and it shall be granted thee: and what is thy request? and it shall be performed, even to the half of the kingdom.

7:3 Then Esther the queen answered and said, If I have found favour in thy sight, O king, and if it please the king, let my life be given me at my petition, and my people at my request:

7:4 For we are sold, I and my people, to be destroyed, to be slain, and to perish. But if we had been sold for bondmen and bondwomen, I had held my tongue, although the enemy could not countervail the king's damage.

7:5 Then the king Ahasuerus answered and said unto Esther the queen, Who is he, and where is he, that durst presume in his heart to do so?

7:6 And Esther said, The adversary and enemy is this wicked Haman. Then Haman was afraid before the king and the queen.

7:7 And the king arising from the banquet of wine in his wrath went into the palace garden: and Haman stood up to make request for his life to Esther the queen; for he saw that there was evil determined against him by the king.

7:8 Then the king returned out of the palace garden into the place of the banquet of wine; and Haman was fallen upon the bed whereon Esther was. Then said the king, Will he force the queen also before me in the house? As the word went out of king's mouth, they covered Haman's face.

7:9 And Harbonah, one of the chamberlains, said before the king, Behold also, the gallows fifty cubits high, which Haman had made for Mordecai, who spoken good for the king, standeth in the house of Haman. Then the king said, Hang him thereon.

7:10 So they hanged Haman on the gallows that he had prepared for Mordecai. Then was the king's wrath pacified.

8:1 On that day did the king Ahasuerus give the house of Haman the Jews' enemy unto Esther the queen. And Mordecai came before the king; for Esther had told what he was unto her.

8:2 And the king took off his ring, which he had taken from Haman, and gave it unto Mordecai. And Esther set Mordecai over the house of Haman.

8:3 And Esther spake yet again before the king, and fell down at his feet, and besought him with tears to put away the mischief of Haman the Agagite, and his device that he had devised *against the Jews.*

*8:4   Then the king held out the golden sceptre toward Esther. So
        Esther arose, and stood before the king,*

*8:5   And said, If it please the king, and if I have favour in his sight,
        and the thing seem right before the king, and I be pleasing in
        his eyes, let it be written to reverse the letters devised by
        Haman the son of Hammedatha the Agagite, which he wrote to
        destroy the Jews which are in all the king's provinces:*

*8:6   For how can I endure to see the evil that shall come unto my
        people? or how can I endure to see the destruction of my
        kindred?*

*8:7   Then the king Ahasuerus said unto Esther the queen and to
        Mordecai the Jew, Behold, I have given Esther the house of
        Haman, and him they have hanged upon the gallows, because
        he laid his hand upon the Jews.*

*8:8   Write ye also for the Jews, as it liketh you, in the king's name,
        and seal it with the king's ring: for the writing which is written
        in the king's name, and sealed with the king's ring, may no man
        reverse.*

*8:9   Then were the king's scribes called at that time in the third
        month, that is, the month Sivan, on the three and twentieth day
        thereof; and it was written according to all that Mordecai
        commanded unto the Jews, and to the lieutenants, and the
        deputies and rulers of the provinces which are from India unto
        Ethiopia, an hundred twenty and seven provinces, unto every
        province according to the writing thereof, and unto every
        people after their language, and to the Jews according to their
        writing, and according to their language.*

*8:10 And he wrote in the king Ahasuerus' name, and sealed it with
        the king's ring, and sent letters by posts on horseback, and*

riders on mules, camels, and young dromedaries:

8:11 Wherein the king granted the Jews which were in every city to gather themselves together, and to stand for their life, to destroy, to slay and to cause to perish, all the power of the people and province that would assault them, both little ones and women, and to take the spoil of them for a prey,

8:12 Upon one day in all the provinces of king Ahasuerus, namely, upon the thirteenth day of the twelfth month, which is the month Adar.

8:13 The copy of the writing for a commandment to be given in every province was published unto all people, and that the Jews should be ready against that day to avenge themselves on their enemies,

8:14 So the posts that rode upon mules and camels went out, being hastened and pressed on by the king's commandment. And the decree was given at Shushan the palace.

8:15 And Mordecai went out from the presence of the king in royal apparel of blue and white, and with a great crown of gold, and with a garment of fine linen and purple: and the city of Shushan rejoiced and was glad.

8:16 The Jews had light, and gladness, and joy, and honour.

8:17 And in every province, and in every city, whithersoever the king's commandment and his decree came, the Jews had joy and gladness, a feast and a good day. And many of the people of the land became Jews; for the fear of the Jews fell upon them.

9:1 Now in the twelfth month, that is, the month Adar, on the thirteenth day of the same, when the king's commandment and his decree drew near to be put in execution, in the day that the enemies of the Jews hoped to have power over them, though it was turned to the contrary, that the Jews had rule over them that hated them;

9:2   The Jews gathered themselves together in their cities throughout all the provinces of the king Ahasuerus, to lay hand on such as sought their hurt: and no man could withstand them; for the fear of them fell upon all people.

9:3   And all the rulers of the provinces, and the lieutenants, and the deputies, and officers of the king, helped the Jews; because the fear of Mordecai fell upon them.

9:4   For Mordecai was great in the king's house, and his fame went out throughout all the provinces: for this man Mordecai waxed greater and greater.

9:5   Thus the Jews smote all their enemies with the stroke of the sword, and slaughter, and destruction, and did what they would unto those that hated them.

9:6   And in Shushan the palace the Jews slew and destroyed five hundred men.

9:7   And Parshandatha, and Dalphon, and Aspatha,

9:8   And Poratha, and Adalia, and Aridatha,

9:9   And Parmashta, and Arisai, and Aridai, and Vajezatha,

9:10 The ten sons of Haman the son of Hammedatha, the enemy of the Jews, slew they; but on the spoil laid they not their hand.

9:11 On that day the number of those that were slain in Shushan the palace was brought before the king.
9:12 And the king said unto Esther the queen, The Jews have slain and destroyed five hundred men in Shushan the palace, and the ten sons of Haman; what have they done in the rest of the

king's provinces? now what is thy petition? and it shall be granted thee: or what is thy request further? and it shall be done.

9:13 Then said Esther, If it please the king, let it be granted to the Jews which are in Shushan to do to morrow also according unto this day's decree, and let Haman's ten sons be hanged upon the gallows.

9:14 And the king commanded it so to be done: and the decree was given at Shushan; and they hanged Haman's ten sons.

9:15 For the Jews that were in Shushan gathered themselves together on the fourteenth day also of the month Adar, and slew three hundred men at Shushan; but on the prey they laid not their hand.

9:16 But the other Jews that were in the king's provinces gathered themselves together, and stood for their lives, and had rest from their enemies, and slew of their foes seventy and five thousand, but they laid not their hands on the prey,

9:17 On the thirteenth day of the month Adar; and on the fourteenth day of the same rested they, and made it a day of feasting and gladness.

9:18 But the Jews that were at Shushan assembled together on the thirteenth day thereof, and on the fourteenth thereof; and on the fifteenth day of the same they rested, and made it a day of feasting and gladness.

9:19 Therefore the Jews of the villages, that dwelt in the unwalled towns, made the fourteenth day of the month Adar a day of gladness and feasting, and a good day, and of sending portions one to another.

9:20 And Mordecai wrote these things, and sent letters unto all the Jews that were in all the provinces of the king Ahasuerus, both nigh and far,

9:21 To stablish this among them, that they should keep the fourteenth day of the month Adar, and the fifteenth day of the same, yearly,

9:22 As the days wherein the Jews rested from their enemies, and the month which was turned unto them from sorrow to joy, and from mourning into a good day: that they should make them days of feasting and joy, and of sending portions one to another, and gifts to the poor.

9:23 And the Jews undertook to do as they had begun, and as Mordecai had written unto them;

9:24 Because Haman the son of Hammedatha, the Agagite, the enemy of all the Jews, had devised against the Jews to destroy them, and had cast Pur, that is, the lot, to consume them, and to destroy them;

9:25 But when Esther came before the king, he commanded by letters that his wicked device, which he devised against the Jews, should return upon his own head, and that he and his sons should be hanged on the gallows.

9:26 Wherefore they called these days Purim after the name of Pur. Therefore for all the words of this letter, and of that which they had seen concerning this matter, and which had come unto them,

9:27 The Jews ordained, and took upon them, and upon their seed, and upon all such as joined themselves unto them, so as it should not fail, that they would keep these two days according to their writing, and according to their appointed time every year;

9:28 And that these days should be remembered and kept throughout every generation, every family, every province, and every city;

and that these days of Purim should not fail from among the Jews, nor the memorial of them perish from their seed.

9:29 Then Esther the queen, the daughter of Abihail, and Mordecai the Jew, wrote with all authority, to confirm this second letter of Purim.

9:30 And he sent the letters unto all the Jews, to the hundred twenty and seven provinces of the kingdom of Ahasuerus, with words of peace and truth,

9:31 To confirm these days of Purim in their times appointed, according as Mordecai the Jew and Esther the queen had enjoined them, and as they had decreed for themselves and for their seed, the matters of the fastings and their cry.

9:32 And the decree of Esther confirmed these matters of Purim; and it was written in the book.

10:1 And the king Ahasuerus laid a tribute upon the land, and upon the isles of the sea.

10:2 And all the acts of his power and of his might, and the declaration of the greatness of Mordecai, whereunto the king advanced him, are they not written in the book of the chronicles of the kings of Media and Persia?

10:3 For Mordecai the Jew was next unto king Ahasuerus, and great among the Jews, and accepted of the multitude of his brethren, seeking the wealth of his people, and speaking peace to all his seed.

****

Did you notice the emphasis on the eunuchs? Did you notice how eunuchs were instrumental in the story and events taking place in the book of Esther?

The book of Esther reveals how all the Jews in the empire were going to be wiped out. Mordecai asked Esther to go to the King and intervene. This act of courage and heroism could have cost Mordecai and Esther their lives and they both knew that. It also shows how Mordecai became second in command under the King. Esther exposed Haman's treachery against the King's interests as well as his manipulation of the King to act out his own corruption and jealousy.

**It is evident Mordecai and Esther
saved the seed of Abraham,
which later came to bless all of God's people of the earth.**

Do you have an ear, are you listening?

A feminine gay man and his daughter prevented the annihilation of the Jews as a race. We would not have the Bible or salvation today if not for the heroism of a feminine gay man and his daughter. The nation of Israel wouldn't have come into existence without the intervention of Mordecai and his daughter Esther.

Genesis 12:2
*12:2 And **I will make of thee a great nation,** and I will bless thee, and make thy name great; and thou shalt be a blessing:*

Genesis 22:18
*22:18 And **in thy seed shall all the nations of the earth be blessed;** because thou hast obeyed my voice.*

Genesis 18:16
18:16 And the men rose up from thence, and looked toward Sodom: and Abraham went with them to bring them on the way.

18:17 And the LORD said, Shall I hide from Abraham that thing which I do;

*18:18 Seeing that Abraham shall surely become a great and mighty nation, **and all the nations of the earth shall be blessed in him?***

*18:19 For I know him, that he will command his children and his household after him, and they shall keep the way of the LORD, to do justice and judgment; **that the LORD may bring upon Abraham that which he hath spoken of him.***

These eunuchs were obviously what we today call the Lgbt community. Eunuchs wouldn't have been any different from the gays of today. They were men and women with husbands and wives of the same gender. They would have had children and families. Eunuchs had the tasks of every day work and life and the joys of social and family love and respect on every level. They were people who had positions as high ranking military officers for the King's armies, judges, religious figures, etc., These positions would not have been given to a class of people that society looked down on in any way.

As intertwined as church and government was in Mordecai's time and the nation of Israel back then the church would not have frowned on them in any manner. They would not have been cast out of their own families or harassed in public places or oppressed. They would not have been victims of hate crimes, lost jobs, or been mistreated in the work place. They would not have been denied civil and human rights that all others in ancient times received. I could go on and on but I think you get the point.

Deuteronomy 23:1 states that a castrated male could not come into the congregation of God. Because of his physical defect and because he would have been viewed as unclean according to the old law covenant. This scripture is talking about a man who is literally castrated. The only castrated men among God's people would have been those rescued from prostitution as children. Or those from pagan nations who converted their religion and moved to live among God's people. Or those visiting from other nations.

Keep in mind if any of God's people took part in any kind of castration they would have been given a death sentence by stoning. They would not have lived to go to church to worship, act as judges, lead armies, provide personal care to the King's wives, or act as church leaders.

Let's be realistic here. If you were castrated as a child and forced into prostitution wouldn't you rather live among a nation, society, and religion where such practices were forbidden and illegal? I know I would. Keep in mind our Heavenly Father told the nation of Israel over and over to go to these pagan nations and rescue the young male prostitutes.

Our Heavenly Father detested these nations and their practices more than all others. Our Heavenly Father told Israel to rescue the male temple prostitutes. He told them to tear down the temples, and kill and disperse the inhabitants of the towns, cities and the nation in it's entirety. God's purpose for killing and dispersing the inhabitants of these nations was to prevent these practices from starting up again in the region of His Israelite children. God did not want these practices anywhere near His precious Israelite children.

These socially labeled eunuchs were in every part of society. They were parents active in family life, served as judges, and were regular church goers, etc. As a matter of fact any person eunuch or otherwise, would have been regarded as an upstanding member of their communities in order to have the positions in church and government that they held. The majority of these eunuchs would have been married. Back in Biblical times if you wanted sex you were required to marry first. Sex before marriage was a death sentence. Stones were everywhere and those generations were more than happy to start throwing them. They would have been married to people of their same gender.

1 Corinthians 7:36 38
7:36 But if any man think that he behaveth himself uncomely toward his virgin, if she pass the flower of her age, and need so require, let him do what he will, he sinneth not: **let them marry.**

7:37 Nevertheless he that standeth stedfast in his heart, having no necessity, but hath power over his own will, and hath so decreed in his heart that he will keep his virgin, doeth well.

7:38 So then he that giveth her in marriage doeth well; but he that giveth her not in marriage doeth better.

1 Timothy 4:2
4:2 **Speaking lies in hypocrisy;** *having their conscience seared with a hot iron;*

4:3 **Forbidding to marry,** *and commanding to abstain from meats, which* **God hath created to be received with thanksgiving of them which believe and know the truth.**

4:4 For **every creature of God is good, and nothing to be refused,** *if it be received with thanksgiving:*

*4:5 For it is sanctified by the **word of God** and prayer.*

Promiscuous sexual behavior was a sin back then and still is today. God's people were instructed to keep themselves free from sexual sin. If you were single and had sexual desires, to keep yourself from engaging in sexual sin or worse, you were advised to marry. Of course remaining single and keeping control of your sexual desires has always been advised in the scriptures as your best choice.

1 Corinthians 7:6-9
*7:6 But I speak this by permission, **and not of commandment.***

7:7 For I would that all men were even as I myself. But every man hath his proper gift of God, one after this manner, and another after that.

*7:8 I say therefore to the **unmarried** and widows, It is good for them if they abide even as I.*

*7:9 But if they cannot contain, **let them marry: for it is better to marry than to burn.***

1 Corinthians 7:32-37
*7:32 But I would have you without carefulness. **He that is unmarried** careth for the things that belong to the Lord, **how he may please the Lord:***

*7:33 But **he that is married** careth for the things that are of the world, **how he may please his wife.***

*7:34 There is difference also between a wife and a virgin. **The unmarried woman careth for the things of the Lord,** that she may be holy both in body and in spirit: but she that is **married careth for** the things of the world, how she may please **her husband.***

7:35 *And this I speak for your own profit; not that I may cast a snare upon you, but for that which is comely, and that ye may **attend upon the Lord without distraction.***

7:36 ***But if any man think that he behaveth himself uncomely** toward his virgin, if she pass the flower of her age, and need so require, let him do what he will, he sinneth not: **let them marry.***

7:37 *Nevertheless **he that standeth stedfast** in his heart, having no necessity, but hath power over his own will, and hath so decreed in his heart that he **will keep his virgin, doeth well.***

God does not ask more of us than we can handle. He expects us to be obedient. But of course not everyone is designed the same. Some can live a life of celibacy without any problem in total peace. Some of us have higher libidos than others and could not live a life of celibacy. Yet, our Heavenly Father expected all of mankind to remain obedient to His Word. God made it quite clear if a person wants sex they should marry. This included eunuchs then and now.

You're probably asking yourself what happened? Your probably wondering why so many people feel the way they do about gay, lesbian, and transgender people today? Your probably wondering how gays, lesbians and transgenders went from being loved and highly respected to loathed and hated? Who has convinced the majority of people to strip away all civil and human rights from God's gay, lesbian, and transgender children? As God is my witness we will get to that.

THE REAL TRUTH BEHIND
SODOM AND GOMORRAH

For generations false Bible teachers have blamed open gay people for the events that took place in Sodom and Gomorrah over 5000 thousand years ago. I cannot count the number of times I have turned on the television and found today's Bible teachers standing before a pulpit with their arm in the air, fist clenched and screaming about today's open gay people and Sodom and Gomorrah. They accuse today's open gay people of being a part of, and living like, the characters of Sodom and Gomorrah. These false Bible teachers have exhausted themselves in an attempt to make today's open gay people look like rapists, child molesters and all around monsters. Let's take a look at what really happened over 5000 years ago in the story of Sodom and Gomorrah. It is an especially important event to reconsider. Considering today's open gay people are accused of the same lifestyle and behavior.

STORY OF SODOM AND GOMORRAH

Genesis 18:20-33

*18:20 And the LORD said, Because the cry of Sodom and
        Gomorrah is great, and because their sin is very grievous;*

*18:21 I will go down now, and see whether they have done
       altogether according to the cry of it, which is come unto me;
       and if not, I will know.*

*18:22 And the men turned their faces from thence, and went toward
       Sodom: but Abraham stood yet before the LORD.*

*18:23 And Abraham drew near, and said, Wilt thou also destroy the
       righteous with the wicked?*

*18:24 Peradventure there be fifty righteous within the city: wilt thou
       also destroy and not spare the place for the fifty righteous that
       are therein?*

*18:25 That be far from thee to do after this manner, to slay the
       righteous with the wicked: and that the righteous should be
       as the wicked, that be far from thee: Shall not the Judge of all
       the earth do right?*

*18:26 And the LORD said, If I find in Sodom fifty righteous within
       the city, then I will spare all the place for their sakes.*

*18:27 And Abraham answered and said, Behold now, I have taken
       upon me to speak unto the LORD, which am but dust and
       ashes:*

*18:28 Peradventure there shall lack five of the fifty righteous: wilt
       thou destroy all the city for lack of five? And he said, If I find
       there forty and five, I will not destroy it.*

*18:29 And he spake unto him yet again, and said, Peradventure
       there shall be forty found there. And he said, I will not do it*

for forty's sake.

18:30 And he said unto him, Oh let not the LORD be angry, and I will speak: Peradventure there shall thirty be found there. And he said, I will not do it, if I find thirty there.

18:31 And he said, Behold now, I have taken upon me to speak unto the LORD: Peradventure there shall be twenty found there. And he said, I will not destroy it for twenty's sake.

18:32 And he said, Oh let not the LORD be angry, and I will speak yet but this once: Peradventure ten shall be found there. And he said, I will not destroy it for ten's sake.

18:33 And the LORD went his way, as soon as he had left communing with Abraham: and Abraham returned unto his place.

Genesis 19:1-29
19:1 And there came two angels to Sodom at even; and Lot sat in the gate of Sodom: and Lot seeing them rose up to meet them; and he bowed himself with his face toward the ground;

19:2 And he said, Behold now, my lords, turn in, I pray you, into your servant's house, and tarry all night, and wash your feet, and ye shall rise up early, and go on your ways. And they said, Nay; but we will abide in the street all night.

19:3 And he pressed upon them greatly; and they turned in unto him, and entered into his house; and he made them a feast, and did bake unleavened bread, and they did eat.

19:4 But before they lay down, the men of the city, even the men of Sodom, compassed the house round, both old and young, all the people from every quarter:

19:5 And they called unto Lot, and said unto him, Where are the men which came in to thee this night? bring them out unto us, that we may know them.

19:6 And Lot went out at the door unto them, and shut the door after him,

19:7 And said, I pray you, brethren, do not so wickedly.

19:8 Behold now, I have two daughters which have not known man; let me, I pray you, bring them out unto you, and do ye to them as is good in your eyes: only unto these men do nothing; for therefore came they under the shadow of my roof.

19:9 And they said, Stand back. And they said again, This one fellow came in to sojourn, and he will needs be a judge: now will we deal worse with thee, than with them. And they pressed sore upon the man, even Lot, and came near to break the door.

19:10 But the men put forth their hand, and pulled Lot into the house to them, and shut to the door.

19:11 And they smote the men that were at the door of the house with blindness, both small and great: so that they wearied themselves to find the door.

19:12 And the men said unto Lot, Hast thou here any besides? son in law, and thy sons, and thy daughters, and whatsoever thou hast in the city, bring them out of this place:

19:13 For we will destroy this place, because the cry of them is waxen great before the face of the LORD; and the LORD hath sent us to destroy it.

19:14 And Lot went out, and spake unto his sons in law, which married his daughters, and said, Up, get you out of this place; for the LORD will destroy this city. But he seemed as one that mocked unto his sons in law.

19:15 And when the morning arose, then the angels hastened Lot, saying, Arise, take thy wife, and thy two daughters, which are here; lest thou be consumed in the iniquity of the city.

19:16 And while he lingered, the men laid hold upon his hand, and upon the hand of his wife, and upon the hand of his two daughters; the LORD being merciful unto him: and they brought him forth, and set him without the city.

19:17 And it came to pass, when they had brought them forth abroad, that he said, Escape for thy life; look not behind thee, neither stay thou in all the plain; escape to the mountain, lest thou be consumed.

19:18 And Lot said unto them, Oh, not so, my LORD:

19:19 Behold now, thy servant hath found grace in thy sight, and thou hast magnified thy mercy, which thou hast shewed unto me in saving my life; and I cannot escape to the mountain, lest some evil take me, and I die:

19:20 Behold now, this city is near to flee unto, and it is a little one: Oh, let me escape thither, (is it not a little one?) and my soul shall live.

19:21 And he said unto him, See, I have accepted thee concerning this thing also, that I will not overthrow this city, for the which thou hast spoken.

19:22 Haste thee, escape thither; for I cannot do anything till thou be come thither. Therefore the name of the city was called Zoar.

19:23 The sun was risen upon the earth when Lot entered into Zoar.

19:24 Then the LORD rained upon Sodom and upon Gomorrah brimstone and fire from the LORD out of Heaven;

19:25 And he overthrew those cities, and all the plain, and all the inhabitants of the cities, and that which grew upon the ground.

19:26 But his wife looked back from behind him, and she became a pillar of salt.

19:27 And Abraham gat up early in the morning to the place where he stood before the LORD:

19:28 And he looked toward Sodom and Gomorrah, and toward all the land of the plain, and beheld, and, lo, the smoke of the country went up as the smoke of a furnace.

19:29 And it came to pass, when God destroyed the cities of the plain, that God remembered Abraham, and sent Lot out of the midst of the overthrow, when he overthrew the cities in which Lot dwelt.

Notice not even ten righteous men were found in the entire District not even ten. There would have been tens of thousands or millions of people living in this area but not even ten were considered righteous by God. Our Heavenly Father found only Lot to be righteous enough to spare from Sodom and Gomorrah's destruction. Why is that?

As you can see the people of Sodom and Gomorrah were horrible. They were corrupt in every way. Had the young and old men who were surrounding Lot's house been able to get in they would have raped the young visitors as well as Lot. Let's face it considering the number of men around the house Lot and his visitors would have been brutally rapped to their death. It sounds like this behavior was a common thing in Sodom and Gomorrah as well as the entire region. This atrocious lifestyle and behavior was too well orchestrated and massive for it to have been the first time these kinds of horrendous rapes took place in Sodom and Gomorrah. The scriptures point out that our Heavenly Father could hear the cries coming from Sodom and Gomorrah all the way up into Heaven.

Brothers and sisters did you notice throughout the entire recorded documentation of Sodom and Gomorrah, not once were the people of the region, or the men around Lot's house ever referred to as Eunuchs? It is logical to believe all kinds of men were involved in this type of behavior at the time. Because this was a form of sexual entertainment for them. It is likely many of these men had wives and children at home. One thing we do know is the Bible writer made a special point NOT to refer to these people as eunuchs when he recorded the events of Sodom and Gomorrah. That could not have been a mistake. Perhaps he was trying to protect the innocent eunuchs of that day or perhaps he was trying to protect open gays of today. Why haven't religious leaders shared this knowledge with the generations of past and present? Were they and are they trying to hide this fact from us?

Considering this sexual violence took place at night throughout the cities, the scriptures suggest that secrecy, or being "in the closet" was involved here. When these men of Sodom and Gomorrah were finished gang rapping their victims, when their sexual violence was over, obviously they had homes they returned to. It is only logical there were wives and children waiting for them there with fresh baked bread and a glass of wine etc. No doubt their wife's had to have asked, "Honey, where have you been all night?" It is hard to realistically believe he said to his wife, "Oh, out gang rapping young boys."

Not once are these men identified by the Bible writers of that time as eunuchs or as any specific sexual orientation. Yet, all throughout the scriptures open gay people are clearly identified as eunuchs. It really wasn't necessary because this was a story about homosexual rape and God has shown us how he feels about that. Notice the story was about the violation of rape as a sex crime, not about a mutual loving act of sexual intimacy, such as a marriage between two people of the same gender. This was a story about massive wide spread gang rape that huge numbers of men took part in on a regular basis. Remember our Heavenly Father said He could hear the cries coming from Sodom and Gomorrah in Heaven prior to sending the angels who were posing as young boys.

This was an entire region of people who were without sexual boundaries or sexual morality of any kind. This was a society where anything sexual was accepted, encouraged and tolerated. This is why the Bible writer did not label these men. Their sexual immorality and violence encompassed both perceived heterosexual, bisexual, and open homosexual men and only God knows what else. The reason I included "heterosexual" is because many of these men would have been viewed socially as such. This Sodom and Gomorrah event looks a lot like the world we live in today. Straight men marrying women and having families while gang raping young boy's and men and sexually pleasing other straight men in public restrooms and rest areas after dark in secrecy. King Solomon said, "there is nothing new under the sun."

All Bible scripture is written to make you think and reason and to teach a lesson. There is a lesson in the story of Sodom and Gomorrah. I hope you received the lesson. No rape of any kind is tolerated by our Heavenly Father.

DO YOU HAVE AN EAR, ARE YOU LISTENING?

BEFORE ANYONE STARTS THROWING STONES AT TODAYS CLOSETED AND STRAIGHT COMMUNITY, LET ME SET SOMETHING STRAIGHT.

There is not one person alive today who is responsible for what happened 5000 years ago in Sodom and Gomorrah. Not one heterosexual, straight, closeted, or openly gay person alive today is responsible for those atrocious events. Not one of us were there. The entire purpose of the destruction of Sodom and Gomorrah was to show mankind how God felt about sexual violence, rape, gang rape, and wide spread corruption. It was not to gang up on or attack any group of straight men, bisexuals or open gay people in today's world.

Modern Bible teachers are the ones who have twisted the meaning of that event to exclusively attack God's open gay children. Every straight preacher I had ever meet when I was younger was all fired up to council me about being openly gay. They would go on and on about what a terrible sin it was to be openly gay. While at the same time making a special effort to let me know gay sex in the dark behind closed doors was the way to handle it. All the while assuring me that this is how all men handle being gay, winking, smiling, grabbing my leg etc. I can assure you if our Heavenly Father could hear the cries coming from Sodom and Gomorrah, He could definitely heard me setting things straight with the last straight preacher who tried to council me on the proper way to be a straight guy. Our Heavenly Father has stated over and over how much He hates a lair.

Destroying Sodom and Gomorrah was a good thing even for us today. Scripture shows these people didn't know God and that's why they had grown to become so corrupt. Let's keep in mind Sodom and Gomorrah were not totally occupied by homosexuals and bisexuals. If heterosexual Lot and his wife lived there it is only logical to believe other heterosexual people lived there as well. Other scriptures in the Bible show Sodom and Gomorrah were beautiful places full of water ways, farming, commerce and trade. Keep in mind God couldn't find ten men righteous enough to save the region over only Lot and his family. If you read further in the Bible on your own you will also find Lot's family had been badly influenced from living in such a corrupt place for so long.

Further Reference
(Ge.13:10-13)(Ge.19:33)(Jude7)

Now here are some details that man has not been aware of for generations. There were eunuchs (or gays) all over the earth at the time when the people of Sodom and Gomorrah were having their hey day and when they were destroyed. If God was out to destroy people for being gay or (eunuch) for their sexual orientation he would have destroyed every city, every country side and town. Or God would have targeted just the eunuchs as a whole and yet he did not. Remember heterosexual and perceived heterosexual people lived in Sodom and Gomorrah as well and were destroyed right along with the others. If God hated homosexual relationships as he does rape He would have made an example out of the eunuchs at that time, not just the gang rapists of Sodom and Gomorrah.

OUR HEAVENLY FATHER
DID NOT AND HAS NOT
TO THIS DAY, SAID SUCH A THING,
OR USED LGBT PEOPLE EXCLUSIVELY
IN SUCH A STORY OR BIBLE EVENT.

The story and lesson of Sodom and Gomorrah was in regard to rape and gang rape of every kind regardless of sexual orientation.

Why was **everyone** destroyed?

Why was the **entire region** destroyed?

The entire region and everyone in it were destroyed because God held all of them responsible. Because most were involved and others tolerated the behavior. Did you notice in the Sodom and Gomorrah story that God felt only Lot was righteous? Did you notice Lot's entire family was spared because of Lot's righteousness? Do you remember in the beginning of the story Lot was standing at the entrance of the city in order to protect travelers from getting gang raped? God saw Lot's heart. My question to you is, Did you see it? God has destroyed multitudes of people and entire regions over rape and gang rape. Rapists and gang rapists are rampant in today's world, heterosexual's, perceived heterosexual's and open gay's, this has become common world wide.

Do you have an ear, are you listening?

This angel is telling me that today's rapists believe they are damned by God for their same gender attraction. They believe they will be destroyed come judgment day regardless so what does their sexual behavior matter. Hopefully at the end of this Bible revelation their hearts will be changed and they will receive salvation and ever lasting life. If their hearts do not change then they know where they stand with God. Their eternal death is by their own free will and conscious choice.

God's anger was directed at the abundant corruption and sin in general as well as all the sexual violence. The people of Sodom and Gomorrah; eunuch, heterosexual, bisexual were all running wild completely out of control. That entire region had become so out of control that these types of horrendous crimes were taking place on a regular basis. These cities would have been corrupt from city leaders all the way down to common folk just like today's world is.

Today's false Bible teachers have said the story of Sodom and Gomorrah was a lesson for all open gay people. As we all know the only time this story is brought up is when they are talking about the open gay population. Let me be the one to say the words: The story of Sodom and Gomorrah is a lesson for all mankind, for each person, whether he or she is heterosexual, openly gay or in between. There's no way today's Bible teachers didn't know the accuracy of that story all these years.

For thousands of years eunuchs lived perfectly happy and respectable lives before and after the destruction of Sodom and Gomorrah. At the time of Sodom and Gomorrah's hey day and destruction people of the earth knew why that region had been destroyed. There were few people on the earth at that time compared to today's world and in those days news traveled fast. The scriptures said God could hear the cries from Sodom and Gomorrah all the way up in Heaven. You can bet the known world at that time heard the cries as well. Keep in mind the destruction of Sodom and Gomorrah was a stage and lesson for the world then and now.

It is my opinion that the translation of the word eunuch had become lost over many generations. Did you know the word homosexual was created in the late 1800's by a doctor to define what a gay person was. The word did not exist before that. In 200 years from now will anyone remember what the word "gay" meant? I have no idea what gay people were called prior to the late 1800's in English cultures. Of course "Spirit and the Flesh" by Walter Williams gives that information about other cultures. A host of other publications also include that information far to many to mention here.

Now that we have set things straight on the Sodom and Gomorrah issue, why have modern Bible teachers come down so harshly and treacherously on **open** gay people, and singled them out as horrible unforgivable sinners for so long?

WHO'S OUT TO HURT GOD'S LGBT CHILDREN?

Some Bible teachers have a lot of God's love and understanding while others are without God's love and understanding altogether. God's wisdom and reasoning powers are not something you can attain on your own by your own efforts. All the Bible and university or seminary training in the world will not educate a person in the reasoning powers that understanding "God's Word" requires.

Understanding the Word of God is a gift from God. Yes I said a gift. The scriptures are designed by God to be that way. I have always felt this has been God's way of protecting His people from Satan's followers. Don't misunderstand me I am an advocate for all the Bible training a person can get in a lifetime. But I cannot count the number of Bible teachers (and when I say Bible teachers I mean any Priest, Pastor, clergy, Bible teacher, or church leader, etc.) that I have met who have had an enormous amount of formal Bible training and education, who I felt did not know God or really understand His Word.

Some of these Bible teachers do love God. They want to know the Word of God with all their hearts. They have worked very hard at that goal yet they do not have understanding. Does God love them? Yes. Will they have God's undeserved kindness, salvation and everlasting life? Yes. God judges a man by his heart not his education or lack of it. Bible understanding is a gift from God and only God. Of course one needs to open a Bible and start reading to get the gift. One does not get the gift in bars, at sports activities, or while drinking alcohol or using drugs. As a matter of fact from what I have seen many people don't receive the gift of understanding when reading the Bible. If your heart is right God will give you the gift of understanding.

Brothers and sisters prior to Oct. 30,1996 I was one of those people. My knowledge of the Bible was completely average. Much of it was over my head. Most of the knowledge I had was nothing more than head knowledge most of it did not reach my heart. When this angel came to me on Oct. 30, 1996 and blessed me with this revelation I am sharing with you now he gave me incredible clarity and understanding that I never had before.

That clarity and understanding has not left me. I knew a lot about God's Word more than many people but nothing like now. I am being guided by that same angel right now as I am writing. This level of Bible clarity and understanding is way beyond what I had before. I am not so bright or intelligent that I could do what I am doing now on my own. I have always considered myself to be below average on the scale of intelligence and I still do. I cannot take any of the credit for this revelation you are reading.

Today's Bible teachers are but mortal men like the rest of us. They are full of sin and imperfection just like the rest of us. Let's keep in mind they didn't know what I am teaching them now about these generations of eunuchs. But I must say to be a man or woman in charge of guiding people to salvation as Bible teachers are many have been reckless. To read the story of Sodom and Gomorrah and a scripture that says: " It's a sin for a man to lie with another man," and walk away with the kind of sermons I have heard on radio and television over my lifetime I am disappointed in them and heartbroken. Heartbroken over their lack of love and tenderness towards open gay people as well as the entire body of Christians world wide.

I am heartbroken over all the open gay people who have gone to their death beds believing God hated them for something they never chose and couldn't change. I am heartbroken over all the lives lost over so many years as a result of a deliberate attack against God's open gay, lesbian, and transgender children. Through Bible teachers exaggeration and twisting of God's Word they have misrepresented God's Word and claim that God said things **that God did not say**.

I've watched Bible teachers shake their fists, tremble, scream at the top of their voice, stomp their feet, point their fingers, and wave their arms accusing today's open gay people of the same behavior that happened in Sodom and Gomorrah. I have heard them tell gay people that same destruction awaits them if they do not turn heterosexual. They have spent much time and energy telling openly gay people if they don't change their ways and become heterosexual today they are going into a burning hell for eternity. They have accused openly gay people of trying to destroy American families undermining the Christian community, etc. They have become obsessed with telling openly gay people God hates them and advising all Christians to do the same. This is not Biblical and it is not God's personality.

Our Heavenly Father did not say these things!

Let's go to God and find out what He has said on the subject of these kinds of church leaders and Bible teachers.

Acts 20:28 - 30
*20:28 **Take heed** therefore unto yourselves, and to all the flock, over the **which the Holy Ghost hath made you overseers,** to feed the church of God, which he hath purchased with his own blood.*

20:29 For I know this, that after my departing shall grievous wolves enter in among you, not sparing the flock.

20:30 Also of your own selves shall men arise, speaking perverse things, to draw away disciples after them.

Ezekiel 22:26-28
22:26 Her priests have violated my law, and have profaned mine holy things: they have put no difference between the holy and profane, neither have they shewed difference between the unclean and the clean, and have hid their eyes from my sabbaths, and I am profaned among them.

*22:27 Her princes in the midst thereof **are like ....wolves ravening the prey, to ....shed blood**, and to........ **destroy souls, to get dishonest....... gain.***

22:28 And her prophets have daubed them with untempered morter, seeing vanity, and divining lies unto them, saying, Thus saith the Lord GOD, <u>when the LORD hath not spoken</u>.

In these scriptures Bible teachers are instructed by God to attend to the flock, God's children. Yet, God points out they will behave like oppressive wolves handling God's children without tenderness while twisting scriptures and Bible events. They will single out certain types of sinners and various groups of God's children and attack them like a pack of wolves. Our Heavenly Father warns that the guardians of the flock will take God's Word and create violence with it like wolves tearing prey. They are destroying the souls of God's openly gay, lesbian, and transgender children for **unjust personal gain**. These Religious leaders are without respect for God or God's precious openly gay children. They sacrifice God's flock in their attempt to **impress the masses.**

Keep in mind brothers and sisters more congregation members means more money, more clout and more prestige. Preaching against openly gay people is an example of human vanity at the cost of so many lives. The lives of God's precious openly gay children. You can take it from this Bible teacher these preachers knew and know full well what they were and are doing. Whatever it takes to bring in that money! They are nothing more than business men and corporate preachers with a greed for wealth and power at any cost!

Stay clear of them!

Additional Reference
(Eze.22:25-31)(Job13:1-5)(Jer.5:21-26)(Ac.20:25-30)(2Co.11:12-15)(2Th.2:6-12)(Ro.1:21-28)(2Pe.2:19-21)(Ps.7:14-16)(Mt.10:5-18)

This revelation from God that I am presenting in this book will bring those false Bible teachers and their financial empires bought by the souls of so many of God's righteous openly gay children to ruin before our very eyes.

1 Timothy 4:1-3
4:1   Now the Spirit speaketh expressly, that in the latter times some shall depart from the faith, **giving heed to seducing spirits, and doctrines of devils;**

4:2 **Speaking lies in hypocrisy;** *having their conscience seared with a hot iron;*

4:3 **Forbidding to marry,** *and commanding to abstain from meats, which God hath created to be received with thanksgiving of them which believe and know the truth.*

Job 13:4+5
13:4 **But ye are forgers of lies, ye are all physicians of no value.**

13:5 **O that ye would altogether hold your peace! and it should be your wisdom.**

Exodus 23:7+8
23:7 **Keep thee far from a false matter; and the innocent and righteous slay thou not: for I will not justify the wicked.**

23:8 **And thou shalt take no gift: for the gift blindeth the wise, and perverteth the words of the righteous.**

2 Peter 2:1-3

*2:1 But there were **false prophets** also **among the people,** even
as there shall be false teachers among you, who privily shall
bring in damnable heresies, even denying the Lord that bought
them, and bring upon themselves swift destruction.*

*2:2 **And many shall follow their pernicious ways; by reason of
whom the way of truth shall be evil spoken of.***

*2:3 And through covetousness shall they **with feigned words make
merchandise of you: whose judgment now of a long time
lingereth not**, and their damnation slumbereth not.*

Well, I think I covered that issue! We'll let God deal
with those false Bible teachers as God has instructed us to do.

Satan uses people to attack God's children

Ephesians 6:10-13
*6:10 Finally, my brethren, be strong in the Lord, and in the power
of his might.*

*6:11 **Put on the whole armour of God, that ye may be able to stand
against the wiles of the devil.***

*6:12 For we wrestle not against flesh and blood, but against
principalities, against powers, against the rulers of the
darkness of this world, **against spiritual wickedness in high
places.***

*6:13 **Wherefore take unto you the whole armour of God, that ye
may be able to withstand in the evil day, and having done all,
to stand.***

How clear was that! God shows mankind who's calling the shots in today's world and who the ruler of today's world really is. Don't be deceived. Satan uses people and our own human weaknesses against us causing us to fall from obedience and stumble in our walk with God.

I listened to a "so called Christian brother" speaking recently. He said: " I hate all these spicks, niggers and faggots! I think they should all be hung! God hates all these spicks, niggers and faggots too! God is going to destroy all of them. I don't want them in my town, in my church, or in my neighborhood. I don't want to work with them or sit next to them in a restaurant and I don't want them around my children! I am sick and tired of hearing these people wine and cry about having equal rights, and faggots wanting to marry each other. Jesus Christ! They are always demanding all kinds of special treatment. These spicks, niggers, and faggots or gays or whatever they call themselves have been shoving this crap down our throats for years now and I'm sick and tired of it!"

I stood there listening to this man spew, huffing and puffing, nostrils flaring in his rage. I truly believe he had more that he wished to share. I felt he was actually trying to hold back. As he was speaking I was thinking about all the married women and the hand-full of men that I knew he had slept with over the years and I knew this for a fact. I couldn't help but notice how impressed so many of the so-called Christian brothers and sisters were by his performance.

I walked away thinking, "What a side show. What a performance. What a grand illusion of Christianity and heterosexuality." Oh, How impressed the majority were. Many of the people had such admiration over his performance. As I looked into the eyes of his audience you would have thought they were listening to God. I could hardly believe the praise and admiration in their eyes as they stood staring at their icon a macho, Christian, and heterosexual man. Or so they thought.

I walked away thinking I wouldn't trade all the lack of respect, lack of equal rights, lack of so called "right skin color," or all the sexual perfection in the world to stand in that mans shoes before God.

If God judges a man by his heart a man would be better off with all his sin and sexual imperfections standing before God than that man will be. Sadly, the world is full of these kinds of people and so are the churches. Stay away from lovers of hatred. Have nothing to do with them because their hatred will infect you.

Romans 2:1
2:1 Therefore you are inexcusable, O man, whosoever you are that judge: for wherein you judge another, you condemnest thyself; for you that judge do the same things.

Matthew 6:14+15
6:14 For if ye forgive men their trespasses, your Heavenly Father will also forgive you:

6:15 But if ye forgive not men their trespasses, neither will your Father forgive your trespasses.

1 John 4:1
4:1 Beloved, believe not every spirit, but try the spirits whether they are of God: because many false prophets are gone out into the world.

I think these scriptures pretty much speak for themselves. Isn't it interesting how Romans 2:1 points out that many will judge and condemn others for the very same things they are doing in secret. We are to forgive **all** those who trespass against us. We are not perfect. We want man as well as God to forgive us for our bad behavior and mistakes. Please do not believe any Bible teacher until you can prove their teachings to be accurate through your careful review of scripture. If you are suspicious of a Bible teacher's teaching, if it doesn't sound forgiving and loving, if it contradicts what you already know to be truth you know where to start reading. **The Bible.** I think we have heard enough of how false teachers have abused God's Word and God's openly gay, lesbian, and transgender children. Let's move foreword.

God's blessings in this revelation just keep getting better and better. Now that we know how the views on eunuchs have changed over the years, I think its time we looked further into the scriptures. Let's see how God felt about the eunuchs of ancient times, and feels about gays, lesbians, and transgender people of today. Now let's turn our attention to the compassionate, forgiving, loving, and righteous openly Lgbt children of God.

Additional Reference
(Mt.6:9-34) (Mt.7:1-29)

WHY ARE LGBT PEOPLE.........LGBT?

For many generations people of every sexual orientation have pondered over this perplexing question. Generations of medical doctors and psychiatrists have made this question their life's work. Many have believed a same gender attraction is a choice as if someone just wakes up in the morning and decides to be gay, lesbian, or transgender for the rest of their lives.

Unfortunately the "Who can I hate next?" Christian mentality that dominates today's world has made being openly gay or being a loved one of an openly gay person very heartbreaking and difficult. Bible teachers have told generations of gay people to just give it up or take up baking for women or playing more football for men.

Generations of Bible teachers have told openly gay people they are disgusting and an abomination before our Heavenly Father. They have been told our Heavenly Father hates them for their same gender attraction. They have been told they will burn in hell for eternity just to mention a few **straight out lies**.

Considering all these myths, straight out lies, misguided theories, and misguided opinions, openly gay people and their loved ones have been bombarded with much heartache.

Unfortunately, all this unfounded information, lies and lack of understanding has made living an openly gay life all but unbearable for many over the generations. Many openly gay people have been made to believe these things are true. Many learn to hate themselves from a very young age. This can also cause much self loathing resulting in sexual disorders, depression, drug and alcohol abuse, and even suicide, common among our openly gay people. These past generations of gay people have found the world to be very unloving in regard to them. I think it is always best to look and see how our Heavenly Father feels about Lgbt people and stick to what He has to say on this issue as well as all issues.

Here at Matthew 19:12 we find Jesus giving instruction to His disciples as He explains why eunuchs are eunuchs, or why Lgbt people are Lgbt.

Do you have an ear, are you listening?

Matthew 19:12
For there are some eunuchs, which were so born
from their mother's womb:
and there are some eunuchs, which were made
eunuchs of men:
and there be eunuchs, which have made
themselves eunuchs
for the kingdom of Heaven's sake.

He that is able to receive it, let him receive it.

Lets take a very close look at this scripture.

Here Jesus is telling the Pharisees, His disciples
and a great crowd that some eunuchs
WERE BORN
eunuchs.(or Lgbt)

Here Jesus is stating eunuchs (or Lgbt people) were born this way from their mothers womb. I wish I had been told this by a competent adult or Bible teacher when I first came to verbalize I had "a same gender attraction" when I was a boy of fourteen years old. I guess that explains why most of us knew that we had a same gender attraction at 3, 4, or 5 years old. Even at that age it was written in our hearts that we were to be with the same gender and yet we knew nothing about sex. This also proves being gay is a mental state not a sexual state. Oh, how I wish people could understand that! When so many heterosexual women and straight men meet or see a openly gay person all they can think about is sex, sex, sex! Many think that is all that we are about. The fact of the matter is sex is all that they are about.

Here at Matthew 19:12
Jesus is also telling them that some eunuchs
<u>WERE MADE THAT WAY BY MEN.</u>

<u>Made that way by men</u> which means: by castration, molestation or forced prostitution in other nations in ancient Biblical times. Many people have experienced abusive childhoods or abusive relationships in adult life preventing them from feeling safe with the opposite gender ultimately preventing sexual intimacy. When the scripture says that eunuchs were " <u>made that way by men</u>," it also means: a person became eunuch or Lgbt as a result of a literal castration or social conditioning. Some Lgbt people were and are forced into sex as children and as adults, therefore victims of people lacking natural affection, including parents or other family members. Environment can play a powerful influence over a persons sexual orientation. Notice: in Matt.19:12 Jesus says: <u>they were made that way.</u>

Keep in mind I am always using the male form as the Bible does in this revelation.

(this includes both male and female here as always)

Here at Matthew 19:12 Jesus is also telling them that

SOME MADE THEMSELVES EUNUCHS

Jesus stated here that some have made themselves eunuchs meaning: some choose to be eunuchs to better serve our Heavenly Father. This would be a Lgbt person who chose a life of honesty in regard to their sexual orientation not living in secrecy. An honest life before God and man to better devote their life in honesty to God.

Notice Jesus stated they did it "for the Kingdom of Heaven's sake." We cannot ignore that all throughout the scriptures we are reminded how much God hates a liar. We cannot ignore the fact that this part of Matthew 19:12 states that honesty is in conjunction with the "sake of Heaven" or salvation.

This could also be a bisexual person who chose to live an open gay life keeping them from sexual promiscuity. Because their sexual attraction leaned more towards their own gender. This is referring to a person with a same gender attraction living an honest authentic life before God and man which we are all instructed to do. These types of people <u>do not choose a same gender attraction</u>, they only have the option to choose to be honest about it.

Notice at Matt.19:12 Jesus is giving instruction to the eunuchs, His disciples, and the large crowd. Teaching them how to stay out of sexual promiscuity and other sexual sin and how to remain faithful within God's law covenant in regards to marriage and sex.

The label "eunuch" has never had anything to do with celibacy. The definition of the label "eunuch" does not apply to heterosexual people in any way or any form. This label would not include a celibate heterosexual person. The Bible only uses the label "eunuch" when referring to a person with a same gender attraction. **Jesus is not** talking about a heterosexual, homosexual or lesbian person who chooses celibacy as a life style.

In this section of the Bible Jesus is talking about God's original state of perfection in the beginning and how eunuchs became eunuchs:

Gender, **in the beginning**
Marriage, **in the beginning**
and Divorce**, in the beginning**..................and how to remain obedient, and stay out of sexual sin.

Jesus makes it very clear to us at Matt. 19:12

* Some gay people **are born gay**.
* Some gay people **are made that way by other people.**
* Some gay people **choose to live a gay life,** to live an authentic life in harmony with the spirit God gave them.

**<u>The definition of the label eunuch is: a person who has a
same gender attraction.</u>**

- Whether Lgbt people chooses a life of marriage and sex, or a life of celibacy, they are in ancient Biblical terms still considered a eunuch.
- If your sexual attraction is for your own gender you are a eunuch or Lgbt.
- In Biblical times if your sexual attraction was for the same gender you were considered a eunuch.
- If you are heterosexual and refrain from using your sexual organs because you can not find a partner this does not make you a eunuch.
- If you are heterosexual and abstain from sex for any reason you are not a eunuch.
- What defines a persons sexual orientation is their sexual identity.
- Sexual orientation is a mental state of mind, an innate sexual identity.

A persons sexual identity is something designed at conception or designed by social conditioning in childhood and in other stages of our lives. We do not get the luxury to choose this ourselves. God has designed our minds for survival and has created an instinct to pursue a life of happiness. When we have been put into unnatural situations such as in the hands of an evil person or a dysfunctional parent these situations can change who we are. For example:

- A son who is raised by a mother who hates men and is full of anger for men causes her son to believe he is not worthy of love from a woman. These males often feel more comfortable with those of their own gender.

- A daughter who is raised by a father who hates women and is full of anger for women causes his daughter to believe she is not worthy of love from a man. These females often feel more comfortable with those of their own gender.

- A son who has a physically or emotionally abusive mother grows up to fear women and will feel safer with those of his own gender.

- A daughter who has a physically or emotionally abusive father grows up to fear men and will feel safer with those of her own gender.

- If a young male or female is molested by a person of their same gender this can make a young person believe that is who they are. They will identify themselves as such from that time on into adulthood.

- If a young male or female is molested by someone of the opposite gender it can be so disturbing to the mind that their view of heterosexuality is altered for life making them draw towards a same gender when it comes to sex and intimacy.

In my lifetime I must say that I feel most people are gay, lesbian, and transgender because they have developed a hatred and distrust towards the opposite gender. If you think I'm wrong just listen to a group of gay or straight men talk about women when there are no women around. Just listen to a group of lesbians talk about men when there isn't any men around. The level of hatred and despise is absolutely disturbing. These types of examples are endless I could go on and on for pages. The point is some are made Lgbt by conditioning after being born heterosexual.

Yes, parents can change the sexual orientation of their children if they are dysfunctional enough. However, I do not believe most parents are aware of the power they have in this area and don't do this on purpose The first instinct a parent has when they find out one of their children is gay is to blame themselves. That instinct is there for a reason. This is there conscience speaking to them. Not every gay person is born gay, many are "made that way by other men." (or women)

As for you gay and lesbian people who are thinking, "Yeah, yeah, my mother or father made me this way," and are thinking of giving one of your parents a call to share this with them, don't even think about it. Allow me to remind you of one of God's commandments, "Thou shall honor thy parents." It does not say, "Thou shall honor thy parents unless thy parents are imperfect." There is not one parent out there who would not like to go back and raise their children over again. Making all the wrongs right and correcting all their imperfections now that they are more experienced with life and older and wiser.

Unfortunately our Heavenly Father has not given any of us that luxury. God expects you to forgive your parents for all their imperfections just as you expect the same from them. You do not know what they have had to deal with and overcome in their childhoods. You only saw the best they had to offer you when you were growing up. I also want you to keep in mind that some people's best looks better than others.

However, do call your parents and invite them out to lunch. During the entire lunch tell them how much you appreciate all the sacrifices they made for you. Tell them how grateful you are for all they went without to provide for you. Tell them how much you appreciate all the hours, days, weekends, and years they dedicated to the raising of you. Putting you first in their lives and putting themselves last. Tell them how much you love and appreciate them and all that they did for you. Love can heal a multitude of mistakes, wounds and imperfections.

As for you parents out there who are gasping for air, clutching your chests, and blaming yourselves, because one of your children are Lgbt you need to forgive yourselves. Our Heavenly Father has not given you the luxury to go back and do it over again. Also keep in mind Jesus said: many gay, lesbian, and transgender people are born that way.

However, call your Lgbt child and invite them out to lunch and all the while tell them how proud you are of them. Tell them how much you accept their honest hearts regarding their sexual orientation and tell them you love them. Love can heal a multitude of mistakes, wounds and imperfections.

I highly doubt that any gay person or parent of a gay person could ever pin point exactly how they became gay. A person could go their entire life without ever having sex yet, they would know without question whether they were attracted to men, or to women, or to both. Just think about a teenager who is still a virgin, it is often obvious to them and everyone around them which gender they are lusting over. Unless they are in the closet and hiding their true sexual desires.

**As King Solomon said:
"there is nothing new under the sun."**

Remember, our Heavenly Father's state of perfection **in the beginning** was intercourse between a married male and female. <u>Jesus is not implying here that anyone can choose their sexual orientation.</u> Sexual orientation is not something anyone gets to choose contrary to popular modern beliefs.

**The label eunuch does not
describe people who choose a life of celibacy.**

A heterosexual or a eunuch could have chosen a life of celibacy. The label eunuch used in the Bible refers to Lgbt people only, a specific sexual orientation. Anyone in Biblical times could have chosen a life of celibacy and would not have been labeled for it. This has been a huge misconception in today's world.

"There is nothing new under the sun."

Do we today label people who are temporarily not having sex? NO, of course not and neither did people of ancient times. If you have been taught that a eunuch was a person who chose a life of celibacy by cutting off their penis you have been lied to. Celibacy is a gift that God has provided for all His earthly children. Some make this choice for a lifestyle and some do not.

God never instructed anyone to cut off their penis or testicles for any reason.

Again read Deuteronomy 23:1

No one who has been castrated may enter the assembly of the LORD this is an abomination.

As I have pointed out in Deuteronomy 23:1 of the Old testament God says it is "an abomination," and people were put to death for it. The only time it happened was when men were castrating little boys for prostitution in pagan nations. A celibate person could be a person of any orientation, heterosexual, homosexual, or lesbian, etc. These people were not labeled for a celibate lifestyle in ancient Biblical times and are not labeled today. Many people who choose a celibate lifestyle live happy successful lives in peace with their celibacy and live in obedience before God.

The Catholic church is a perfect example of what happens when a sexual person tries to live a life unnatural to the spirit that God gave them. The generations of millions of victims are more than enough proof of that. They are a living example of what happens when man goes against the spirit God gave him. God created most people to be sexual. The Catholic priests and nuns have been trying to claim this "name in Heaven" for generations. Because they have been deceived into believing eunuchs were celibate people. The "name in Heaven" simply does not belong to them and never has. Unless they have a same gender attraction of course and are in line with what God considers to be obedient.

If you have a same gender attraction and you are molesting children this "name in Heaven" does not pertain to you, whether Catholic, Protestant, Baptist, or whatever. These kinds of crimes against God, against children, against nature, and against society are way outside of the lines of obedience.

The Catholic priests and nuns teach the myth that eunuchs were celibate, they give the illusion they are celibate, and claim this "name in Heaven." The priests and nuns know full well this "name in Heaven" does not belong to them. They have been deceived and many deceive themselves. The millions of victims the Catholic church has violated is proof of that. The trillions of dollars the Catholic church has in the bank and holds on to so diligently and uses to protect these monsters with contribution money is proof of that. Many have financially supported crimes against children and support the harboring of child molesters. This is despicable in the eyes of our Heavenly Father. It has not gone unnoticed.

Our Heavenly Father will not excuse your deception, ignorance or complacency. He will not excuse your love for your religion. Our Heavenly Father gave each one of you a brain, a heart, and the power of reason and he expects you to use it. If you choose not to use the gifts God gave you, you have made your choice before God. Do keep in mind, not every Priest is a child molester. Not every Nun has turned a blind eye to child molestation. Many Priests and Nuns are celibate and that is perfectly fine. Let me also state; many denominations are guilty of these same atrocities. To wrap this up this "name in Heaven" the Bible speaks of is not referring to celibates. The label "eunuch" means: a person sexually attracted to their own gender.

The Catholic church and their "so called celibates" are a perfect example that most people are created to be sexual. I could go on and on but I will spare you all that ugliness. Just watch the news and observe their abominations before our Heavenly Father and the world.

Remember brothers and sisters everyone has a sexual orientation. Most of mankind are sexual and have a strong sex drive this is natural and the way God created mankind to be. Some people are only a little sexual with almost no desire for sex at all and yet some " A" sexual people still identify themselves as gay because their sexual attraction is for their same gender.

Regarding a same gender attraction Jesus said:

- **They were born that way.**
  Because it was written in their hearts at conception.

- **They were made that way by other men.**
  Because of child prostitution and social conditioning.

- **Some choose it for the kingdom.**
  Because they choose a life of honesty about their sexual orientation.

These people with a same gender attraction still deserve God's blessings of sex, love, companionship, tenderness, joy, fun, intimacy, marriage, children, etc. God did not provide these blessings for only the heterosexual people.
Don't ever let one of them tell you that again!

- Don't forget these eunuchs had all their sexual organs and most would have been sexual people.
- At the time Jesus made this statement eunuchs were already marrying those of their same gender.
- Eunuchs in Biblical times were parents of biological and adopted children.
- Many eunuchs did not have a choice whether to live a heterosexual or gay life style. In remote areas then and now Lgbt men and women were and are forced to procreate to preserve their villages or tribes.
- Jesus knew they were not suddenly going to change their orientation.

- Jesus had the power to change them at that time and chose not to. He left them in the Lgbt state they were in.
- If Jesus could raise the dead and heal the sick He could have turned Lgbt people heterosexual at the blink of an eye yet, He chose not to.
- Eunuchs were Lgbt people and Jesus gave them the same instruction on obedience as He did the heterosexual people.
- Jesus knew eunuchs were Lgbt people and He did not expect eunuchs to be with the opposite gender regarding intimate relationships.
- Generations of men and women and their victims are proof of how destructive it can be for mankind to live a life against the sexual spirit God gave them.

I KNOW EVERY LGBT PERSON ON THE PLANET JUST UNDERSTOOD WHAT JESUS SAID HERE.

I am praying the heterosexual people do as well.

Do you have an ear, are you listening?

Brothers and sisters did you comprehend all that? There is a wealth of information in those verses.

- **Jesus said, <u>some were born that way.</u>**
  That would mean this was God's plan for them. No one chooses to have a same gender attraction.
- **Jesus said, <u>some were made this way by other men.</u>**
  Through molestation, prostitution, abuse from the opposite gender, social conditioning etc. No one chooses to have a same gender attraction.
- **Jesus said, <u>some choose it for the kingdom of Heaven sake.</u>** A true authentic life of honesty. No one chooses to have a same gender attraction.

The ancient term eunuch refers to a person who did not use his or her sexual organs in a heterosexual or procreative way.
A eunuch was a person with a same gender attraction.

The boys who were literally castrated for prostitution would not have necessarily been gay prior to their castration. Keep in mind many of these boys were royalty and citizens from defeated nations. Some boys would have been chosen for their prettiness and attractiveness. Castrating a child would change a child's sexual orientation. If a boy were heterosexual before he was castrated, he would have become gay after a period of time, he would have identified himself as gay, because of the life he was forced to live. Considering he was used for same gender prostitution as a child.

These boys were castrated at puberty or before and used for sex. In most cases these boys would have become gay because gay sex would have been all they knew and experienced. These literally castrated boys would have identified themselves as eunuch, or as a woman trapped in a mans body, and likely been transgender considering these boys would have been forced to cross dress for their clients.

Furthermore, their inability to perform heterosexual intercourse, or to reproduce, would have ruined their chances for a heterosexual life in ancient times considering reproduction was so vital and necessary. The twisted, demonic, sick perverts that did this to them knew this. Be advised most of these eunuchs would have only lived a short time in most cases. They would have died from sexual disease and sexual abuse very quickly.

If you are naive enough to think this only happened thousands of years ago and doesn't happen anymore, I recommend you take a good look at society among males in America, South America, the Middle East, Asia, Europe etc. Although castration has become banned in the world today modern child molesters are still here actively seeking new boys to turn gay for their violent and perverted appetites. Most pedophiles identify and label themselves as "Straight."

If you are heterosexual and past the bloom of life and have lost your sex drive you are not a eunuch. If you were heterosexual before you lost your sex drive you still have the same orientation.

I hope I'm not making this complicated. Whatever the reason a person might have become a eunuch in Biblical times it is clear that God was not condemning of them.

If you are sexually attracted to your own gender you are a eunuch.

God made you this way for a reason.

This is God's plan for you and your orientation has a purpose.

Go in peace rejoicing.

Go in peace rejoicing.

Go in peace rejoicing.

How Does God Feel About Gay Marriage?

Preachers have claimed that our Heavenly Father and His son Jesus Christ are against gay marriage. They have exhausted themselves and spent huge amounts of money in their efforts to deny gay and lesbian people this blessing. They have repeatedly pronounced that gay marriage is absurd and completely against God's standards.

I would like to share a little Bible story with you about Jesus. Jesus lead a teaching giving instruction about marriage, regarding heterosexual, homosexual, and lesbian people of ancient Biblical times and those people of today. Jesus takes something the Pharisees said and leads the conversation right were He wanted it to go. In Matthew 19, Jesus prepares today's modern world for an earth shaking statement. Although this information was common knowledge at the time Jesus walked the earth it will shock and amaze today's world. Notice the beginning of the conversation posed to Jesus by the Pharisees.

Matthew 19:3-5
*19:3 The Pharisees also came unto him, **tempting him,** and saying unto him, Is it lawful for a man to put away his wife for every cause?*

*19:4 And he answered and said unto them, Have ye not read, that he which made them **at the beginning** made them **male** and **female**,*

*19:5 And said, For this cause shall a man leave Father and mother, and shall cleave to his wife: and they twain **shall be one flesh?***

Notice how odd it is that the Pharisees asked Jesus a question about divorce and Jesus answered by bringing up male and female in the beginning. Here Jesus is answering the Pharisees and giving council to the disciples and the large crowd at the same time. Jesus is stating the fact that God created male and female to be together **in the beginning.** Remember now the Pharisees asked a question about divorce. Keep in mind the Pharisees were constantly looking for ways to stumble Jesus in His teachings. The Pharisees were jealous of Jesus and relentlessly sought to harm and kill him. Notice the Pharisees chose this subject to try to cause Jesus to stumble in His teachings.

Notice Jesus has now brought up the subject of:

gender, **in the beginning,**
and responding to marriage and grounds for divorce.

Matthew 19:9+10

19:9 And I say unto you, Whosoever shall put away his wife, except it be for fornication, and shall marry another, committeth adultery: and whoso marrieth her which is put away doth commit adultery.

*19:10 His disciples say unto him, If the case of the man be so with his wife, **it is not good to marry.***

Now the disciples are asking Jesus, "If people get divorced should marriage itself be avoided?" Wondering if they should avoid marriage and stay single because some marriages end in divorce. Jesus is still responding to the challenge made by the Pharisees and leading the Pharisees, the disciples, and the great crowd of people following Him right were He wants them. Keep in mind the subject of marriage and divorce had been well covered in the scriptures long before Jesus' ministry.

Jesus continues to teach on the subject of:

Gender,............... **in the beginning**
Marriage, ... **in the beginning,**
and, Divorce,...............**at the time of Jesus' ministry.**

Jesus responds at *Matthew 19:11*
But he said unto them, All men cannot receive this saying, save they to whom it is given.

What did Jesus say here? "Save they to whom it is given" this means: only those with the gift of understanding, will understand what He is about to say.

Notice here Jesus is covering an age old subject. Why would anyone suddenly need a <u>gift</u> to understand an age old topic that had been around since Adam and Eve. This subject of divorce had been resolved by Moses for over a thousand years. Why would anyone suddenly need some kind of special **"gift of understanding"** about a subject that had already been covered many times and resolved for over a thousand of years?

Do you have an ear, are you listening?

Now remember the topic of conversation has not changed. Jesus is saying only those who have a special **"gift of understanding"** will understand what He is <u>about to tell them.</u> We all know that the Pharisees did not have the gift of understanding.

At Matthew 19:4 Jesus is speaking to all the people about marriage, gender in the beginning, and divorce. Jesus deliberately included the eunuchs in His instruction at Matthew 19:11. Jesus begins by stating only those with the "gift of understanding" would understand. Notice Jesus wasn't worried about the eunuchs, or disciples, or the majority of people in the crowd not understanding what He was about to say. He knew the eunuchs, and disciples, and many others in the crowd were going to get it, just like God and Jesus knows the majority of Lgbt people and others today will get it.

Matthew 19:11+12

*19:11 But he said unto them, **All men cannot understand** the*
*word of God, **therefore give these words to those with***
understanding.

19:12 For there are some eunuchs,
which were so born from there mother's womb:
and there are some, eunuchs,
made that way by other men:
and there are some eunuchs,
which have made themselves eunuchs
for the kingdom of God, for Heavens sake. Glorious is he who
understands the word of God, let him receive understanding.

Remember, the Pharisees originally asked Jesus a question about divorce. Jesus responded by making a statement that, **"In the beginning**, marriage was between a **male** and **female**." Then to conclude his answer he brings the eunuchs (or gays) into the topic of conversation. If the eunuchs did not have genitals, or have sex, or have marriages or divorces, or have the privileges of sex, marriage, and divorce, <u>Jesus would not have brought the multitude of eunuchs into this conversation,</u> and given the eunuchs instruction on:

gender,............ **in the beginning,**
marriage,......... **in the beginning,**
and divorce,........... **at the time of Jesus' ministry.**

If gender was not an issue worth bringing up, and if marriage and divorce was not something the eunuchs took part in, or something that did not involve the eunuchs, Jesus would not have brought them into the conversation. Nor, was Jesus expecting them to suddenly turn heterosexual. Nor, was Jesus going to suddenly turn them heterosexual, which Jesus had the power to do if He had chosen. Jesus raised the dead, healed the sick, made the blind see, made the lame walk, turned water to wine, etc. Had He felt the need to turn these gay and lesbian people heterosexual, He certainly could have and would have. It would have been easy for Him to do.

Matthew 13:9-19
13:9 **Who hath ears to hear, let him hear.**

13:10 And the disciples came, and said unto him, **Why speakes thou unto them in parables?**

13:11 He answered and said unto them, Because it is **given unto you** *to know the mysteries of the kingdom of Heaven,* **but to them it is not given.**

13:12 For **whosoever hath, to him shall be given,** *and he shall have more abundance: but whosoever hath not, from him shall be taken away even that he hath.*

13:13 Therefore speak I to them in parables: **because they seeing see not; and hearing they hear not, neither do they understand.**

13:14 And in them is fulfilled the prophecy of Esaias, which saith, **By hearing ye shall hear, and shall not understand; and seeing ye shall see, and shall not perceive:**

13:15 For this people's **heart** *is waxed gross, and* **their ears are dull of hearing, and their eyes they have closed;** *lest at any* *time they should see with their eyes and hear with their ears, and should understand with their heart, and should be converted, and I should heal them.*

13:16 **But blessed are your eyes, for they see: and your ears, for they hear.**

13:17 **For verily I say unto you, That many prophets and righteous men have desired to see those things which ye see, and have not seen them; and to hear those things which ye hear, and have not heard them.**

13:18 Hear ye therefore the parable of the sower.

13:19 When **any one heareth the word of the kingdom,** *and* **understandeth it not, then cometh the wicked one,** *and catcheth away that which was sown in his heart. This is he which received seed by the way side.*

Do you have an ear, are you listening?

Matthew 19:4

*19:4 And he answered and said unto them, Have ye not read, that he which made them **at the beginning** made **them <u>male</u> and <u>female</u>**,*

In Matthew 19:4 Jesus points out **in the beginning,** God created male and female for marriage and yet, at the time Jesus walked the earth things had changed. People of the same gender were marrying each other. **In the beginning,** God forbid divorce all together without exception. But, because the people complained so much because they were in unhappy marriages Moses allowed them to divorce. Moses with God's blessing made it become the law of the land after that. Yet, **in the beginning,** God forbid divorce for any reason.

Matthew 19:8

*19:8 He saith unto them, Moses because of the hardness of your hearts suffered you to put away your wives: **but from the beginning it was not so.***

Matthew 19:11

*19:11 But he said unto them, **All men cannot receive this saying, save they to whom it is given**.*

At Matthew 19:11 Jesus makes the eunuchs the focal point of His conversation pointing out again that things have changed from God's original state of perfection, regarding

<u>males and females in the beginning in regard to marriage.</u>

Jesus goes on in Matthew 19:12 to explain how that came to be. Some eunuchs were born that way, some eunuchs were made that way, and some eunuchs chose that way. In the verses prior to Matthew 19:12, Jesus is pointing out that the eunuchs are expected to uphold to the same standards of obedience as the heterosexual people were expected to live up to. You did not read at any point Jesus saying the laws on obedience had changed in any way for the eunuchs. When it came to sex, marriage, divorce, and obedience, all were held to the same laws, whether heterosexual or eunuch (gay).

If you are gay and you want sex you should marry. The laws about marriage and sex are the same for heterosexuals and gays and everyone in between. If these laws on marriage and sexual obedience were only for the heterosexual people, Jesus would not have brought the eunuchs into His instruction during His topic of,

**gender..... in the beginning,
marriage..... in the beginning,
and divorce..... in the beginning, and at the time of Jesus ministry.**

**Jesus brought the eunuchs into this conversation
for a purpose,
He wanted His statements about eunuchs
(or gays) on record for mankind <u>then and now</u>.**

Do you have an ear, are you listening?

There's no way Jesus would tell those gay people to be heterosexual. Jesus would not have brought the eunuchs into the conversation of;

gender.....in the beginning
marriage.....in the beginning
and divorce .....in the beginning

....if the eunuchs were not people who had such privileges.

Jesus gave them the same instruction as He gave the heterosexual males and females when it came to sex and marriage. Keep in mind Jesus was teaching His disciples at the same time as well as a huge crowd of people. The disciples knew a time was coming when they would go out to the world and teach without Jesus. Jesus was preparing them to do that.

There is no way Jesus would tell them to fake a heterosexual life, or heterosexual orientation, or to live a lie, not true to the spirit that God had put in them. Jesus would never instruct anyone to deceive themselves or their fellow brothers and sisters.

This is modern man's twisted and deceptive understanding. Jesus would not have set eunuchs up for a lifestyle of failure, frustration and deception. A lifestyle that many could not live up to or a life always sexually frustrated and unsatisfied. A life of depression, lying to oneself, and hiding the truth of ones own true spirit that God created in them.

There are many gay people who are not comfortable or capable of having sex with the opposite gender. Sex with the opposite gender is totally unnatural to them, just as unnatural as a heterosexual person having sex with someone of the same gender.

Some gay people are totally and completely gay. It is only logical that many of them were in ancient Biblical times. God created them this way and Jesus knew this. Jesus would not have asked them to live a life of lies and deception. This is totally against everything God stands for and Jesus knew that.

THERE IS NO WAY JESUS WOULD EVER ADVISE ANYONE TO LIVE A LIE IN ANY SITUATION!

I don't care what today's preachers have told you!

As you all well know it is today's preachers who are teaching a lie and encouraging others to do the same!

For generations false Bible teachers have encouraged men to live this deceptive lifestyle of keeping their same gender attraction secret. This is why public rest rooms and rest areas are full of straight men sexually pleasing each other after dark in secret. This is why married women for the last 20 years have been diagnosed with aids at the fastest rate. This kind of deception is of Satan not of God.

Jesus knew that many eunuchs were eunuchs at birth while others were made that way by men and still others chose it as an honest life-style for the sake of salvation. Jesus was telling the eunuchs they were expected to be in line with the same obedience and regulations when it came to sex, marriage and divorce just as the heterosexual people were.

- No fornication

- No adultery

- No lying

- No cheating

- No divorcing without just cause, etc.

**Jesus also instructed them to marry
if they were inflamed with lust.**

**Our Heavenly Father expects all of us to live a life of
obedience in spite of our sexual
imperfections or differences.**

Jesus did not need to say, "God created **male** and **female in the beginning**," if He was only giving instruction to the heterosexual people. Everyone knew it was Adam and Eve in the beginning. Jesus was deliberately trying to clear up this issue on behalf of the eunuchs of His day and the gays of today. The heterosexual people, and the eunuchs, and the disciples, and the great crowd, knew the laws on heterosexual marriage. It is quite possible the Pharisees were looking for a group to single out as terrible sinners to attack and oppress at that time. They were so corrupt. Do the Pharisees remind you of anyone today? They look very similar to many of today's Bible teachers to me.

The question was,

"How does God feel about gay marriage?

The answer is,
our Heavenly Father and His Son Jesus Christ
instructed Lgbt people to marry if they wanted sex.

For those of you who didn't understand this,
that's okay, pray to God for the gift of understanding.

Additional Reference
(Mt.19:9-17)(1Co.7:1-40)

Matthew 19:11
But he said unto them, All men cannot receive this saying, save
they to whom it is given.

GOD DOES HAVE A PLAN FOR US.

I think God's plan for us is too glorious for us to even begin to imagine. There have been times in history when it was a protection that not all people could understand God's Word. The scriptures tell us God will reveal more knowledge when the end is near. He instructed Daniel to write a book, and then instructed Daniel to seal it up for the time of the end, when the time is right.

THAT TIME IS NOW!

1 Corinthians 2:9+10
*2:9 But as it is written, **Eye hath not seen, nor ear heard,** neither have entered into the heart of man, the things which **God hath prepared for them that love him.***

*2:10 But **God hath revealed them unto us by his Spirit:** for the Spirit searcheth all things, yea, the deep things of God.*

Daniel 12:3
And they that be wise shall shine as the brightness
of the firmament; and they that turn many to
righteousness as the stars for ever and ever.

Daniel 12:4
But thou, O Daniel, shut up the words,
and seal the book, even to the time of the end:
"Many shall run to and fro, and knowledge shall be increased."

Additional Reference
(Mt.13:9-19)(1Jo.5:19+20)(Pr.1:1-9)(De.29:29)

We are living in the last days the Bible has spoken of for thousands of years. Let's face it this book you are reading, is full of an abundance of truth and Bible secrets, that the current world hasn't known for many generations. God has made it very clear to all people whether heterosexual or gay,

NO MARRIAGE, NO SEX.

If your state doesn't respect marriage get married before God. Your promise to God is greater than any promise to a church or state. No, you will not have the benefits that married heterosexual people have, but God will bless you, and make it up to you for your obedience. Please be intelligent and wise in marriage and love.

**Our Heavenly Father will change the hearts
of those who oppress us. Gay marriage will become legal
in America and many others nations
just be patient and wait on God's timing.**

God's greatest gift to mankind in this life is a happy marriage and children. The joys this kind of life has to offer are beyond words. All of the achievements one can accomplish in a life time will not compare to the simple joys of a happy marriage and the joys of raising children. Statistics repeatedly show this to be the case. Unfortunately, we are living in the last days and times are hard to deal with as the Word of God has foretold.

To often these dreams are shattered for many due to complicated people and complicated times. In spite of this our Heavenly Father recommends marriage to everyone who desires a life with sexual pleasure. Be wise in choosing a mate and be committed to your spouse for life. Use God's Word for direction. Divorce should be a last resort and only under extreme circumstances. Children are the most wounded in divorce and regardless of what you do you can not fix those wounds.

Don't marry for sex, money, social appearances or any of today's silly nonsense. The more you follow the ways of the world the more problems your going to have in all aspects of your lives. Marry someone deserving of you, someone who loves you, loves God and loves obedience. The scriptures are full of good instruction on choosing a good husband or wife. Don't be a complicated person and don't become complicated after you are married.

Our Heavenly Father has taught us a lesson about marriage through penguins. Some mate for life. They are simple and uncomplicated when it comes to a life long bond. Penguins are migratory birds. When migrating sometimes pairs get to far apart from each other and separate into different migratory patterns and loose each other for years. During their time apart they are always looking for each other. When they find each other again they do not hold a grudge against each other for getting separated and lost. They instantly forgive each other for loosing their way. As soon as they see each other again they both straighten their backs, lift their beaks straight up, and flap their flippers in excitement and both very loudly sing to the Heavens in joy. Penguins are uncomplicated and very forgiving of each other.

Yes, our Heavenly Father created mankind to be this simple, this uncomplicated, this loving and this forgiving. This is how we should be in marriage and in life. Our Heavenly Father didn't intend for only rocket scientists to have happy and successful marriages. Don't forget about the blessing of singleness God has provided for us.

Our Heavenly Father created us. He alone knows what is best for His earthly children. He put these laws in writing for mankind to maintain law and order in our lives and our societies. Our bodies were not designed to have sex at an early age. Our bodies were not designed to have sex with multiple partners. Our minds and bodies were designed to marry one person and have sex with that one person for a lifetime. This was for our mental and physical wellness. The marriage arrangement was designed for the well being of the children created by marriage.

There is nothing more heartbreaking for children than to experience the break up and separation of their parents. The mental and emotional pain and anguish of a child who is forced to be split up by parents causes damage to a child for a lifetime. Parents breaking the bond of marriage hurts children to the very inner core of their fragile hearts and it is not reparable. Divorce is the most unnatural and hurtful act of mankind I have ever seen. It deeply hurts everyone involved for a lifetime. Of course it is the treacherous acts of the parents that warrant divorce and these are treacherous times.

Our Heavenly Father has created all things to have perfect order. The stars shine in perfect order. The sun, moon, and the earth all move in perfect order. The earth doesn't move to fast or to slow. The sun rises and the sun sets in perfect order. The weather patterns on earth move in perfect order. The earth after all these years is still a beautiful garden. The wildlife on the planet function in perfect order. God gave the wildlife instinct to follow. Migratory birds for example do not need to be told when to fly south for the winter. Our Heavenly Father's wildlife moves in perfect order.

Jesus created mankind to function in perfect order. After creating Adam and Eve Jesus raised them from infancy. After raising them Jesus came each evening to teach them how to live a perfect life in perfect order. After they were deceived by Satan Jesus provided a book of instructions so we could live in perfect order and have harmony throughout our lives.

After thousands of years the stars are still shinning in perfect order. The sun, moon, and earth are still moving in perfect order. The sun still rises and the sun still sets in perfect order. The weather still moves in perfect order. The earth is still a beautiful garden. The wildlife is still functioning by instinct in perfect order.

The question I pose to you is, What happened to mankind. What has happened to us. Mankind moves further from order with each passing day. Why is mankind so out of order when everything else Jesus created is still moving in perfect order.

Here is the answer to that question. Mankind no longer knows God. Mankind no longer knows God's laws which are written in the Bible. Most people world wide today do not own a Bible. Most people today have never opened a Bible and have no idea what God's instructions are for mankind. Mankind today doesn't know right from wrong or truth from fiction. This will continue to be the case for the majority of mankind world wide. Fewer and fewer people will know or understand God's Word.

Be wise and stay as close to God's Word as you can. Be as obedient as you can. These are the last days and treacherous times are upon all of us. One reckless move in today's world could cost you your life because today's world has become so wicked. The majority of men, women, and children today are evil to the core. The majority of the worlds population will soon be destroyed for their wickedness and evil corrupt hearts.

Matthew 7:13+14
Enter you in at the strait gate: for wide is the gate,
and broad is the way, that leads to destruction,
and many there be which go in thereat:
Because strait is the gate, and narrow is the way,
which leads unto life, and few there be that find it.

Salvation or destruction is a choice that each person on the earth will make each day. Whichever choice you make you will reap the benefits and reward or the everlasting destruction.

Only you can make this choice.

Brothers and sisters
I know its hard to believe but God's blessings only get better and better in this revelation.

Let's continue with God's gift to the world.

BROTHERS AND SISTERS, YOU NEED TO VOTE

People who hate and disapprove of gays, lesbians, and transgender people are **voting**. People who single openly gay people out as the only sinners in the world are **voting**. This is why gay marriage is not legal in America. This is why we openly gay people have had to struggle for so long, to get the few human and civil rights that we have today.

I know many of you feel politicians are corrupt, are liars, only catering to the rich, promising to back gay issues, but never following through. This is all true. I have felt this way most of my life as well and for many years I did not **vote**. However, the only way you will be heard and have your agendas met is through the power of your **votes**. The only thing politicians care about is a **vote.** If you do not **vote,** they do not care about you or your issues. They are business men and women who are out to get rich and richer, not the sweet, humble, caring, and sensitive people they claim to be. They emulate all these characteristics to win **votes**. Politicians look at **vote**s like a drug addict looks at their drug. They care more about a **vote** than they do poverty, hunger, crime, gay rights, jobs, homelessness, etc. All of these things have already been proved to be the case.

Politicians send their people into cities ahead of them to find out what the **voters** in the next area are interested in. Notice I said the **voters** in the area. Then their people write and format speeches on those issues to win their **votes.** These politicians don't even know what their speech entails until they are on their way to the location. If their annalists come to your city and find gay **voters** are abundant, **as God is my witness**, their format and agenda, will be about gay issues, and the needs of gay people. Most of Americans do not **vote** for the reasons I have mentioned. Less than 20% of Americans

vote. Less than 20% of the population are calling all the shots for the entire country. (This does not include the Obama election, but of course that was a historical election.)

With this being the case it pushes many important issues under the rug in politics not only gay issues but many other important issues. Politicians cater first to the corporations that put them into office and everyone and everything else comes second if at all. By the time a politician's name or face ever comes to you in print or on television they have already accomplished their mission in life: to get rich. They have already been bought and sold by corporations in America and abroad.

Corporations know the best way to sway **votes** in America is to use the gay agenda as a platform. It works every time. Only in America does the hatred for openly gay, lesbian, and transgender people have this kind of power and influence over **votes**. American corporations are masters at manipulating the masses. Corporations could care less who is, and who is not gay, or what rights they do, or do not have. Why do corporations do this at the cost of so many of God's openly gay children? They do it for money due to an unnatural desire of greed.

The people who hate open gays are **voting,** and the rich are **voting**. Corporations are financially supporting these politicians and as you can see their needs and wants are met. The rich have become richer and the poor have become poorer. American corporations have benefited by the trillions. I cannot stress enough, "Go out and **vote**." Become informed and stay informed. Your **votes** do have power in this country and always will. Your power and confidence as an adult is by **voting.**

All corporations, companies, small businesses, unions, politicians etc. that do not support civil and human rights for gay people should be boycotted world wide for life. These politicians, corporations and their subsidiaries, their products and those who sell them, as well as their unions should be boycotted for life.

Churches who do not support all civil and human rights for open gay, lesbian, and transgender people should be boycotted world wide for life. Set up websites and agencies to monitor their dealings and list them accordingly, and stand behind your word, using your money and **votes** wisely. The only thing corporations and politicians and most churches care about is money. If you hit them in their bank accounts, you will suddenly become important to them, and not until then. It is my understanding all the bills passed in the House and Congress are designed and written by the worlds largest corporations. These bills are designed to be so wordy and lengthy, members of the House and Congress don't even read all of them before they pass them through.

If corporations are writing these bills who's interests are in those bills?

The days of oppressing, and using gay people as pawns in politics are OVER!

If gay people in America are ever going to obtain equal rights we can not ignore this reality. **And this is a reality.** I'm not just sitting here making these statistics up. Do your own investigation you will find I have only touched on this subject.

Openly gay, lesbian, and transgender people have been on this planet since the beginning of time and look at the state we are in today. If you are still waiting for the "all powerful and wonderful majority" to give it to you, you will never get it, you will be waiting forever. They have already proved that. The people doing the **voting** in this country have made their feelings about open gay people and **voting** direction quite clear.

Brothers and sisters,
get out and <u>vote</u> in every election and get your power back.

SOUND BIBLICAL REASONING

Was Jesus a eunuch?

No, Jesus was not a eunuch. For years many have speculated that Jesus was a eunuch, or gay, or had a secret female wife. There is not one scripture that validates that kind of thinking. There is not one scripture that classifies Jesus as a eunuch. Jesus would not have been classified as a eunuch in ancient times or today. He chose to abstain from sex to better serve the Lord. The scriptures do not mention any sex life for Jesus at all. If Jesus ever had any sexual experiences of any kind they are not mentioned in the scriptures. The scriptures do not mention a wife and therefore we can only conclude Jesus was a virgin.

The scriptures state that Jesus was without sin. The label eunuch was used to identify a person with a same gender attraction just as the label gay is used today. In Biblical times a heterosexual person who chose to abstain from sex for God or any other reason would have been classified as a regular guy. Because a heterosexual orientation is natural there was no need to label these people. These people would have been the majority so they did not need labels for the majority just like today's world.

My understanding is Jesus loved everyone male and female and did not act on any sexual feelings He may have had. It is only logical Jesus would have had a sex drive in His mortal body but he chose not to act on it. What his sexual orientation was on earth is currently unknown and has no importance. When we see Jesus again and we will, he will be a spirit person, an angel and angels are not sexual beings they do not reproduce.

If you are going to have a Bible discussion, or a Bible debate, you must stick to the scriptures. It is not wise to make more out of the scriptures or more out of Bible characters than what God has clearly presented. I find people tend to let their minds wander to far from what is written. This has hurt a multitude of people over history open gays for one example.

It is logical to believe Jesus would have had imperfections (or sins) while in his fleshly body. However the scriptures say he did not. To muse on or speculate on possible sins Jesus may have had would be very unloving for us to do. Jesus died a brutal death on a cross for our sins because he loves us like his own children. Jesus did the best he could do while on earth and completed his mission for our Heavenly Father on our behalf. To try to conjure up sins or imperfections of any kind in regard to Jesus would be brutally unloving. Jesus doesn't muse on or remember our sins so why wouldn't we return that same kind of love and respect for him?

For years the gay community has tried to identify King David and Jonathan as gay.

Of course I am the last person who can criticize anyone for wanting to find any shred of evidence about gay people in the scriptures. However, the scriptures do not mention homosexual behavior and King David or Jonathan together. The Bible does not label either one of them as eunuchs. Many men, heterosexual and gay, have friends they love like brothers and those men have never had sex together and never would. The kind of love that was between Jonathan and King David is not the kind of love you find with someone you are having an intimate relationship with.

The kind of love between two friends like Jonathan and King David is a brotherly love. If any of you have siblings you know that love is strong. This kind of friendship is even stronger than the love between siblings. This kind of friend ship is a gift from God. You are blessed if you have a friend you love this much.

The scriptures regarding King David and Jonathan do not prove King David and Jonathan were sexually involved with each other. Jonathan was more than thirty years older than David. Jonathan was a great warrior and David gained Jonathan's love and admiration after killing Golliath. King David and Jonathan went off to battle together many times in their lives. In these types of situations men do pour their hearts out to one another. Men who fight together are often very aware of their love and appreciation for each other, especially male friends who fought in war together. War is brutal and terrifying for men.

King David had many wives and he still lusted for other women so badly that he had Bathsheba's husband murdered in war in order to have her. **This was definitely a man who loved women.** Keep in mind at no time are either of them identified as a eunuch in scripture. Satan had not been cast down to the earth at that time and had not created the gay closet arrangement. Eunuchs or gay people were honored and respected in Biblical times. There was no need to fear being open about your sexual attraction in those days.

King David's lust for women was so intense that he committed murder to have another mans wife. His lust drove him to do something that horrible against God. A God who King David loved more than anyone or anything else.

King David's lust became so overpowering that he couldn't control himself anymore. This was definitely a man who developed a serious problem and like most mental and emotional problems it was expressed through destructive sexual behaviors. King David had many wives. Many wives were given to him. He had his choice of many woman. He may have become arrogant and haughty regarding his prowess and collection of women.

However, "There is nothing new under the sun." We cannot ignore today's military or the military of nations in history who nurtured and seduced younger men and boys during times of battle. I cannot ignore the nature of men I have seen in my 52 years of life either. It has been my experience that men who have abnormal heterosexual behavior like this also participate in homosexual sex. However, there is no Biblical proof that King David or Jonathan were sexually involved with each other or with any other men. I have found that the Bible does not beat around the bush when mentioning sexual activity regarding anyone.

Sexual promiscuity is a sign of an inner mental problem. Having sex with many people, with anyone at any old time, is always a red flag that a person does not respect their body or soul, or the bodies and souls of others. This kind of behavior is a form of sexual abuse. Abusive towards yourself and others. Genuine intimacy and love for other people means nothing to these types of people. They are looking for a fix like a drug addict. A fix to ease the pain that is going on inside of them like an addition. Women on the other hand give their bodies for sex due to their desperate desire to be loved. Most women do not have orgasms and therefore do not enjoy sex or have the sexual satisfaction that men do.

I must say I don't know what would be worse. Having the sexual libido that men do, or having the strong desire to be loved as women do. Both seem like a blessing and yet a curse at the same time.

However, God did use King David for a grand purpose. A fact that I have always found interesting and evidence of God's great love. The Bible has so many scriptures referring to the love King David had for our Heavenly Father. There are so many scriptures referring to all the love our Heavenly Father had for King David that I'm not going to show you any of them. They are to numerous to mention. This is something I will let you investigate on your own. If I were to start talking about the love between our Heavenly Father and King David this book would be 800 pages long.

What I will share with you is the tremendous love a person is capable of having for our Heavenly Father in spite of their many sins or imperfections. King David was proof of that. God is capable of having a tremendous love for someone with many sins or imperfections as well. God proves this when in spite of King David's sins and imperfections God still loved him tremendously.

That is good news for all of us heterosexual or gay. God can still love all of us in spite of all our sins. God welcomes our love in our imperfect and sinful state whatever our sins may be. It is also a testimony to show us that we should have that same unconditional love for others. A love that covers a multitude of sins, regardless of who we are, regardless of what we have done, regardless of our emotional and mental problems. Of course remorse and repentance should be a factor. A person who goes through life without any regard for their general, or sexual behavior, is not walking with God and you should keep yourself distant from these types and out of harms way.

I can not end this subject without clarifying that God **did** punish King David severely for what he did to Bathsheba's husband. This is proof that God will punish us for our sins right here and now if they are severe enough. God's grace and Jesus sacrifice does have their boundaries and limits as the story of King David makes very clear.

The moral of the story is:

- King David let lust get out of hand.
- King David manipulated his own thinking and power of reason to sin against God to get what he wanted.
- King David had a man murdered for lust.
- King David thought he could outsmart God by having someone else do the killing for him.
- God punished King David for what he did.
- King David lost the throne.
- King David's children fell into murder and sin over it.
- King David lived in caves for many years running for his life from his own son.
- King David asked for forgiveness for what he did and God did forgave him.
- King David loved God, and God loved him back.
- How loving is that?
- How loving are we?

I think this story of King David is a huge lesson for mankind today. How often do we manipulate our own reasoning abilities to have what we want. Do we manipulate ourselves when truth and reality is staring us straight in the face? Do we cheat a little here and lie a little there? Do we follow corrupt instructions from our bosses even when we know we are doing something corrupt or illegal? Do we place ourselves in sexual situations and tell ourselves, "Well it all just happened?" Just how much do we manipulate ourselves into believing it was out of our control? Do we really know what we are doing, and worst of all, do we try to pass that over God's head?

This story of King David shows us our Heavenly Father will not excuse this type of manipulative behavior or self manipulation. Most of all God will not tolerate His children trying to manipulate Him. God teaches us in this story of King David He will punish us <u>here and now,</u> for this kind of deception against ourselves and against Him.

Were King David and Jonathan gay lovers? It is highly unlikely yet we will never really know. **Nor, does it matte**r. King David and Jonathan will be resurrected and we will not ask them if it is true or false. Asking such a question of them will be inappropriate and unloving. All of their past behavior died when they asked our Heavenly Father to forgive them. Our Heavenly Father does not and will not remember their past imperfections or sins and neither should we.

For years the gay community has tried to identify Paul as gay.

There aren't any scriptures that refer to Paul as a eunuch. Paul often spoke about a thorn in his side. That thorn in his side could have been anything. A physical ailment or any multitude of things that could have bothered him. The scriptures tell us Paul was celibate. Paul stated himself that he was quite happy with his decision to be celibate. Throughout all the scriptures that Paul wrote, and they are many, Paul never once mentions any struggle with his sexual desires. As a matter of fact Paul makes it quite clear that he was very much at peace about his sexuality and decision to be celibate. Again, it does not matter whether he was or not. When Paul is resurrected we will not ask him because we will not care about such things at that time. Considering there isn't any Biblical evidence that Paul was gay it is best not to assume that he was. Let's always hope for the best in people even those who are now deceased.

A NAME IN HEAVEN

For many generations Bible teachers have said some of the most hurtful things about openly gay, lesbian, and transgender people. They have declared from the roof tops that God hates these people. They have lead others to believe if they want to remain in good standing before the congregations they must hate and despise these people as well. They have twisted scripture to back their personal hatred. Bible teachers have divided families and broken a multitude of hearts and are responsible for the spiritual and mortal death of many.

God's loving Words to Lgbt people were declared long ago by our Heavenly Father and His son Jesus Christ and His Bible writers. Today is the day of reckoning for our Heavenly Father. Today God's true feelings about Lgbt people will ring from the roof tops. Never again will Satan's followers be able to stand before any gay, lesbian, or transgender person, or congregation, and spew their nonsense with any kind of credibility. Today is God's day of reckoning with these false teachers who pretend to follow Christ. What a glorious day this is for all of God's children.

HALLELUJAH!

Just a reminder, all the scriptures used in this revelation are from the original Hebrew, Greek, and Aramaic manuscripts. The scriptures you have read till now, and will read throughout this revelation, are the first English translation of the original manuscripts. Before I introduce the following scriptures be advised the word "sabbaths" means: "all of God's commandments," including attending church on the sabbath. The word "sabbaths" encompasses all of God's instruction, commandments, and direction.

Let's start by reading Isaiah 56:1-8

Isaiah 56:1-8
*56:1 Thus saith the LORD, Keep ye judgment, and do justice: for my salvation is near to come, and **my righteousness to be revealed.***

*56:2 Blessed is the man that doeth this, and the son of man that layeth hold on it; **that keepeth the sabbath** from polluting it, and keepeth his hand from doing any evil.*

*56:3 Neither let the son of the stranger, that hath joined himself to the LORD, speak, saying, **The LORD hath utterly separated me from his people: neither let the eunuch say, Behold, I am a dry tree.***

*56:4 For thus saith the LORD unto the **eunuchs that keep my sabbaths, and choose the things that please me,** and take hold of my covenant;*

*56:5 **Even unto them will I give in mine house and within my walls a place and a name better than of sons and of daughters: I will give them an everlasting name, that shall not be cut off.***

*56:6 Also the sons of the stranger, that join themselves to the LORD, to serve him, and to love the name of the LORD, to be his servants, **every one that keepeth the sabbath from polluting it,** and taketh hold of my covenant;*

*56:7 **Even them will I bring to my holy mountain,** and make them joyful in my house of prayer: their burnt offerings and their sacrifices **shall be accepted** upon mine altar; for mine house shall be called an house of prayer **for all people.***

*56:8 The **Lord GOD,** which **gathereth the <u>outcasts</u> of Israel** saith, Yet will I gather others to him, beside those that are **gathered unto him.***

Notice in Isaiah 56:1-3 our Heavenly Father is instructing the eunuchs to live in righteousness and keep His commandments and to remain in obedience. Notice our Heavenly Father is speaking directly to the church leaders and congregations in regard to the eunuchs. These are God's Words, God's instruction, God's promises to the eunuchs, and the eunuchs only. In Isaiah 56:3 our Heavenly Father is stating that not one Preacher, not one church, and not one person, should deprive the eunuchs from worship or attending church services. Our Heavenly Father commanded His church leaders and followers that these are His blessings and promises to the eunuchs for eternity.

Isaiah 56:4 points out our Heavenly Father is speaking exclusively about the eunuchs. Our Heavenly Father is saying: "keep my sabbaths" which means: keep my commandments and remain pleasing in His eyes with worship, obedience, and righteousness.

Isaiah 56:4
For so saith the LORD unto the EUNUCHS,
that keep my sabbaths, and choose the things that
please me, and take hold of my covenant;

Isaiah 56:5
I will even give to them in my house
and within my walls a
MONUMENT AND NAME,
something better than
SONS AND DAUGHTERS.
A NAME TO TIME INDEFINITE
I shall give them, one that will not be cut off.

Isaiah 56:4+5 states that eunuchs who "keep my sabbaths" meaning those who choose to be obedient will be given a "name," in His house, in "Heaven." The word "place," in modern translations is, "monument," as well as the cross reference scriptures. The scriptures go on to state: "something better than sons and daughters." Now that you understand these promises from our Heavenly Father, I recommend that you go back and read Isaiah 56:4+5, again.

How long did God say?
"TO TIME INDEFINITE."

The reason eunuchs (or gays) were given this special name in Heaven, a name greater than son or daughter, and a monument in their honor to time indefinite, is because eunuchs (or gays) have an imperfection that many were born with. An imperfection that is beyond their choice. An imperfection beyond their control. Yet, eunuchs were and gays are expected to remain obedient regardless. This is an added burden that heterosexual people do not have to bear as they live throughout their lives. Our Heavenly Father knew this. That is why He has provided us with this special privilege of a name in Heaven greater than son or daughter, and a monument in Heaven in our honor to time indefinite. Our Heavenly Father is especially proud of His Lgbt children whom are obedient for this very reason. God's obedient gay, lesbian, and transgender children are an honor to Him, a cause for boasting, a reason for a myriad of angels to stand in applause.

Now that you know how the scriptures, the "Word from God," clearly shows the world how God really feels about Lgbt people, you can better understand why Satan has worked so hard against us. Satan spends his time tirelessly trying to destroy God's obedient heterosexual children. How much more so has he tried to stumble and destroy God's open Lgbt children. Our Heavenly Father will not let Satan harm us with a lightning bolt, or an earth quake, or to stand before us and physically harm us. God will not give Satan that kind of power over anyone. Satan can only get to us by way of his people, his followers, those who he has deceived with his lies. Satan has created many lies to destroy God's heterosexual and eunuch (Lgbt) children. The lie that God hates open Lgbt people is just one of many.

If you are having a vision of a Satanic cult with a fire burning in the back ground or a human sacrifice allow me bring you back to reality. Satan is far too intelligent for tactics as primitive as that. I suggest instead you envision a beautiful church. Beautiful church going people marching into churches, Bibles in hand, bumper stickers on cars, Jesus pins, and smiles on their faces. Making many pronouncements such as "Glory be to God," and "God bless us all," quoting scripture etc. This is where Satan's work is most productive. Our Heavenly Father has already warned us of Satan's tactics and how he deceives people to do his dirty work for him.

Satan's followers have already exposed themselves and the churches they worship in. Our Heavenly Father has already exposed these vicious, violent lovers of the lie to His obedient Lgbt children. Those whom have a name in Heaven and a monument in Heaven in their honor for eternity. These wolves cannot hide in sheep's clothing anymore. Our Heavenly Father has exposed them. Yet, I warn you to be cautious because Satan is relentless. He will find new tactics, new decoys, new ways to deceive God's children, by using his followers.

Now brothers and sisters I want to take a moment to pause here.

Do you have an ear, are you listening?

- Eunuchs were gay people.
- God said the eunuchs who are obedient shall have a name in Heaven.
- A name greater than son or daughter.
- To time indefinite.
- Does God love Lgbt people?
- YES HE DOES!
- Oh yes he does, and look how much he loves us.
- I want you to say out loud, "GOD LOVES ME!"
- Go ahead and say it 100 times out loud. I'll be happy to wait.

All these years we thought God had forgotten and forsaken us. We were told God hated us. Today God reveals He did not forget or forsake us. He shows us His Lgbt children are all over the Bible from Genesis to Revelation! Today we are told a truth that hasn't been heard for many generations. Today is our Heavenly Fathers day of reckoning on behalf of His eunuch (Lgbt) children before the world.

**Please take a moment
to thank our Heavenly Father.**

Matthew 10:5-18

*10:5 These twelve **Jesus sent forth, and commanded them,** saying, Go not into the way of the Gentiles, and into any city of the Samaritans enter ye not:*

10:6 But go rather to the lost sheep of the house of Israel.

*10:7 And as ye go, preach, saying, The kingdom of **Heaven is at hand.***

10:8 Heal the sick, cleanse the lepers, raise the dead, cast out devils: freely ye have received, freely give.

10:9 Provide neither gold, nor silver, nor brass in your purses,

10:10 Nor scrip for your journey, neither two coats, neither shoes, nor yet staves: for the workman is worthy of his meat.

10:11 And into whatsoever city or town ye shall enter, enquire who in it is worthy; and there abide till ye go thence.

10:12 And when ye come into an house, salute it.

10:13 And if the house be worthy, let your peace come upon it: but if it be not worthy, let your peace return to you.

10:14 And whosoever shall not receive you, nor hear your words, when ye depart out of that house or city, shake off the dust of your feet.

*10:15 Verily I say unto you, **It shall be more tolerable for the land of Sodom and Gomorrha in the day of judgment,** than for that city.*

10:16 Behold, I send you forth as sheep in the midst of wolves: be ye therefore wise as serpents, and harmless as doves.

10:17 But beware of men: for they will deliver you up to the

councils, and they will scourge you in their synagogues;

10:18 And ye shall be brought before governors and kings for my sake, for a testimony against them and the Gentiles.

Hebrews 10:19-26
10:19 Having therefore, brethren, boldness to enter into the holiest by the blood of Jesus,

10:20 **By a new and living way,** *which he hath consecrated for us, through the veil, that is to say, his flesh;*

10:21 And having an high priest over the house of God;

10:22 **Let us draw near with a true heart in full assurance of faith,** *having our hearts sprinkled from an evil conscience, and our bodies washed with pure water.*

10:23 **Let us hold fast** *the profession of our* **faith without wavering;** *for he is faithful that promised;*

10:24 **And let us consider one another to provoke unto love and to good works:**

10:25 **Not forsaking the assembling of ourselves together, as the manner of some is; but exhorting one another: and so much the more, as ye see the day approaching.**

10:26 **For if we sin wilfully after that we have received the knowledge of the truth,** *there remaineth no more sacrifice for sins,*

Isaiah 65:13-25
65:13 Therefore thus saith the Lord GOD, Behold, my servants shall eat, but ye shall be hungry: behold, my servants shall drink, but ye shall be thirsty: behold, **my servants shall rejoice,** *but ye shall be ashamed:*

*65:14 Behold, **my servants shall sing for joy of heart,** but ye shall cry for sorrow of heart, and shall howl for vexation of spirit.*

*65:15 And ye shall leave your name for a curse unto my chosen: for the Lord GOD shall slay thee, **and call his servants by another name:***

*65:16 That he who blesseth himself in the earth shall bless himself in the God of truth; and he that sweareth in the earth shall swear by the God of truth; **because the former troubles are forgotten, and because they are hid from mine eyes.***

*65:17 For, behold, I create new Heavens and a new earth: **and the former shall not be remembered, nor come into mind.***

*65:18 But **be ye glad and rejoice for ever in that which I create:** for, behold, I create Jerusalem a rejoicing, and her people a joy.*

*65:19 And I will rejoice in Jerusalem, **and joy in my people: and the voice of weeping shall be no more heard in her, nor the voice of crying.***

*65:20 There shall be **no more thence an infant of days,** nor an old man that hath not filled his days: for the child shall die an hundred years old; but the sinner being an hundred years old shall be accursed.*

*65:21 **And they shall build houses, and inhabit them; and they shall plant vineyards, and eat the fruit of them.***

*65:22 **They shall not build, and another inhabit; they shall not plant, and another eat: for as the days of a tree are the days of my people, and mine elect shall long enjoy the work of their hands.***

*65:23 **They shall not labour in vain,** nor bring forth for trouble; for they are the seed of the blessed of the LORD, and their offspring with them.*

*65:24 And it shall come to pass, **that before they call, I will answer;** and while they are yet speaking, I will hear.*

*65:25 **The wolf and the lamb shall feed together, and the lion shall eat straw** like the bullock: and dust shall be the serpent's meat. They shall not hurt nor destroy in all my holy mountain, saith the LORD.*

Genesis 8:19-22

8:19 Every beast, every creeping thing, and every fowl, and whatsoever creepeth upon the earth, after their kinds, went forth out of the ark.

8:20 And Noah builded an altar unto the LORD; and took of every clean beast, and of every clean fowl, and offered burnt offerings on the altar.

*8:21 And the LORD smelled a sweet savour; and the LORD said in his heart, **I will not again curse the ground any more for man's sake;** for the imagination of man's heart is evil from his youth; neither will I again smite any more every thing living, as I have done.*

*8:22 **While the earth remaineth, seedtime and harvest, and cold and heat, and summer and winter, and day and night shall not cease.***

Is it a sin to be LGBT?

This question has been debated and misunderstood for many generations by Bible teachers and common folk alike. I cannot tell you how many times I have asked open gay and lesbian preachers if a same gender attraction is a sin. They have all but held up a cross and stabbed me in the heart with a wooden stake to avoid answering that question. To this day not one gay or lesbian preacher has ever answered that simple question.

I can not tell you how many times I have asked that same question to straight mainstream preachers. Only to see them suddenly attain a gleam in their eyes and jump on a tangent blowing Bible scripture and God's Word way out of proportion.

Needless to say I am a preachers worst nightmare. When I ask one of them a question they better have an answer because I will turn them every way but loose until I get one. If they can't give me a concrete answer they better honestly tell me they simply don't know.

It is my understanding that open gay and lesbian preachers do not want to answer this question because they feel gay and lesbian people have been through enough. Gay and lesbian preachers are often dealing with brothers and sisters who are on the verge of suicide and desperate for a kind Word from our Heavenly Father.

It has been my experience that most straight mainstream preachers love to hate. Just give them an opportunity to conjure up hatred, violence, and oppression and they're suddenly full of zeal and enthusiastic energy.

However, there is one true answer to this question and gay and lesbian people deserve to hear the truth of God's Word. You can not sugar coat or lie to anyone when it comes to God's Word. We do no justice or favors for anyone by lying to them. In order to live a level headed life firmly grounded and mature as our Heavenly Father wants all of us to do, one must always be willing to face God's truth. Whether it makes us feel all warm and fussy inside or not. The answer to this question has gone from one extreme to the other leaving everyone in a false state of reality when it comes to God's true feelings and His true Word on this subject.

Deceived Bible teachers have taught that gay people:

- Are going to hell.
- Make a conscience choice to be gay.
- Have entertained the thought of being gay and fell to the desires of it.
- Brought this upon themselves.
- Became gay by watching talk shows about gay people when they were heterosexual to begin with.
- Were made gay by other gay people, such as hanging out with the wrong crowd.
- Are possessed by the Devil.
- Are child molesters.
- Are perverts.
- Are infectious.

- Are immoral.
- Do not love our Heavenly Father.
- Do not know our Heavenly Father.
- Are not Christians.
- Worship the Devil.
- Are trying to destroy America by being gay.
- Are trying to destroy American families.
- Are trying to destroy and infect American children.
- Are trying to force the gay lifestyle on everyone.
- Are trying to destroy heterosexual marriage.
- Are trying to destroy the institution of marriage as a whole.
- Are trying to destroy the fabric that America is founded on.
- Are living in sin because they do not hide their same gender attraction while acting on it in secret.

I could go on and on. My favorite one has always been the belief that watching talk shows about gay people will turn a heterosexual person gay. I was at a Christian convention years ago. One of the preachers gave a sermon stating that he knew a brother who watched a talk show with gay people on it and has been gay ever sense. This preacher spent an hour teaching about 10,000 Christians the dangers of watching talk shows and how the wrong type of show could turn a person gay.

I do believe a brother saw the show the preacher talked about. However, he would have been gay before he saw the show. If closeted people watching talk shows about gay people brings them out of the closet then I recommend it to everyone.

Straight men in today's world have had it beat into their heads for generations that they must keep their same gender attraction secret. This mindset has created a terrible existence for God's straight men. They have had no other choice but to date and marry women. They have had no other choice but to congregate in public restrooms and Rest Areas for same gender intimacy. Risking their safety and lives with dangerous strangers with no chance of a normal healthy and Godly existence. No chance to live the life that God had originally intended for them. The reason I classify gay men who date and marry women as straight is because this is the label they live throughout their lives with. This is the label they identify themselves with.

I was working on my car in the driveway one warm afternoon when a neighbor who was a politician came walking up to me. St. Paul schools were hiring gay counselors because the suicide rate of gay children in the St. Paul schools system was sky-rocketing.

The dominate mind set of Minnesotans is that all people should be on the down low. Keeping their same gender attraction secret. This is the dominate mindset among the male and female population. This is pretty much the dominate mind set world wide for that matter.

She had a petition in her hand and asked me to sign it. She said: "We need to stop this. They are putting gay counselors into the schools." I said: "What is your problem with this? Don't you think this would be beneficial for gay children to bring down or stop the suicide rate?" She proceeded to tell me how this would turn many heterosexual school children gay. If the school system allowed gay counselors to come into the schools. She believed the gay counselors would turn the school children gay with their examples as human beings and with their tricky voodoo.

She continued to tell me how her nephew turned gay a few years back because he started hanging around with open gay children at school. I said: "Don't you think there was a possibility your nephew was gay to begin with?" She stated: "Oh no! He was totally heterosexual before he started spending time with those gay kids." I asked her if all of her friends were lesbian women could they possibly turn her into a lesbian? She said: "Oh no! I'm totally heterosexual. The thought of being with a women sexually makes me sick. I could never be gay not in a million years." I said: "Well, don't you think if a teenage boy is totally heterosexual the case would be the same for him?" She said: "I can see I'm wasting my time here with you." As she walked away I said: "Shame on you Julie!" She turned around and said: "What!" I said: "Shame on you! You're putting your homophobic fears and hateful beliefs before the welfare of innocent children." Her last words as she stomped away were, "All I know is I don't want my five sons turned gay by those gay councilors!" Unfortunately she is representative of most straight women.

Sadly most women are completely clueless when it comes to men with a same gender attraction. Often when I am sitting around socializing or interacting with straight men and women while the women are talking together, their straight boyfriends or husbands are winking, licking their lips, and checking out my body in places that they shouldn't. While the women are totally oblivious to what their men are doing.

I am often reminded how Satan deceived Eve so easily back in the beginning. Some people just need to get a clue. Some people just need to get a real meaningful life with a productive purpose. I guess my neighbor Julie was a living breathing example why the down low community (straight community) exists in the first place. After all I have just said let me say there is nothing wrong with a man or woman whom has a same gender attraction marrying someone of the opposite gender as long as they are happily monogamous. The promiscuous straight community has always been so annoying and shameful.

The misrepresentation of open Lgbt people for generations has been quite damaging. Not only for straight people but for open Lgbt people and their loved ones as well.

I want you to remember that our Heavenly Father directed the Bible writers to single out the eunuchs as different from everyone else over and over throughout the Bible. The reason they labeled the eunuchs was because their sexual orientation was different from the majority. We do the same thing today with gay people. Yet, Jesus did include the eunuchs (Lgbt people) right along with the heterosexuals when giving instructions on obedience and how to live.

Additional Reference
(1Ti.4:1-16)(Ro.6:1-23)(1Jo2:1-29, 3:1-24, 5:3)(1Pe.1:5-25
(Ec.12:8-14)(Pr.2:1-22)(Mt.6:9-34, 7:1-29)

Our Heavenly Father, Jesus, and the disciples did not forget that the eunuchs had a same gender attraction. After all that's why they were labeled as eunuchs because they had a same gender attraction. Jesus did mention and include them when it came to instruction on what was pleasing to God. They were not left out. As so many have been told for generations.

I am hoping by this point you realize the same instruction applied to heterosexuals and eunuchs alike. Our Heavenly Father, Jesus, and the disciples knew that not one of these eunuchs were suddenly going to turn heterosexual. They knew eunuchs were born that way, and made that way by other men, and that their orientation was permanent. Unchangeable even by their own desire. I know there is not gay or lesbian person alive who does not know his or her sexual orientation is unchangeable. Unchangeable due to their own efforts and abilities anyway.

Now I'm going to define what sin is and it is quite simple. Sin: is a human imperfection, short of perfect. Any behavior that is different or against what our Heavenly Father put into place at the beginning of man's creation is an imperfection or to use the Biblical term ....sin.

Here is a list of just a few sins or human imperfections many live with as children of God on earth:

- fornication
- adultery
- idolatry
- male prostitution
- female prostitution
- homosexuality or gay
- stealing
- greed
- drunkenness
- gossip
- reviling
- extortion, and many many more

Brothers and sisters stay with me here.
Gay and heterosexual
people have had a hard
time with the subject we are about to enter.
This subject has closed the hearts of
many people over the years because it has been
misinterpreted in so many ways
over the generations. That misrepresentation has hurt
many, and broken many hearts.

Keep in mind, I love you, God loves you, and we are going
to take you by the hand and lead you to God's truth,
salvation and everlasting life.

<u>No one is going to tell you to turn heterosexual.</u>

Leviticus 18:22
Thou shalt not lie with mankind,
as with womankind: it is abomination.

FACING OUR IMPERFECTIONS
WILL MAKE US STRONG

We cannot change God's Word to suit us. God's Word is there to educate and protect us and to keep us out of harms way. These Words from our Heavenly Father have been misunderstood and misrepresented for many generations.

Yes, a same gender attraction is a sin.

It is outside of God's original state of perfection. God created everything and everyone "perfect," **in the beginning**. Things started to change from the beginning. Eve was deceived. Adam disobeyed to follow Eve's example. Cain killed his brother. Men and women were being born gay. God's people wanted to divorce, etc., etc., etc.

Anything that deviates from God's original state of perfection is a sin. No one man or woman has ever been able to live up to God's original state of perfection which was established **in the beginning.** Not Adam or Eve, not one person, not ever, not you, and not me have ever been perfect.

If our Heavenly Father's love and acceptance or obtaining salvation depends on anyone being perfect, totally without flaws, or imperfections we are all doomed. If this is the case every man and woman who has ever lived is doomed before our Heavenly Father. Now you know that is not the case just keep reading. This is not how our Heavenly Father operates.

Over the years I have listened to God's young open gay children on talk shows, and in person, state they hate themselves for having a same gender attraction.

I have heard God's open Lgbt children say:

- They think a same gender attraction is disgusting.
- It is the worst thing in the world.
- It is the worst sin in the Bible.
- They make themselves sick because of this same gender attraction.
- They would rather be **dead,** than have a same gender attraction.
- They want to kill themselves over this same gender attraction.
- They have tried to kill themselves because of their self loathing over a same gender attraction.

Why have so many young Lgbt people felt this way?

The reason our Heavenly Father's Lgbt children feel this way is because they have been lied to. They have been lied to about sin and lied to about the gay issue and lied to about our Heavenly Father.

I have **never** heard anyone say these types of things over any others sins.

Have you ever heard anyone say:

- I would rather be dead, than be a fornicator.
- I would rather be dead, than be a adulterer.
- I would rather be dead, than be a idolater.
- I would rather be dead, than be a prostitute.
- I would rather be dead, than be a thief.
- I would rather be dead, than be a greedy person.
- I would rather be dead, than be a drunkard.
- I would rather be dead, than be a gossiper.
- I would rather be dead, than be a reviler.
- I would rather be dead, than be a extortioner.

NO!....WE DO NOT HEAR PEOPLE SAY THESE TYPES OF THINGS OVER ANY OTHER SINS.

Why do people with a same gender attraction feel this way over this particular sin above all others? Why is a same gender attraction the end of the world for these people and for many others who do not have a same gender attraction? What is it about this particular sin that makes so many feel this way? Millions of God's gay and heterosexual children have walked away from God and churches over the misunderstanding of sin and this scripture at Leviticus 18:22.

It is because many have been lied to about this particular sin.

God teaches His children what is, and what is not, a sin or imperfection all throughout the Old Testament and New Testament. God states in the Old Testament the penalty for **all** sin is death. The generations prior to the arrival of Jesus were waiting for Jesus to come for this very reason. They knew they needed Jesus' sacrifice to redeem them from their sins or imperfections. If not for the sacrifice of Jesus we are all destined for eternal death before God.

Only through the sacrifice of Jesus can anyone be forgiven for any sin or imperfection. All of God's children with the right **heart** from the Old Testament days are forgiven for all their sins or imperfections today. All of God's children with the right **heart** today are forgiven through Jesus Christ for all of their sins. Providing they come to Jesus and ask for forgiveness and accept Jesus as the son of God. Without accepting Jesus as the sacrifice for our sins His death on the cross for our sins means nothing.

Does anyone from the Old Testament days or today deserve forgiveness? No. God says it is through His undeserved kindness that He forgives all mankind through His Son Jesus Christ. All mankind is born guilty of sin. According to God we inherit sin from Adam the first man who sinned against God. Before any of us have a chance to do anything wrong or make any mistakes we are guilty of sin in God's eyes because of Adam and Eve's original sin.

Our Heavenly Father feels the same intense love for us at fifty years old as He did for us at six months old. Mankind's sins or imperfections and all of our bad behavior is no surprise to our Heavenly Father. Our Heavenly Father says He judges a man by his **heart**. He says He judges mankind on their **hearts** and that only. Not by his multitude of various sins or imperfections. Nor does God judge man on any **one** particular sin. As the Lgbt community has been told for generations.

The problem with God's children when it comes to the scripture at Leviticus 18:22 is that they tend to incorporate the lie that they have been taught with this scripture. The lie that they have been taught is that a "same gender attraction" is the worst sin or imperfection in the world. They are taught that this is the worst sin or imperfection in the Bible. They have been taught that this sin or imperfection is so horrific that God couldn't possibly forgive or pardon it. They have been taught that God hates people with a same gender attraction. They read Lev. 18:22 and incorporate these lies with it and are stumbled. Most people today cannot separate God's Word from Satan's lies they have been taught. Most people today do not know the difference between God's loving Word and Satan's viscous evil lies.

Over the years I have watched open gay and heterosexual preachers and their followers try their best to twist Leviticus 18:22 in so many different ways. In their desperate attempt to make those words mean something **other than what it clearly says**. The heart of man is treacherous but the heart of man is also loving, fragile and breakable. It is our intense love for God, and our desire to be loved by God, and strong desire to be obedient, that makes these words at Leviticus 18:22 so painful for so many people to read and except. I have seen gay and heterosexual people read Leviticus 18:22 and say:

"Well I don't care, I don't believe it!"

If you are a Christian you must believe the scriptures are the truth from God. If you do not believe that all of the scriptures are true you have nothing to stand on in your faith. If you take one scripture and decide to believe it, because it tickles your ear, and makes you feel all warm and fussy, and take another scripture and decided not to believe it, because it doesn't tickle your ear, and doesn't make you feel all warm and fussy, you are creating your own God. Your own make believe God in your head. A God that does not exist.

Either the Bible is true or the Bible is false. There are many scriptures that are open to many interpretations. However, Leviticus 18:22 is not one of them. Leviticus 18:22 could not be more to the point, or more clear, as to what our Heavenly Father was saying. **AND.........DO NOT** make more out of this scripture than what it says. It says "a same gender attraction" is a sin or imperfection. Nothing more. Nothing less.

It does not say God hates people with a
same gender attraction.

It does not say people with
a same gender attraction
are the only sinners in the world.

It does not say this sin or imperfection
is worse than other sins or imperfections.

It does not say this sin is unforgivable.

Now.....brothers and sisters those of you who are
heterosexual and those of you with a same gender
attraction, listen up!

Do you have an ear, are you listening.

Read the following scriptures, God's Word,
that I have presented here and read them well.

Isaiah 44:22
44:22 **I have blotted out, as a thick cloud, thy transgressions, and,
as a cloud, thy sins: return unto me; for I have redeemed
thee.**

Acts 10:43
*10:43 To him give all the prophets witness, that through his name
whosoever believeth in him shall **receive remission of sins.***

1 Kings 8:46
*8:46 If they sin against thee, **for there is no man that sinneth
not,** and thou be angry with them, and deliver them to the
enemy, so that they carry them away captives unto the land of*

the enemy, far or near;

Matt7:1-3

7:1 **Judge not, that ye be not judged.**

7:2 For with what judgment ye judge, **ye shall be judged***: and with what measure ye mete, it shall be measured to you again.*

7:3 And why beholdest thou **the mote that is in thy brother's eye,** *but considerest not the* **beam that is in thine own eye?**

Hebrews 10:16+17

10.16 This is the covenant that I will make with them after those days, saith the Lord, **I will put my laws into their hearts,** *and in their minds will I write them;*

10:17 And their sins and iniquities will **I remember no more.**

Acts 10:34+35

10:34 Then Peter opened his mouth, and said, Of a truth I perceive that **God is no respecter of persons:**

10:35 But in every nation **he that feareth him, and worketh righteousness,** *is accepted with him.*

Romans 3:21-24

3:21 But **now the righteousness of God without the law** *is manifested, being witnessed by the law and the prophets;*

3:22 Even the righteousness of God which is by faith of Jesus Christ unto all and upon all them that believe: **for there is no difference:**

3:23 **For all have sinned, and come short of the glory of God;**

3:24 Being **justified freely by his grace** *through the redemption that is in Christ Jesus:*

Luke 5:31+32

5:31 And Jesus answering said unto them, They that are whole need not a physician; but they that are sick.

5:32 **I came not to call the righteous, but sinners to repentance.**

Romans 10:4

10:4 For **Christ is the end of the law** *for righteousness to every one that believeth.*

Isaiah 1:18

1:18 Come now, and **let us reason together,** *saith the LORD: though* **your sins be as scarlet, they shall be as white as snow;** *though they be red like crimson, they shall be as wool.*

Acts 13:38+39

13:38 Be it known unto you therefore, men and brethren, that through this man is preached **unto you the forgiveness of sins:**

13:39 And by him all that believe **are justified from all things,** *from which ye could not be justified by the law of Moses.*

Romans 8:33+34

8:33 **Who shall lay any thing to the charge** *of God's elect? It is God that justifieth.*

8:34 **Who is he that condemneth?** *It is* **Christ** *that died, yea rather, that is risen again, who is even at the right hand of God,* **who also maketh intercession for us.**

John 1:12

1:12 **But as many as received him, to them gave he power to become the sons of God, even to them that believe on his name:**

Romans 4:4-8

*4:4 Now to him that worketh is the reward **not reckoned of grace, but of debt.***

*4:5 But to him that worketh not, but believeth on him that justifieth the ungodly, **his faith is counted for righteousness.***

*4:6 Even as David also describeth the blessedness of the man, unto whom God imputeth **righteousness without works,***

*4:7 Saying, Blessed are they whose iniquities are forgiven, and **whose sins are covered.***

*4:8 Blessed is the man to whom the Lord **will not impute sin.***

Romans 8:1+2

*8:1 There is therefore **now no condemnation to them** which are in Christ Jesus, who walk not after the flesh, but after the Spirit.*

*8:2 For the law of the Spirit of life in Christ Jesus hath made me **free from the law of sin and death.***

*8:3 **For what the law could not do,** in that it was weak through the flesh, God sending his own Son in the likeness of sinful flesh, and for sin, **condemned sin in the flesh:***

Every person who has ever walked the face of the earth has had many sins to deal with in their lifetime. God created mankind in a perfect state knowing we would fall to imperfection to make us realize how much we needed Him and His Son Jesus. All people have various sins or imperfections of some sort. All sins or imperfections are equal to God. God says, "If you have committed one sin you are guilty of all sin." For example, if a heterosexual person commits the sin of gossip they are guilty of all sins. This includes the sin of "a same gender attraction," as well as all other sins listed in the Bible according to God's Word.

The reason many people read Lev.18:22 and become so hurt, so heartbroken, and so enraged, is because Satan has taught them that this sin or imperfection of "a same gender attraction" is worse than other sins, and is not worthy of forgiveness. Many people have been deceived by Satan's lies.

Do you remember who deceived Eve?

**Do you remember who has deceived
the entire inhabited earth?**

Do you remember who the creator of the lie is?

**Do you remember who taught you
this lie about a same gender attraction?**

**Was he dressed in red, with a pitch fork, or was he wearing a
suit, standing before a pulpit, in a beautiful church?**

Think about it.

Let me give you an example. Eve was walking about the garden minding her own business and trying to be as obedient as she could to the God that created her. Her heart was full of joy, and blessings, and love for the God that created her.

When suddenly a deceptive person crept up to her and began to tell her a lie about God. This person was familiar to her. Someone Eve trusted in the garden. He told her that God did not want her to eat from the tree because if she did she would have the same wisdom and knowledge that God had.

This deceptive person deceived Eve into believing God was keeping something from her. He deceived Eve into believing she would be better off by going against God's commandment. As you know, Eve ate from the tree and realized she had been deceived, lied to by the deceiver and lost her grace before God for her disobedience.

Let me give you another example. In 2009 a person attracted to her own gender was walking about the garden minding her own business and trying to be as obedient as she could to the God that created her. (Let me remind all of you that we are all standing in that same garden right now) Her heart was full of joy, and blessings, and love, for the God that created her.

When suddenly, a deceptive person crept up to her and began to tell her a lie about God. This person was familiar to her. Someone that she trusted in the garden. He told her that "a same gender attraction" was a far worse sin than all other sins and God would certainly destroy her for this horrible sin and imperfection. He deceived her into believing God couldn't possibly forgive or pardon her for this same gender attraction. Because he said it was so horrific in the eyes of the God that created her. He deceived her into believing God hated her for this imperfection. He deceived her into believing she had to change this imperfection or God would surely destroy her.

This person attracted to her same gender believed she could not please the God that created her. Because of the lie she had been told and came to believe. She tried her best but could not change this same gender attraction and then she became heartbroken. She was deceived into believing that God hated her for this same gender attraction. Believing she could no longer please the God that created her, she could not cope each day, believing she was a disappointment to the God that created her. She finally walked away from God. She walked away from God's Word. She walked away from church and tried to wipe God from her memory and lost her grace and salvation before God.

Eve and the person attracted to her own gender were born about 6000 years apart. What is the common factor between these two children of God?........The same "lover of the lie" that deceived Eve also deceived the person attracted to her own gender. That same deceptive person is still here today. Still up to his business of deceiving and destroying God's precious Lgbt children.

Did this "lover of the lie" walk up to Eve with flames and a pitch fork looking all scary?....NO. He came up to Eve in a presence that she was familiar with and trusted in her environment, an arch angel.

Did this "lover of the lie" walk up to the person attracted to her own gender with flames and a pitch fork looking all scary?....NO. He walked up to her in a presence that the she was familiar with and trusted in her environment, a preacher.

Eve and the innocent girl were enjoying a perfectly beautiful sunny day. Their hearts were full of joy, and all of God's blessings, and their hearts were light, and full of love for the God who created them. Until someone cunningly came up to them and stole all that God had given them. Was this deceptive person out to intentionally hurt Eve, and the girl,...you bet he was. Does he have a name.....YES. His name is Satan and he is still here doing the same thing to mankind today that he did 6000 years ago.

Now that I have reminded you who taught you that lie take a deep breath and relax. God loves you. God forgives you for all of your sins or imperfections just as He forgives everyone else for their sins and imperfections. You are no different! You are no less worthy than anyone else to receive God's forgiveness. Accept your imperfections and get over it. Go do something productive for God. Satan would love nothing more than for you to be stagnant and bogged down in spirit engulfed by his lies. I'm going to say it again. God loves you, and forgives you, in spite of your sins and imperfections. If I were you I would be more concerned over the sins you do have a choice over and work on those.

At this moment I would like to speak directly to people with a same gender attraction.

People who never had a choice in regard to a same gender attraction. Basically, no one has ever had a choice about a same gender attraction. No one chooses to be gay, no one, not ever, chooses this. If anyone says they chose it, they are trying to look strong and hiding the fact their hearts are breaking. Because this is something they do not have control over and they believe this makes them weak.

For example, a heterosexual person who has endured emotional or sexual abuse by someone of the opposite gender, or many people of the opposite gender, gets to a point where they are afraid of the opposite gender. They can no longer enjoy intimacy with the opposite gender. This can last a lifetime for many people. Often these people get involved with someone of their own gender. Did these people choose to be gay in this instance? **Absolutely not**. These people are still living breathing human beings. They are still filled with love and sexual desire just as our Heavenly Father has created all of us to be. Our Heavenly Father created these types of coping skills for mental health, survival, and happiness.

These people started out in life with the best intentions. To be pleasing to God. To be as obedient as they could. But life's circumstances or environment changed

<u>who they were</u> ....in the beginning.

They did not suddenly make a choice to be gay. After this change in lifestyle they had just as many sins as they did before. Our Heavenly Father still loves them just as much. They have not changed God's love for them. Not one iota.

Unfortunately, they are often accused of suddenly choosing to turn gay by others. This has been very unfair for them. This happens to both men and women. Most people do not understand the Lgbt issue. Not even a little bit. This has made a same gender attraction all the more difficult. It's hard enough to be openly gay and part of a small minority, feeling left out of life and the mainstream majority. In every direction they turn no one understands what they are going through emotionally or socially. This has been the root of many suicides in our community. God bless all of our brothers and sisters who deceived by Satan's lies haven't survived this unloving world.

Our Heavenly Father has come
to bring an end to that forever, to time indefinite.

The reason Leviticus 18:22 is so painful for Lgbt people is because they can't understand how it is possible they are accused sinners over something they did not have a choice about. When looking at sins such as gossip, lying, stealing, fornication, murder etc., we know these sins are a choice one makes before hand.

All sins are something we have control over except a same gender attraction. For example, a person who has a weakness with gossip, often does it without really thinking about it. Later they see the damage it caused, realizing or remembering that gossip is a sin, then tries to make a conscious decision to never do it again. Normally most people are capable of success at overcoming the desire to gossip as well as all other sins.

When it comes to a same gender attraction this is not the case. You did not get to choose this, or make a choice about it, and you can not make it go away, no matter what you do. Only God has the power to do that. Nobody knows this better than our Heavenly Father. God knows when the appropriate time is, and when that time comes, he will change us. This change will come when God feels the time is right and not one minute before. Our Heavenly Father is not disappointed in us over our same gender attraction.

God does not want to see you out there thinking and saying, "Oh, why God why. Oh, when God when?" This is our state of sexual orientation right now. It is not going to change, so we need to make peace with it, make the best of our lives, embrace all of God's blessings, and get on with our beautiful lives.

If our Heavenly Father loves us unconditionally as He says He does, how much more so should we <u>forgive ourselves</u> and <u>love ourselves</u> in the same way.

The angel is telling me to repeat this.
<u>Forgive yourselves</u> for being imperfect,
and <u>love yourselves</u>, just as God loves you.

IMPERFECT

Over the years I have watched gay people read Leviticus 18:22 and I have seen the joy drain right out of their faces and spirits. Their hearts breaking before my very eyes. They become heartbroken over this sin and those words because they never chose this sin. They believe the lies that Satan has taught them. The lie that this sin is unforgivable. They never had a choice to make in regard to this sin. What makes this sin or imperfection so painful for many is because it is the only sin mankind does not get to make a choice about. That just seems so unfair.

This scripture makes it quite clear that sex between two people of the same gender in any context or form is a sin or imperfection. This includes eunuchs of ancient times and gays of today. Regardless of how healthy or loving you or your relationships are. Regardless of your level of obedience or how strong your obedient walk with God may be. If you are attracted to the same gender sexually you are guilty of the sin of "homosexuality" mentioned in Leviticus 18:22.

Yes, brothers and sisters homosexuality, gay, eunuch, lesbian, whether male or female, a same gender attraction is a sin, an <u>imperfection</u>. Nature teaches us this as well as God. Whether you were born that way or not. A same gender attraction is a sin just like all the other sins listed in the Bible and there are many sins the Bible mentions. Every single person on this planet has sin of some sort. People with a same gender attraction are not the only sinners. They are not the worst sinners on the planet. We have been lied to for generations.

In the beginning God created intercourse to be between a male and female. For the purpose of procreation and pleasure, **before,** Adam and Eve sinned. Remember, it was the first sin by Adam and Eve that broke the bond of perfection between man and God. If it weren't for their mistake there wouldn't be any sin on earth at all today. You do not need to be a rocket scientist to see that a penis was designed to go with a vagina for the purpose of procreation and pleasure. Any kind of sex outside of intercourse between a biological male and biological female is a deviation from God's original plan. Therefore any sin or imperfection in the eyes of God is a deviation from His original plan and purpose for His creations.

This sin is always going to be a sin and nothing is going to change that nor should it be changed. God's laws are just, righteous, and wise, and for our protection, because of His intense love for His children.

<u>No one gets to be perfect.</u>

Every man, woman, and child who has ever lived has been full of sin. So let's clear up a fact: all sin is the same, on the same level of badness, wrongness, the same level of imperfection. A same gender attraction is not more of a sin than any other sin. Remember the hundreds of years of false Bible teachers I taught you about earlier. The Bible does not say one sin is worse than another. The Bible says if you are guilty of one sin you are guilty of all of them.

Let's take a look at what God says about sin.

Luke 13:1-5

13:1 There were present at that season some that told him of the Galilaeans, whose blood Pilate had mingled with their sacrifices.

*13:2 And Jesus answering said unto them, Suppose ye that **these Galilaeans were sinners above all the Galilaeans,** because they suffered such things?*

*13:3 I tell you, **Nay: but, except ye repent,** ye shall **all likewise perish.***

13:4 Or those eighteen, upon whom the tower in Siloam fell, and slew them, think ye that they were sinners above all men that dwelt in Jerusalem?

*13:5 I tell you, **Nay:** b**ut, except ye repent**, ye shall **all likewise perish.***

Romans 3:21-24

*3:21 But now the righteousness of God **without the law is manifested,** being witnessed by the law and the prophets;*

*3:22 Even the righteousness of God which is by faith of Jesus Christ unto all and upon all them that believe: **for there is no difference:***

*3:23 **For all have sinned, and come short of the glory of God;***

*3:24 Being justified **freely by his grace through the redemption that is in Christ Jesus:***

1 Timothy 1:8-10

*1:8 But we know that the **law is good, if a man use it lawfully;***

*1:9 Knowing this, **that the law is not made for a righteous man,** but for the lawless and disobedient, for the ungodly and for sinners, for unholy and profane, for murderers of Fathers and murderers of mothers, for manslayers,*

*1:10 For whoremongers, **for them that defile themselves with mankind,** for menstealers, for liars, for perjured persons, and if there be any other thing that is contrary to sound doctrine;*

1 Timothy 1:14

*1:14 **And the grace of our Lord was exceeding abundant with faith and love which is in Christ Jesus.***

*1:15 **This is a faithful saying, and worthy of all acceptation, that Christ Jesus came into the world to save sinners; of whom I am chief.***

Brothers and sisters I wish I could tell you being gay was not a sin but that would be a lie. I wish I could tell you that Jesus never mentioned gay people in the scriptures but that would be a lie. I am so sorry you had to hear these words from me. No one knows the heartache of those words better than I do. We are not an accident of birth. God intended for us to be gay. God has a plan and purpose for us. Don't ever let a demon take God's promises and blessings, that I have revealed away from your heart and mind. Obedient eunuchs or Lgbt people are God's pride. He has boasted about us to His angels in Heaven and now to man on earth. He has given us a name in Heaven greater than son or daughter, and a monument in Heaven in our honor. He is so proud of us and He loves His Lgbt children very much.

Our Heavenly Father knows we didn't choose our orientation. He knows if we had a magic wand we would have changed ourselves the instant we realized we had a same gender attraction. But the person with the magic wand is our Heavenly Father. When His time comes to change us He will. It is God's choice to leave us in this state for now. I have no doubt that He has a plan and purpose for us.

Do you have an ear, are you listening?

The sin of "a same gender attraction" is different than other sins. For example;

Jesus did not say anyone was born a:

- fornicator
- adulterer
- idolater
- prostitute
- abuser
- thief
- covetous (greedy)
- drunkard
- gossiper
- reviler (abusive speech)
- extortioner

<u>**or was made that way by other men, or born with any of the multitude of sins the Bible makes reference to. Jesus said only eunuchs were born that way.**</u>

Jesus stated only eunuchs were born that way or made that way by other men. We are responsible for making a decision to lie, to steal, to gossip, etc. All other sins are a personal conscious choice. But we know having a same gender attraction isn't something we have ever had a choice about. If that were the case Lgbt people would be far and few between. God knows this imperfection wasn't a choice for us. Yet we would have to endure this burden for a life time. In this life anyway. God expects us to live up to the same regulations of obedience as the heterosexual people were instructed to.

If you are attracted to both genders <u>equally</u> you only have one **choice** to make. That is to be with the opposite gender. If sex with both genders is pleasing for you, you are making a choice to sin if you have sex with your same gender. Many people are quite satisfied with both genders sexually. If you are one of these people you should remain with the opposite gender. To stay within obedience in the sight of our Heavenly Father.

I am not talking about gay people who are capable of having sex with the opposite gender. There are millions of gay people having sex with the opposite gender for appearance sake in order to appear to be heterosexual. It is possible to have sex with the opposite gender and yet have no attraction to them. Only you and God know your heart and only you and God know your true sexual orientation.

Remember, God says He looks at a man all the way down to his kidneys. If you have read all the scriptures up to now you will know what that means. You cannot walk with God and live a life based on lies and deception. Our Heavenly Father wants all of His children to live an authentic life true to ourselves, true to others, and true to Him.

Additional Reference
(Mt.19:9-17)

If you have a same gender attraction and you are thinking you won't have sex and you won't be guilty of a same gender attraction, let's clear that up.

Jeremiah 17:9+10
*17:9 The **heart is deceitful** above all things, and desperately wicked: who can know it?*

*17:10 **I the LORD search the heart**, I try the reins, even to give every man according to his ways, and according to the fruit of his doings.*

The point is that God sees our hearts. We can't hide our hearts from Him. Many are desperately trying to be pleasing and obedient for the sake of our Heavenly Father for His love and approval. This also shows God your heart.

If you have a same gender attraction and you are thinking of a life of abstinence that is fine. If you have a same gender attraction and are thinking of seeking out the opposite gender in an attempt to be obedient this is not always wise. Whatever you choose to do in this instance, and notice I said, "**what you choose**," keep in mind God sees the heart.

If you are with the opposite gender and fantasizing or lusting for the same gender you have a same gender attraction and our Heavenly Father sees that. In this instance you need to follow your heart. Many gay people for generations have lived a heterosexual lifestyle even though they knew they were gay. God does not have a problem with this as long as you are not lusting for and chasing after the same gender at the same time. Let me remind you that God requires all people to be monogamous in marriage.

Far to often gay men have married women as decoy's and the result is a treacherous lifestyle leaving many hearts and lives shattered. A lifestyle of lies, deception and secrecy. A lifetime of many sexual partners in rest areas, public rest rooms, state and city parks, etc.

I met a young woman in the work place and we fell madly in love. We were married for many years. I was gay and open about it before we met although I was always monogamous. I was perfectly content sexually with my wife because my love for her was so deep. This was possible for me even though I had always been gay. This had been my sexual identity from the age of four. Does that make me bi-sexual? No.

One of the many lessons I learned in that marriage was whether my same gender attraction was from God, nature, or a result of my environment, it was there as a protection. It was a part of me for my well being. Would I marry again? No, not to a man or woman. I have come to love the blessing of singleness far too much.

Do I recommend gay people marry heterosexual people? Do I recommend heterosexual people marry gay people? I recommend people only marry the person they fall madly in love with. If that person has fallen madly in love with them in return. After the angel showed me the big picture of the universe and God's plan for mankind I can assure you God doesn't care who we marry. Who we marry is just a tiny minute detail in the big scope of things.

Let me give you an example. Look into the face of your child and ask yourself what you want foremost for that child. Most people would say all they really want for their children is a happy healthy life. They want the same intense love that they feel for their children returned to them. This is foremost what our Heavenly Father wants from us. What our Heavenly Father wants from us is all of our love and devotion. Our Heavenly Father wants His children to love Him with the same intensity that He has for us. Our Heavenly Father wants His children on earth to be happy above all things. Notice the first of the ten commandments is:

"Love no other God."......HELLO!!!!!!!!!

Whether you live a life exclusively gay or heterosexual we are all guilty of sin or imperfections. A gay man who marries a man or woman still looks the same in the eyes of God. Are you getting this? God falls in love with our hearts. This is not dependent of what particular sins we have or do not have. There is not one parent on earth who looks into the face of their child and thinks of their imperfections. Parents do see the imperfections in their children and love them tremendously anyway. This is the same way our Heavenly Father feels about us. After our Heavenly Father sees our hearts all the rest is details, details, details.

Additional Reference
(1Sa.16:5 7)(Jer 17:9-12)(Ro.10:4-14)

I'm sorry brothers and sisters we can't change what we are. It is written in our minds and hearts. Our Heavenly Father knows us better then we know ourselves. He is the one who made us this way and that's why He gave us a special privilege,**a name in Heaven, greater than Son or Daughter, and a monument in Heaven in our honor.** He did this to let us know He is aware of our hardship and imperfection and to let the angels in Heaven and man on earth see how proud He is of His Lgbt children.

He also gave us Jesus, and salvation through Jesus, as a sacrifice for our sins. Not just for the sinning heterosexuals but for the sinning Lgbt people as well.

A day is coming when God will relieve us from this burden. Until then be as obedient as you can. Live a happy and productive life. Let your heart be light with joy and happiness. Get all the joys and blessings out of life that our Heavenly Father has to offer you.

Brothers and sisters this revelation is nothing but good news for all gay, lesbian, and transgender people. If your heart is heavy and sad right now there may be areas you did not comprehend. This revelation is deep and immense. I recommend you read this revelation many times to ensure that you understand every loving word of it.

LET YOUR HEART BE LIGHT
IN GOD'S EMBRACE
AND GO IN PEACE REJOICING!

Additional Reference
(2Co.5:11-21)(Ro.3:23-26)(Ac.10:34+35, 43-48)
(1Jo.1:7-10)(1Ki.8:46)(1Ch.6:36)

What obedience means for gays and heterosexuals is to: stay as close to God as you possibly can and to follow His direction and instruction. (His commandments) God knows you are never going to be perfect. You know right from wrong. If you don't know right from wrong open your Bible and start reading. Right from wrong is all over the Bible.

God is our Father and we are His children. How do parents feel about their children? They want them to know right from wrong and to be as obedient as they can be. When our children do as we ask we are so pleased with them. When they do the wrong thing or make a mistake do we stop loving them? Of course not. We love them anyway and continue to encourage them to do better the next time. If we had a child born with a deformed leg would we be angry at him for not being able to run? Would we stop loving that child? Of course not. As a matter of fact we would love that child even more because of his infirmity. That's the same way our Heavenly Father feels about His eunuchs or should I say His Lgbt children.

Obedience means giving our Heavenly Father the best behavior we have to offer. Just like all children <u>our obedience improves with time.</u>

A day is coming when God will take this sin away from us. As we all know it will take the power of God to do that. Because we can't get rid of a same gender attraction on our own.

Additional Reference
(1Ti.4:1-16)(Mt.8:13-17)(Mark1:30-34)(Luke4:38-41)
(Mt.10:5-18)(Mt.13:9-19)(1Jo.5:19+20)(Pr.1:1-9)(De.29:29)

Let's take a look at our Heavenly Fathers blessings and promises at 1 Corinthians 6:9-11.

1Corinthians 6:9-11

(9) What! Do you not know that unrighteous persons will not inherit God's kingdom? DO NOT BE **MISLEAD**. *Neither;*

- *fornicators,*
- *nor idolaters,*
- *nor adulterers,*
- *nor effeminate, (meaning men who have a same gender attraction)*
- *nor abusers,*
- *(10) not thieves,*
- *nor covetous, (meaning greedy persons)*
- *nor drunkards,*
- *nor revilers, (meaning people whom are violent in their speech)*
- *nor extortioners...............will inherit Gods kingdom.*

*(11)**AND YET THAT IS WHAT SOME OF YOU WERE**. But you have been **washed clean**, but you have been **sanctified** but you have been **declared righteous** in the name of our Lord Jesus Christ and with the spirit of our God.*

Notice it says these kinds of people will not inherit God's kingdom. Notice in verse 11, God says;

And yet, that is what some of you WERE, but you have been washed clean............DECLARED RIGHTEOUS.

God says we once were these kinds of sinners at one time in our past. Sometime between now and the time we enter Heaven God is going to change our same gender attraction. Maybe it will be in an instant when He makes the blind see, the lame walk, and the deaf hear. Maybe it will be a gradual change over the 1000 year millennium we are about to enter. The Word of God at 1 Corinthians 6:9-11 is a promise to us. You can depend on God's Word.

The fact of the matter is all mankind have sin,
and if not for God's undeserved kindness,
mercy, and grace through Jesus Christ we are
all going to be destroyed come judgment day.

God's grace is greater than our sin.

Isaiah 65:17
For, behold, I create new Heavens and a new earth: and the former shall not be remembered, nor come into mind.

Matthew 8:14
And when Jesus was come into Peter's house, he saw his wife's mother laid, and sick of a fever.

8:15 And he touched her hand, **and** *the fever left her: and she arose, and ministered unto them.*

DOES GOD WANT LGBT PEOPLE IN THE CHURCH?

False Bible teachers have told a multitude of God's open gay, lesbian, and transgender children that they are not welcome in their churches. They have been told if they want to come to their churches, and accept Jesus as their savior, or get baptized they will need to turn heterosexual first. Many churches won't even go that far because they don't want our type there at all. They see an honest homosexual or lesbian as infectious. They are afraid we will encourage other church members to give up the lie which binds the men and women in the church.

These churches and religious organizations have classes, seminars, and all kinds of propaganda aimed at turning open gay and lesbian people into perceived heterosexuals. What a pack of lying devouring wolves. They teach the utterances of demons from their pulpits, intoxicated with the lie, embracing it like a drug addict embraces their drug. They are comforted by the lie because they have been deceived. The heterosexual women deceive themselves into believing they are better than open gay people because they don't carry that burden as we do. The men deceive themselves into believing they are better because their same gender activity is done in secrecy. All the while living as sexual predictors. Creating an unsafe environment for churches, workplaces, and neighborhoods.

In today's world male children are not safe using a public rest room or safe with teachers or coaches. There are countless reports of high school sports teams committing gang rape against new players in hazing. Young boys are raped on school buses etc. Satan has even convinced God's own open gay and lesbian children to live in secrecy deceiving others and themselves. These "church leaders" are corrupt in every way. They are responsible for the lives of so many open gay and lesbian people.

Out of those 25 church leaders I contacted after October 30, 1996 only one invited me and my family to come to his church. After 6 weeks of attending his church, at his invitation which I thought was so-loving of him. He had two guest speakers come and give an 8 hour seminar based on the premise that God hated gay and lesbian people. It was heartbreaking. Because they had such a distorted understanding of God's Word and misunderstanding of gay people and the gay experience. I did know this revelation at the time. I did all that I could do to keep my mouth shut. They were recommending that gay boys play more football and baseball, and recommended that lesbian girls spend more time baking and sewing. **I kid you not.** They truly believed this would turn people heterosexual. This team is known all over America as experts in the field of turning gay and lesbian people into heterosexuals.

At the end of this seminar I asked the husband and wife team what made them feel they were equipped to council gay and lesbian people. They said, they had a gay son and that's what made them experts in the field of turning people heterosexual. I asked them, "Where is your son now?" They proceeded to tell the audience and me that their son committed suicide at the age of 16. At that moment my heart just broke for them. My heart broke for their son, and for every one in the conference, as well as every one left on their traveling agenda. They had many more churches on their schedule. They traveled all over the U.S. trying to help people like their son. But their efforts were so misguided. God help them and God help everyone that they have come in contact with.

As the 75 or so people exited the conference room of the church where the seminar was held, I stood at the exit telling everyone I could that everything the team had said was a lie and that God did love them. Most of the young people had tears in their eyes, looking down towards the floor, looking so beaten down and sad. A couple of children looked at me with a gleam of hope and relief as the parents glared at me with tremendous anger.

I stood there with the crowd passing me on both sides telling the head pastor, and assistant pastor, I couldn't believe they had that team come to teach such nonsense. They said, "They were shocked, they thought of all people, I would have approved of it." I realized at that moment the pastor did not understand one word I told him about the Bible revelation I had shared with him weeks earlier. Apparently the assistant pastor and his wife were the ones who set up the contract for the seminar. Through the entire seminar the assistant pastor couldn't take his eyes off me. He squirmed through the entire seminar because he had an erection. An erection that his wife was fulling aware of I might add. I felt like I was dealing with business men or politicians not Christian preachers. I also felt it was their way of telling me to embrace the closet like all the other fine gay Christians in the church or get out." I couldn't get out of there quick enough!

Heavenly Father,
Please forgive them, for they know not what they do.

Let's use the scriptures again to set things straight.

Isaiah 56:3
56:3 Neither let the son of the stranger, that hath joined himself to the LORD, speak, saying, **The LORD hath utterly separated me from his people: neither let the eunuch say, Behold, I am a dry tree.**

Let's focus on the statement:

"Neither let the eunuch say Behold! I am a dry tree."

Now, what happens to a dry tree? A dry tree that isn't getting any water dries up and **it dies.** As you can see here, God is commanding His Shepard's not to be found guilty of doing such corrupt and evil things to His eunuchs.

Our Heavenly Father has instructed them <u>not</u> to discourage or reject His eunuch children from worship or from the church. In this illustration the scripture is talking about making sure that the eunuchs have the freedom of worship and freedom of salvation. Here our Heavenly Father is specifically speaking about the eunuchs.

Our Heavenly Father is commanding His Shepard's not to forsake the eunuchs, or deprive them from worship, or to deprive the eunuchs from any of God's blessings that He has promised them. There is not one eunuch (or gay) person walking the face of this earth today who has not been a victim of this kind of atrocity. The majority of churches in America are guilty of this abomination in the eyes of God. Today is God's day of reckoning with America's church leaders and their followers. Bring it on Father!

John 1:9
That was the true Light, which lighteth every man that cometh into the world.

Notice the words here,

" EVERY MAN THAT COMETH"

John 1:12
*1:12 But as **many as received him**, to them gave he power to become the sons of God, **even to them that believe on his name:***

*1:13 Which were born, not of blood, nor of the will of the flesh, nor of the will of man, **but of God**.*

Notice how those who received Jesus became God's children because they were exercising FAITH. Notice He didn't say because they were without sin or imperfection. Notice in verse 13 God says they are "OF GOD."

1Corinthians 7:24
Bretheren, let every man, <u>wherein he is called</u>, therein abide with God.

Notice He says, "wherein he is called" this means: "<u>come in whatever condition you were called, let him remain in it with God</u>" It doesn't say make any changes. It doesn't say to turn heterosexual before you come to God. God doesn't say to make any other changes nor does He say to pretend to be something that you are not.

1 Corinthians 7:26
*7:26 I suppose therefore that this is **good for the present** distress, I say, **that it is good for a man so to be.***

Notice God says, "this is good for the present" meaning, continue as you are."That is good for a man so to be" means: it is in mans best interest to remain as he is. This scripture does not say any prerequisites are required such as turning heterosexual or hiding the truth that you are gay or lesbian.

Acts 10:43
10:43 To him give all the prophets witness, that through his name <u>whosoever believeth</u> in him shall receive remission of sins.

Notice the word **"whosoever"** is used here. It doesn't say "just the heterosexual people," and it doesn't say "everyone-**EXCEPT** the eunuchs,"

IT SAYS!
"Whosoever."

Additional Reference
(2Co.5:11-21)(Ro.3:23-26)(Ac.10:34+35, 43-48)(1Jo.1:7-10
(1Ki.8:46)(2Ch.6:36)(Mt.10:5-18)

Brothers and sisters our Heavenly Father does want to see all of us in church worshiping Him. He wants to see all of us singing praises to Him and full of enthusiasm for His Word and His instruction. Our Heavenly Father has instructed us to gather together so we can encourage and build up each other as we progress in our walk with Him. Gathering together is a commandment from God. It is for our spiritual growth and protection. Remember, all of God's requirements and commandments are for our benefit. Not for God's benefit.

Our Heavenly Father does realize that there are many who have been terribly hurt and wounded by Bible teachers and church goers. Deceived Christians and wolves have left a tremendous trail of tears as they slaughter their way to and from church every Sunday.

If you are in driving distance of a gay, lesbian, and transgender friendly church I urge you to attend. Get involved. Be an encouragement for others. They need you there as much as you need them.

If you are thinking the last time you attended church people were cold, rude and unfriendly. Then you go there and show them how a real Christian should behave. Be an example for them to follow. Most of all keep in mind, I said a gay, lesbian, and transgender friendly church. A church who publicly declares God's open Lgbt children are welcome.

If it turns out not to be the case go find another church. I have found churches that are on the registry as gay, lesbian, and transgender friendly list and have turned out to be quite the opposite. After this revelation is released I think most churches will be afraid not to be on that list for fear of being boycotted. If they are only speaking lip service make sure you notify the proper Lgbt agencies.

Our Heavenly Father realizes there are many of you who have been badly hurt by today's church leaders and members. You would rather die than go into another church as long as you live. He also realizes there are many of you who are not within driving distance of an open Lgbt friendly church. Our Heavenly Father realizes for many church simply isn't an option at this time. He understands your predicament and He sees your heart. I must say walking with God all by yourself can be lonely. Keep up your spirits. Stay in God's Word and remember to be a blessing for those less fortunate than yourselves. Our Heavenly Father has said, "Generosity towards others covers a multitude of sins."

Remember, our Heavenly Father, Jesus, and a myriad of angels are always with you. Keep your spirits up and stay productive in your walk with God blessing others as best you can. It is possible to grow in the Lord without going to church. However I do not recommend it. You are missing out on to many good friends and lots of joy.

Above all things embrace
our Heavenly Father as best you can
and go in peace rejoicing.

WHAT IS FAITH?

Many people today believe faith means: BLIND FAITH. People today think they can have faith when they don't know anything about the Bible and God. Many today think if they just say they believe in God that is the faith God and the Bible are talking about. They could not be more wrong. That kind of faith will not get you anywhere with God. Let me give you an example of that kind of faith.

I have an Uncle named Burt. I have never meet him or spoken to him. He lives 1000 miles away from me. I've heard he is a wonderful man. My family members and neighbors have told me many different things about him over the years. I have heard some very loving things about my Uncle Burt. I have also heard some very disturbing things about him. I suppose the reason I've heard so many different things about him is because no one in my family or neighbors have ever meet him.

Well I've decided he is a good man and I'm going to do whatever I think he wants me to do. Just jump right in there trust the law of chance and hope everything works out for the best. I can't wait to learn more about my Uncle Burt from family members and neighbors in the future.

Are you getting the point here.

How ridiculous it is to have faith in someone you do not know. You can not rely on the beliefs and interpretations by others about someone whom you do not know. With this kind of blind faith you will never make it through hard times. You will never make it through tragedies. You will never make it through a demon standing in front of you with a Bible in hand, Jesus pin and bumper sticker. When it comes to our Heavenly Father we are talking about life and death for yourself and your children. Think about it!

Do you have an ear, are you listening?

Brothers and sisters if any of you are wondering what faith is and how to get it I'll show you. Let's look into faith.

Hebrews 11:1
*11:1 Now faith is the substance of things **hoped for,** the evidence of things **not seen.***

11:2 For by it the elders obtained a good report.

Notice the words, "evidence of things not seen," or you could say "convincing evidence proved by realities." The way to get faith is through God from His written Word. Therefore the scriptures. Faith is in <u>knowing</u> our Heavenly Father and His Son Jesus Christ. The only way to know God and His Son Jesus Christ is through the scriptures. The "things hoped for" are God's promises revealed in scripture. The things "not seen" are our Heavenly Father and His Son Jesus Christ in person.

The scriptures DO NOT contradict themselves.

The Word of our Heavenly Father has been proved accurate over and over in history and today. Through reading God's Word you will be able to see and prove logical reality through the power of reason over and over. The written Word of God has great power. Rather than try and explain the miracle of that power I would prefer that you start reading the scriptures and experience that power first hand.

When you read the scriptures you will see the truth and logic in them. Once this miracle begins to take place you will be able to clearly see the difference between truth and deception. Hence with each Word confirming they are truth and no one can persuade you otherwise. You will come to trust God's Word and the power of His Word. At that time you will come to realize what a loving Heavenly Father He is to mankind. You will come to trust God and trust His Word.

You will then come to know our Heavenly Father. You will come to know Him so well you will be able to say, "Our Heavenly Father says this, or He says that." You will be firm in what you know to be our Heavenly Father feelings, opinions and promises. You will firmly know the dept of His love and the dept of His anger and wrath. You will then have faith in someone you know very well. Your Faith will be strong and confident. In these last days that we are living in you will need this kind of strong unwavering faith and relationship with God to make it through successfully.

THIS IS FAITH

Hebrews 11:6

11:6 But without faith it is impossible to please Him: for He that comes to God must believe that He is, and that He is a rewarder of them that diligently seek Him.

Ephesians 2:8+9

2:8 For by grace are you saved through faith; and that not of yourselves: it is the gift of God:

2:9 Not of works, lest any man should boast.

Habakkuk 2:4

2:4 Behold, his soul which is lifted up is not upright in him: but the just shall live by his faith.

Since the beginning of time man has relied on blind faith with nothing to back up their faith or beliefs. That is how gay people became lost in God's scriptures for so many years. Mankind loves to let others do their thinking for them. That has been such a safe place for so many weak lazy religious people for thousands of years. Those weak, lazy, religious people are always wanting man's approval rather than our Heavenly Father's approval and truth. Therefore proving God's Word accurate again. While multitudes head right down a crowded road to everlasting destruction. Completely ignorant and blind with deception.

BROTHERS AND SISTERS,
TAKE THE TIME TO GET TO KNOW OUR CREATOR
DO YOUR OWN THINKING,
AND YOUR OWN BELIEVING!

Check the scriptures out for yourselves. If a Bible teacher says God says this or that go to the scriptures and check it out for yourselves. If you know the Word of God, and you see contradictions, then you know you have been lied to again. Be well versed in God's Word so Satan and his demons cannot trick or lie to you and others again. Get to know the Heavenly Father who created you and you will see everything in the world around you through God's eyes. All the glorious people, and all the beautiful nature around you that you see every day, didn't just come together by the law of chance. Everything in the universe was put together by a master planner. Come to know God. Come to learn how He feels about the universe and the population He has created. Relying on intelligence and ingenuity will not be sufficient as we continue moving forward into these last days.

YOU CANNOT HAVE FAITH IN SOMEONE
OR BELIEVE IN SOMEONE
WHOM YOU DO NOT KNOW.
IF YOU WANT TO KNOW OUR HEAVENLY FATHER,
OPEN YOUR BIBLE AND START READING.

Our Heavenly Father
is not just a whimsical figure
sitting on a cloud.
He is a living, breathing soul,
the creator of all things in existence,
including mankind.

He has the ability to suppress
the selfish and hateful tendencies of greed,
power, and lust,
that rule the major parts of our lives.

If you cannot accept
our Heavenly Father and His Son
Jesus Christ on faith,
then you are doomed to a life
dominated by doubt.

Brothers and sisters you will know our Heavenly Father when you are done reading this revelation. But don't let your growth end here. Purchase A Name In Heaven Bible, or A Name In Heaven Bible Revised, and continue to strengthen your relationship with our Heavenly Father and His Son Jesus Christ and continue build your faith.

This is for your benefit. Not for God's benefit.

THE BIBLICAL BAPTIZING
OF A TRANSGENDER

The past few generations have thought poorly of our Heavenly Father's transgender people. Transgender people in today's world suffer horrendous harassment, hostility, violence, and even death. Today's church leaders and their congregation members are responsible for this oppression and hatred. False Bible teachers have taught for generations that a person who dresses in attire normally worn by the opposite gender is sinful and an abomination in the eyes of God.

These false Bible teachers have lead their congregations to believe these types of people are a part of Satan's world and all should reject and stay clear of them. I for one would not want to be responsible for this type of teaching before God. Depriving anyone from worshiping and gathering together with fellow believers is an enormous abomination before God. Separating God's children from the church and worship is an abomination in the eyes of God, as you have already learned.

I once knew a Christian brother who was very active in his church and was part of a community service agency that provided Christian counseling. I asked him if he ever had a transgender person ask for help from his service. He said, "Oh, Lord no! I'm sure people like that don't care anything about God or Christianity. We never get any people like that." The tone of his voice sounded appalled that I had the very audacity to suggest such a thing. He went on to state that he felt someone who would cross dress would be very disturbed and quite demonic in behavior and lifestyle. He said it with great authority in his voice.

Sadly not only are church leaders deceiving church members, but their influence trickles out to main stream society as well. Because of this "Who can I hate next?" type of Christianity, our Christian society has become so heartless and cold and their thinking so corrupt and polluted towards so many people. Even the majority of gay and lesbian people have rejected these brothers and sisters. Much of the mainstream gay and lesbian community desperately seek the approval of homophobic society in their desperate attempt to be accepted. Our own gay and lesbian people sell out and reject their own kind because their desire to please man is greater than their desire to please God.

Our Heavenly Father's transgender people have been forced to live in an underworld type of environment for generations. Our Heavenly Father's transgender children are often forced into prostitution because most companies will not hire them. Many companies have the mentality that surely no one in our decent society would be anything but appalled dealing with these types of people.

Let's take a look at what the creator of all things has to say about these transgender brothers and sisters.

Matthew 10:5-11
10:5 These twelve Jesus sent forth, and commanded them, saying, **Go not** *into the way of the Gentiles, and into any city of the Samaritans* **enter ye not:**

10:6 But go rather to the **lost sheep of the house of Israel.**

10:7 And as ye go, **preach,** *saying,* **The kingdom of Heaven is at hand.**

10:8 Heal the sick, cleanse the lepers, raise the dead, cast out devils: **freely ye have received, freely give.**

10:9 Provide neither gold, nor silver, nor brass in your purses,

10:10 Nor scrip for your journey, neither two coats, neither shoes, nor yet staves: for the workman is worthy of his meat.

10:11 And into whatsoever city or town ye shall enter, **enquire who in it is worthy;** *and there abide till ye go thence.*

Here Jesus is giving instruction to the His disciples. Instructing them to find His lost sheep, preach to them, heal the lame, and raise the dead. Jesus is also telling them that the millennium is approaching. They are told to search out **all who are worthy of salvation and everlasting life.**

*10:15 Verily I say unto you, **It shall be more tolerable for the land of Sodom and Gomorrah** in the day of judgment, than for that city.*

This scripture shows the people of Sodom and Gomorrah stand a better chance on judgment day than those who reject God's Word, God's instruction, God's gay, lesbian, and transgender children today. The reason the people of Sodom and Gomorrah have not been judged and will be resurrected in the millennium (at the second coming of Christ) is because they never knew God prior to their destruction.

Jesus said the same thing to the Pharisees for their hard hearts, for lying and twisting God's Word, and for their corrupt behavior. Remember the Pharisees were the foremost educated and respected preachers and Bible teachers of <u>their</u> day. They look and sound just like today's foremost educated and respected preachers and Bible teachers.

Matthew 23:13+14

*23:13 But **woe** unto **you,** scribes and Pharisees, **hypocrites! for ye shut up the kingdom of Heaven against men**: for ye neither go in yourselves, neither suffer ye them that are entering to go in.*

*23:14 **Woe** unto **you,** scribes and Pharisees, **hypocrites!** for ye devour widows' houses, and for **a pretence make long prayer:** therefore ye shall receive the greater damnation.*

Matthew 23:27+28

*23:27 **Woe** unto **you,** scribes and Pharisees, **hypocrites!** for ye are like unto whited sepulchres, which indeed **appear beautiful outward,** but are within full of dead men's bones, **and of all uncleanness.***

*23:28 Even so ye also **outwardly appear righteous** unto men, but within ye are **full of hypocrisy and iniquity.***

Matthew 12:30+31
*12:30 **He that is not with me is against me;** and he that gathereth not with me scattereth abroad.*

*12:31 Wherefore I say unto you, **All manner of sin and blasphemy shall be forgiven unto men:** but the blasphemy against the Holy Ghost shall not be forgiven unto men.*

AN ANGEL

sent these disciples out. Let's see who they found.

Acts 8:26
*8:26 And the **angel** of the Lord spake unto Philip, saying, Arise, and go toward the south unto the way that goeth down from Jerusalem unto Gaza, which is desert.*

Acts 8:27
*8:27 And he arose and went: and, **behold**, a man of Ethiopia, an **eunuch** of great authority under Candace queen of the Ethiopians, who had the charge of all her treasure, and had **come to Jerusalem for to worship,***

Keep in mind who sent Philip to the Ethiopian eunuch. It was the angel. Notice an angel told Philip to go down the road towards Gaza. Notice Philip says; "BEHOLD!" An Ethiopian eunuch. Behold means: to look at, to look suddenly, to suddenly see a surprise vision. The way "BEHOLD!" is used here it appears the eunuch was identifiable by sight. It is Philip speaking here. How would Philip know this man was a eunuch by sight? Considering we are talking about eunuchs, (or gay people) it's likely the man was in some kind of apparel that identified him as a eunuch by a first glance.

He was likely in unusual apparel or drag.

The eunuch was on his way back from one of the biggest events of the year. The festival in Jerusalem was an annual event. The biggest event of the year at that time and the entire known world knew about it. It would be comparable to the academy awards of today. That Ethiopian eunuch was representing the empire of Ethiopia while in Jerusalem as well as a culture of eunuchs.

You can bet he was dressed to impress, --- with chariot!

Considering the gay culture I have known in my lifetime most transgender people tend to stand out in a crowd. Transgender people are often quite flashy in apparel especially at special events. History has documented that transgender people were not any different in Biblical times. The scriptures make it very clear that this eunuch was identifiable by sight. This eunuch was returning from the biggest event of the year and logic tells us he was dressed in all his glory.

Either I am accurate here or that eunuch was in that chariot completely naked. Displaying that he didn't have a penis for everyone to see. God through the scriptures has already taught us that the majority of eunuchs did indeed have their penises. God has also taught us at Deuteronomy 23:1, "the castration of oneself or others," was not happening among God's people. This sin was punishable by death. Even if this eunuch was one of the few who were literally castrated he would not have been driving that chariot nude.

Keep in mind God's Word has already shown us that the majority of eunuchs did have their penises. We are talking about gay, lesbian, and transgender people here. The eunuch was logically dressed in attire that identified him as a eunuch. If you see a man driving a car do you say, "Oh, look a gay person," No, not unless the man is displaying in some way that he is gay, or **dressed** in a way that identifies him as gay. Keep in mind, "there is nothing new under the sun." Let's move forward.

Acts 8:28

*8:28 Was returning, and **sitting in his chariot reading** Isaiah the prophet.*

Notice the eunuch was reading the scriptures of Isaiah.

Acts 8:29

8:29 Then the Spirit said unto Philip, Go near, and join thyself to this chariot.

Notice the angel instructs Philip to approach the eunuch. Notice who is calling the shots here. It's not Philip.

It's the angel.....Who sent the angel?......God did.

Acts 8:30

8:30 And Philip ran thither to him, and heard him read the prophet Esaias, and said, Understandest thou what thou readest?

The eunuch is reading Isaiah 53:8 where it talks about Jesus dying for our sins. Philip asks if he knows what he is reading. The eunuch says; No.

Acts 8:31-35

8:31 And he said, How can I, except some man should guide me? And he desired Philip that he would come up and sit with him.

8:32 The place of the scripture which he read was this, He was led as a sheep to the slaughter; and like a lamb dumb before his shearer, so opened he not his mouth:

*8:33 In his humiliation his judgment was taken away: **and who shall declare his generation?** for his life is taken from the earth.*

*8:34 **And the eunuch answered Philip,** and said, I pray thee, of* *whom speaketh the prophet this? **of himself, or of some other man?***

*8:35 **Then Philip opened his mouth, and began at the same scripture, and preached unto him Jesus.***

These scriptures show that the eunuch was reading Isaiah. But the eunuch didn't understand what he was reading. Philip explained to him how Jesus was a sacrifice for <u>his</u> sins and **the eunuch was concerned about who would tell the details of his generation** now that Jesus had died.

Acts 8:36
*8:36 And as they went on their way, they came unto a certain water: and the eunuch said, See, here is water; **what doth hinder me to be baptized?***

*8:37 And Philip said, **If thou believest** with all thine heart, thou mayest. And he answered and said, I believe **that Jesus Christ is the Son of God.***

*8:38 And he commanded the **chariot** to stand still: and they went down both into the water, both Philip and the **eunuch; and he baptized him.***

This shows Philip baptized the Ethiopian eunuch. Don't forget who has been calling all the shots since

Acts 8:26.................the angel.

Acts 8:39
*8:39 **And when they were come up out of the water, the Spirit of the Lord caught away Philip, that the eunuch saw him no more: and he went on his way rejoicing.***

I do not even want to know what most of today's Bible teachers would do, or say, if they saw one of our Heavenly Fathers transgender children sitting in their car reading Isaiah.

- God doesn't love you.
- You couldn't possibly understand the scriptures.
- Oh, your going to need to go in the closet before God would ever hear your voice.
- Oh, you would need to turn heterosexual before God would ever listen to you.
- Oh, God will require you to turn heterosexual before He would give you Bible understanding.
- I'm afraid God finds your lifestyle very sinful.
- Oh, don't you know that cross dressing is the worst sin in the Bible.
- Oh, God would never accept a transgender person, I wouldn't waste your time.
- Oh, before you start reading Isaiah, I recommend a complete 8 hour seminar about how God feels about gay, lesbian and transgender people.

Notice in Acts 8:39 they both came out of the water and the angel quickly led Philip away. This angel did not come to Philip in a human form. Neither Philip or the eunuch saw the angel. Philip only felt his presence and heard his voice and knew that he was there directing things. This was also the case when the angel came to the disciples earlier. This was also my experience on Oct. 30, 1996. This is also the experience I am having now as I write this revelation.

It's important to take a close look at what God said in Acts 8:26-40. The angel came to Philip at Acts 8:26 and directed every step using Philip. After the angels mission was complete, the baptizing of an obvious eunuch, an obvious gay, lesbian, transgender person the angel quickly left.

The angel saw to it that not one tiny detail was missing in his mission. Every detail from the way the eunuch was pointed out to be identifiable by sight. The fact that the eunuch was a lover of God. The eunuchs acknowledgment of Christ and ultimately the eunuchs baptism. Let us also appreciate the fact that the eunuch went away rejoicing. The eunuch wasn't required to change his orientation, or jump through any kind of hoops to be worthy of coming to Christ in baptism or to obtain salvation. The eunuch was never instructed to turn heterosexual or change his attire.

Now I have shown you many things thus far. You didn't hear the angel or Philip say at any time, "You need to turn heterosexual first. You need to dress differently. You're not worthy because you are a eunuch. You must quit smoking, loose 20 pounds,"etc.

God, the angel, and Philip accepted the eunuch as he was and baptized the eunuch just as he was. He was not instructed to give up his sexual orientation, any lifestyle, a husband, his children, etc. The Ethiopian eunuch was loved and accepted just as he was an obvious eunuch. A eunuch who was identifiable by sight from a distance.

THE EUNUCH WENT ON HIS WAY REJOICING!

This eunuch was still a eunuch before and after his baptism. He didn't suddenly turn heterosexual. He went on his way rejoicing, still a transgender person, living the same obedient lifestyle he was living before his baptism. Surely you would not walk away rejoicing if you were told to do something that was out of your power to do. Such as turn heterosexual or to dress heterosexual, act heterosexual, give up your spouses, walk away from your children, etc. Not many churches today would baptize a transgender person. Today's churches are so far removed from our Heavenly Father's love and understanding. Most of today's churches no longer show any resemblance of God's personality.

It is insanity to believe tens of thousands of men were running around castrating themselves in ancient times for God or any other reason. Not one of us would! It is insanity and an abomination to our Heavenly Father to castrate ourselves or pretend to be heterosexual to obtain God's favor and salvation!

I knew a Preacher years ago who I thought was a brilliant and level headed man. We will call him Joe, he was a scientist. He had many years of education as a scientist. He had twenty five years of Bible education and Bible teaching under his belt. I respected this man because I always found him to be down to earth and realistic on all subjects. One day I had given a sermon to the congregation. A particular format had been given to me on a specific subject matter. In my sermon I used a scripture that included a eunuch even though I didn't have a clue what a eunuch was.

After my sermon this preacher whom I had always respected came to me and expressed how much he enjoyed my sermon. I asked him, "What was a eunuch anyway?" I was always full of wonder and questions. An attribute that my church and many church members hated by the way. This highly intelligent preacher, whom I had always admired for his maturity and level head, when it came to life and his understanding of God, suddenly began to turn into someone I had never seen before. His brain turned into pudding before my very eyes.

He responded by lowering his voice to a soft whisper and stretched out his words, saying; "Oh, the eunuchs were men of ancient times who really loved God a lot. Oh, these men loved God so much they would cut off their penises. That's how much they loved God. Men way back then really loved God a lot."

Needless to say seeing this preacher behave and react this way was so strange. Of course, the entire time the very subject was making me cringe. I wanted to hold my crotch. I was thinking; "I could never love God that much." For years after that I never gave my question another thought. I just walked away from the question thinking, "Well I guess man doesn't get to know everything about the Bible." Since my visit from the angel I can not count the number of times I have seen preachers respond the same way when it comes to eunuchs.

**If it looks ridiculous, sounds ridiculous,
and people start to stretch out their words
as if something mystical happened,
it is often ridiculous.**

Additional Reference
(Mt. 10:5-18) (Mt.13:9-19)(1Jo.5:19+20)(Pr.1:1-9)(De.29:29
(1Sa.16:5-7)(Jer.17:9-12)(Ro.10:4-14)

Revelation 4:11
4:11 Thou art worthy, O Lord, to receive glory and honour and power: for thou hast created all things, and for thy pleasure they are and were created.

If you look at any Bible you will find Acts 8:37 has been omitted. From my research I have learned that the first modern English Bible translation was written through the direction of King James back in 1611. To my knowledge prior to 1611 all they had were original manuscripts, written in ancient Hebrew, Aramaic and Greek. There were some German translations prior to 1611. Considering the attitudes of the Spanish explorers who came to America in 1542, it is my belief that Acts 8:37 was omitted from the original manuscripts back then as well.

It is logical to me in reading the book of Acts that the Bible writer Luke was told by the angel guiding him to omit what was originally said at that point. It is very possible that the Ethiopian eunuch, or Philip, said something that clearly identified the eunuch as being transgender.

Acts 8:37 was omitted by God's direction for a reason. Considering eunuchs had a name in Heaven greater than son or daughter, and a monument in Heaven representing their honor, it is likely, had this fact been apparent all these years, many people would have claimed being eunuch for arrogant reasons. Perhaps today's false Bible teachers would have wanted that glory for themselves. Rather than the everyday common imperfect worshipers like the rest of us.

WHATEVER!
A TRANSGENDER PERSON
WAS BAPTIZED, JUST AS HE WAS,
BY GOD'S DIRECTION,
and that you can bet was for a reason.

Do you have an ear, are you listening?

Lgbt brothers and sisters let's run through a list of what I have revealed to you so far......

- Scripture is for setting things straight.
- Eunuch, is the ancient slang term for gay, lesbian and transgender.
- Most eunuchs had all their sexual organs.
- Most would have been sexual.
- Lgbt people are mentioned from Genesis to Revelation.
- Lgbt people were all over the planet, and the Bible does speak of them loving.
- It would be absurd to believe there weren't any gay, lesbian, and transgender people in ancient times.

- Eunuchs were loved by God.
- Eunuchs were loved and trusted by Kings.
- In Biblical times eunuchs were loved and respected by all people.
- They had the same types of jobs in ancient times as they do today.
- Eunuchs had children.
- Mordecai raised Esther.
- If not for Mordecai and Esther, Abraham's seed would have been wiped out.
- Mordecai, the eunuch, a gay Father, wrote the book of Esther.
- Eunuchs went to church and worshiped just like everyone else.
- Eunuchs were just like everyone else, some good, some bad.
- Most eunuchs who were married, were married to the same gender.
- Sodom and Gomorrah had heterosexual and Lgbt people living there.
- Sodom and Gomorrah were destroyed because of extreme lawlessness, sexual violence and sin.
- Sodom and Gomorrah was not a lesson about being Lgbt.
- Sodom and Gomorrah was not about a multitude of people who had or have a same gender attraction.
- There were eunuchs all over the earth at the time of Sodom and Gomorrah's destruction.
- Bible teachers have been wrong to exclude Lgbt people from worship, marriage, and salvation.

- The word for "eunuch" has changed many times since Biblical times.
- Bible teachers have been wrong to single out Lgbt people as sinners.
- Many Bible teachers have behaved just like the scriptures said, like devouring wolves.
- God will deal with those false teachers.
- Many of today's Bible teachers are liar's speaking the utterance of demons.
- We need to forgive those who transgress against us.
- God can see a persons heart.
- God judges a person by their heart.
- We should appreciate the heterosexual people who have treated us fairly and with kindness.
- A same gender attraction is the only sin a person is born with, or made that way according to scriptures, i.e. God.
- Only God can change a persons sexual orientation.
- Eunuchs and heterosexuals should choose singleness as a first choice.
- If you are inflamed with lust, then you should marry.
- Not all people understand the Bible.
- Bible understanding comes from God.
- People have gone to church for 50 years and still do not have Bible understanding.
- There are Bible teachers who do not have Bible understanding.
- Not all people will understand this revelation from God.
- We are living in the last days, just before the millennium.

- The time has come for God to reveal an abundance of knowledge to His Lgbt children.
- All people should be as obedient as they possibly can.
- God has a name in Heaven, greater than son or daughter, for obedient gay, lesbian, and transgender people with faith.
- God has a monument in Heaven, in honor of obedient gay, lesbian, and transgender people.
- The reason God gave this name and monument, is because Lgbt people were given a sin they didn't choose and couldn't change, and were still expected to be obedient.
- Satan is responsible for today's views about Lgbt people.
- False Bible teachers are responsible for today's views about Lgbt people.
- The scriptures give the same instruction for gays and heterosexuals.
- Sin means: human imperfection.
- All people are sinners.
- All sin is the same to God.
- It is man's idea that one sin is worse than another.
- Being gay is not a choice, and we must wait on God's timing to see Him change our sexual orientation.
- Obedient people with faith are forgiven for their sins through Jesus Christ.
- Gay, lesbian, and transgender people are God's children.
- God loves Lgbt people who try to be obedient.
- All of God's scriptures are a promise to mankind.
- We can count on God.

- Every sort of man or women can come to God.
- God is calling us in the condition we are in.
- God knows you are Lgbt, and he knows all of your other sins.
- **God is calling us.**
- **God's great harvest has begun.**
- **God is gathering all his Lgbt children under his wing, because the end is near.**
- God has decided now is the time to tell the details of these generations of eunuchs.
- God gave special attention to see to it that a transgender eunuch was baptized.
- He knew what the future would hold for them.
- Lgbt people of today are no different than the eunuchs of ancient times.
- The Ethiopian eunuch was accepted by God, the angel, and Philip just as he was.
- The Ethiopian eunuch didn't have to make any changes after he was baptized, such as turning heterosexual.
- The only way to know God is through the scriptures.
- The only way to have faith in God and His Son Jesus is through knowing them through the scriptures.

You can not believe in, or have faith in, someone you do not know.

Matthew 11:28
Come unto me, all ye that labour and are heavy laden, and I will give you rest.

Lgbt brothers and sisters do you have an ear, are you listening? God has given you such a blessing and such an abundance of knowledge through this revelation. God has shown you through this revelation how much He loves you.

GOD IS CALLING YOU!

**He is standing in front of you,
arms wide open, waiting for you to run into them.
Just like a Father embraces his child when he has
been hurt and injured. He loves you so much.
Go to our Heavenly Father just like the Ethiopian
eunuch did and tell Him you love Him. Ask Him to forgive
you for all your sins, in the name of His Son Jesus Christ,
and go rejoicing!**

I'm going to give you some good advice now. Do not walk away from this revelation beating yourself up over the law or your imperfections.

**Change the things you can change,
and forgive yourself for the things you cannot change.**

Give the things you can not change over to God and patiently wait on His timing to change it. God will change you when He is ready and not before. Go-rejoicing! Our Heavenly Father wants to see you rejoicing tomorrow, next week, next year, right into the millennium.

Additional Reference
(Mt.9:13)(Ac.22:12-16)(Neh.1:9-11)(Mt.13:30)(Isa.65:13-25
(Isa.35:3-10)(Ro.10:4-14)(Lu.5:32)(1Co.7:1-40)

Lgbt brothers and sisters it is that simple.

This angel is telling me some of you don't believe you are worthy of forgiveness. You believe you have to many sins under your belt. Let me tell you a little about the apostle Paul. He was a Pharisee. He killed many of Christ's followers. He was corrupt, arrogant, and zealous in his persecution of Christians.

Our Heavenly Father changed his heart and put him in line with obedience. Paul went on to write most of the new testament. Not only did he bring many to salvation when he was alive, but since, his writings have brought many millions to salvation. If our Heavenly Father can forgive Paul for all he did against IIim, and IIis Son, He can forgive you for what you have done in the past. As a matter of fact God used Paul as an example for those of you who feel you had to many sins to ever be forgiven.

**Ask God to forgive you,
in the name of His Son Jesus Christ,
forgive yourselves, and go rejoicing!**

Go out with this revelation and all of God's blessings. Share this revelation with the multitude of lost and wounded, gay, lesbian, and transgender people, who haven't heard God's blessings as of yet. Show our Heavenly Father your appreciation for this blessing.

Baptism is a public declaration of the words you just read. Go to your nearest Lgbt friendly church and make your public declaration, just like the Ethiopian eunuch did, and so many millions of eunuchs before you have. No, you don't need to be in drag! Remember, many eunuchs were military officers and not all were feminine. Go in peace, rejoicing, God's precious children.

Additional Reference
(Lu.15:7,10)

2 Timothy 3:16 +17
3:16 All scripture is given by inspiration of God, and is profitable for doctrine, for reproof, for <u>correction</u>, for instruction in righteousness:

Notice the word
"CORRECTION."

3:17 That the man of God may be perfect, throughly furnished unto all good works.

Matthew 19:11+12
*19:11 But he said unto them, All men cannot receive this saying, **save they to whom it is given.***

*19:12 For there are **some eunuchs**, which were **so born from their mother's womb**: and there are **some eunuchs**, which were **made eunuchs of men**: and there **be eunuchs**, which have **made themselves eunuchs for the kingdom of Heaven's sake.** He that is able to receive it, let him receive it.*

These scriptures show us only some
will understand God's message.
The Bible was written to be this way
on purpose.
It isn't a mistake.
More than likely it is for our protection.

Additional Reference
(Mt.13:9-19)(1Jo.5:19+20)(Pr.1:1-9)(De.29:29)

Gᴏᴅ'ꜱ ɢʀᴇᴀᴛ ʜᴀʀᴠᴇꜱᴛ ʜᴀꜱ ʙᴇɢᴜɴ

Brothers and sisters,
"Do you have an ear, are you listening?"

GOD IS CALLING YOU!

Our Heavenly Father has revealed the existence and details of Biblical generations of Lgbt people to us through these scriptures and this revelation. We are living in the last days. God's knowledge is coming to mankind in an abundance.

Daniel 12:3+4
12:3 And they that be wise shall shine as the brightness of the firmament; and they that turn many to righteousness as the stars for ever and ever.

12:4 But thou, O Daniel, shut up the words, and seal the book, even to the time of the end: many shall run to and fro, and knowledge shall be increased.

I want you to notice the words **"run to and fro."** The only time the Bible uses that term, "run to and fro," is when referring to angels roving about on the earth. You are reading the inspirations of the angel that is guiding me right now.

Do you have an ear, are you listening?

DID YOU NOTICE THE WORDS, "UNTIL THE TIME OF THE END?"

Colossians 1:13+14

*1:13 Who hath **delivered us from the power of darkness,** and hath translated us into the kingdom of his dear Son:*

*1:14 In whom we have redemption through his blood, **even the forgiveness of sins:***

Ephesians 1:2-6

1:2 Grace be to you, and peace, from God our Father, and from the Lord Jesus Christ.

*1:3 Blessed be the God and Father of our Lord Jesus Christ, who hath **blessed us with all spiritual blessings in Heavenly places in Christ:***

*1:4 According as **he hath chosen us in him before the foundation of the world,** that we should be holy and without blame before him in love:*

*1:5 Having **predestinated us unto the adoption of children by Jesus** Christ to himself, according to the good pleasure of his will,*

*1:6 To the praise of the glory of his grace, **wherein he hath made us accepted in the beloved.***

Did you notice at Ephesians 1:4 it states:

"he hath chosen us"

Before the foundation of the world
HE HAS CHOSEN YOU.

Our Heavenly Father has chosen you.

HE IS NOW CALLING YOU

He is calling you to come under His protection. Because the end is drawing near. Our Heavenly Father does not want to see any of His children lost when He brings in the new order. A new order that will be dominated by His Son Jesus Christ here on earth. Our Heavenly Father wants to see all of His children there to enjoy all the blessings He has in store for us. These scriptures clearly show that Jesus is the ransom for our sins. That is why Jesus died on the cross, FOR US. His shed blood fulfilled the old law covenant for sins. Mankind waited for thousands of years for Jesus to come for that purpose.

Romans 3:19-24,

3:19 *Now we know that what things soever the law saith, it saith to them who are __under the law;__ that every mouth may be stopped, and __all the world may become guilty before God__.*

3:20 *__Therefore by the deeds of the law__ there shall __no flesh be justified in his sight;__ for by the law is the knowledge of sin.*

3:21 *But now the righteousness of God __without the law__ is manifest, being witnessed by the law and the prophets;*

3:22 *Even the righteousness of God which is __by faith of Jesus Christ__ unto all and upon all them that believe; for there is no difference;*

3:23 *<u>For all have sinned, and come short of the glory of God;</u>*

3:24 *Being justified <u>freely</u> by his grace through the redemption that is in Christ Jesus.*

- **Notice in verse 19, it states; "UNDER THE LAW"**
- Notice in verse 20, it states; **"THEREFORE BY DEEDS OF LAW, NO FLESH WILL BE JUSTIFIED RIGHTEOUS."**
- Notice verse 21, states; **"WITHOUT THE LAW"** meaning we are not accused by it anymore.

The purpose of the law is to show us our sin.
Not to crucify us with it.

- Notice in verse 22, it states; **"by faith in Jesus Christ,"** through **"faith"** we are forgiven for our sins.
- Notice in verse 24, it states; it is **"freely"** given.

This is a FREE GIFT.

Can you get this free gift by living up to one or all of the laws? NO! Can you get this free gift through lots and lots of volunteer work or hours of prayer? NO! You cannot earn or pay for this gift. It is undeserved and it is free from our Heavenly Father. This is God's undeserved kindness towards us. You could live up to every law and commandment in the Bible and it will not buy your forgiveness. Only "faith" in Jesus gives us forgiveness for our sins and salvation.

**IT IS THAT SIMPLE.
DO YOU REMEMBER HOW I TOLD YOU
HOW TO GET FAITH?
YOU CAN NOT BELIEVE IN SOMEONE
OR HAVE FAITH IN SOMEONE
<u>WHOM YOU DO NOT KNOW</u>.
THE ONLY WAY TO KNOW OUR HEAVENLY FATHER
AND HIS SON IS THROUGH THE SCRIPTURES.**

Never again is anyone going to lead us to believe if we turn heterosexual, or pretend to be heterosexual, we are somehow going to earn that "free gift" of forgiveness from God!

NEVER AGAIN!

Romans 1:16-19

*1:16 For I am not ashamed of the gospel of Christ: for it is the power of God unto salvation to **every one that believeth**; to the Jew first, and also to the Greek.*

*1:17 For therein is the righteousness of God revealed from **faith to faith:** as it is written, **The just shall live by faith.***

*1:18 For the wrath of God is revealed from Heaven against all **ungodliness and unrighteousness** of men, who hold the truth in unrighteousness;*

*1:19 Because that which may be known of God is manifest in them; **for God hath shewed it unto them.***

Romans 3:23
For all have sinned, and come short of the glory of God;

GOD IS GATHERING HIS LGBT CHILDREN TOGETHER FOR SALVATION.

Isaiah 65:15-25

*65:15 And ye shall leave your name for a curse unto my chosen: for the Lord GOD shall slay thee, **and call his servants by another name:***

*65:16 That he who blesseth himself in the earth shall bless himself in the God of truth; and he that sweareth in the earth shall swear by the God of truth; because the **former troubles are forgotten,** and because they are hid from mine eyes.*

*65:17 For, behold, I **create new Heavens and a new earth**: and the **former shall not be remembered, nor come into mind.***

*65:18 But **be ye glad and rejoice for ever in that which I create:** for, behold, I create Jerusalem a rejoicing, and her people a joy.*

*65:19 And I will rejoice in Jerusalem, **and joy in my people**: and the voice of **weeping shall be no more** heard in her, **nor the voice of crying.***

65:20 There shall be no more thence an infant of days, nor an old man that hath not filled his days: for the child shall die an hundred years old; but the sinner being an hundred years old shall be accursed.

*65:21 **And they shall build houses, and inhabit them; and they shall plant vineyards, and eat the fruit of them.***

65:22 They shall not build, and another inhabit; they shall not plant, and another eat: for as the days of a tree are the days of my people, and mine elect shall long enjoy the work of their hands.

65:23 They shall not labour in vain, nor bring forth for trouble; for they are the seed of the blessed of the LORD, and their offspring with them.

*65:24 And it shall come to pass, **that before they call**, I will answer; and **while they are yet speaking, I will hear.***

*65:25 **The wolf and the lamb shall feed together,** and the lion shall eat straw like the bullock: and dust shall be the serpent's meat. **They shall not hurt nor destroy in all my holy mountain, saith the LORD.***

Doesn't this new world order that Jesus is bringing in sound too good to be true. What a glorious time it will be for all mankind. Our Heavenly Father feels the same kind of love, compassion, and concern for us, as earthly parents feel about their children. Perhaps more so considering His love is so tremendous and overwhelming. He created all mankind out of love in the first place. Now, I would like to share a beautiful Bible story with you about the love a father had for a son at;

Luke 15:11-24
15:11 And he said, A certain man had two sons:

15:12 And the younger of them said to his father, Father, give me the portion of goods that falleth to me. And he divided unto them his living.

15:13 And not many days after the younger son gathered all together, and took his journey into a far country, and there wasted his substance with riotous living.

15:14 And when he had spent all, there arose a mighty famine in that land; and he began to be in want.

15:15 And he went and joined himself to a citizen of that country; and he sent him into his fields to feed swine.

15:16 And he would fain have filled his belly with the husks that the swine did eat: and no man gave unto him.

15:17 And when he came to himself, he said, How many hired servants of my father's have bread enough and to spare, and I perish with hunger!

15:18 I will arise and go to my father, and will say unto him, Father, I have sinned against heaven, and before thee,

15:19 And am no more worthy to be called thy son: make me as one of thy hired servants.

15:20 And he arose, and came to his father. But when he was yet a great way off, his father saw him, and had compassion, and ran, and fell on his neck, and kissed him.

15:21 And the son said unto him, Father, I have sinned against heaven, and in thy sight, and am no more worthy to be called thy son.

15:22 But the father said to his servants, Bring forth the best robe, and put it on him; and put a ring on his hand, and shoes on his feet:

15:23 And bring hither the fatted calf, and kill it; and let us eat, and be merry:

15:24 For this my son was dead, and is alive again; he was lost, and is found. And they began to be merry.

This story is so heartbreaking and full of joy at the same time. I will bring this story to life for those of you who need that little extra clarification.

The father and the son had a falling out. The son may have felt there was a world out there that his father was depriving him from. Perhaps the son desired the world and sinful living. The son came to believe working on the farm with his father and serving God was a waste of his time and talent. He had desires for a sinful life. A life that offered various types of sin he was unable to indulge in while living with his father and serving his father's God. The end result was the son asked for all of his inheritance. Immediately after he left his father's farm and God and went to a foreign land. There he squandered his inheritance and lived in disobedience to his father and God.

Notice in Luke 15:20 his father looked out to the distance and saw his son coming home. I'll bet that father was looking out at the hills over the horizon often throughout his work day. Looking for his precious son to come over that horizon. His heart was surely heavy and missing his much loved and spiritually lost son.

Notice in Luke 15:20, when his father saw him coming from a far distance over the horizon. Notice he didn't keep working. He didn't wait for his son to come to him. He ran to meet his son on the road, embraced him, falling on his neck and kissing him.

Back in those days people were not as reserved and sophisticated as people today. These men were rural people and would have been even more simple than the city people of that time. This father would have ran towards his son with his arms stretched forward crying his heart out. He would have been crying so hard that running towards him would have been overwhelming.

If you can imagine how a small child runs towards a parent with their arms stretched out when crying this is how this father would have greeted his son. Back in those days if a child left home to live in a far away land they rarely saw each other again if ever. People traveled on foot and such journeys were difficult. His father had waited with an aching and heavy heart for who knows how long for his son to come over that horizon to return to him and to God. What joy must have filled his heart when he saw that precious boy of his coming over that horizon.

This father could have waited for his son to come to him. He could have greeted his son with harsh words such as, "What do you want! I suppose your broke now! I suppose you want food and money from me now!" Yet, he didn't. He welcomed his beloved son home with open arms. No, "I told you so's," no criticisms, not one harsh word. He was so happy to see his son again and to hold him in his loving embrace.

Notice in Luke 15:22 his father told his servants to bring his son one of his best robes, and a ring, and to put shoes on his feet. Notice that even though the father should have believed he would never see his son again, he still bought gifts for him, when he saw something that he thought his son would like. Such as a ring. His father had his fattest calf prepared for his hungry and tired son and had a big celebration. What a loving father this son had.

Our Heavenly Father feels the same way about you. You have a Heavenly Father who loves you just as much as this father loved his son. Our Heavenly Father's heart has been heavy and aching for you for such a long time. He has been watching for you with a heavy heart. He has been looking for you from a distance to come over that horizon. He has been missing you. Just like that father was missing his lost son. Our Heavenly Father is calling you with this revelation. He is calling all of His gay, lesbian, and transgender children home to His loving embrace. He is standing before you with open arms waiting to embrace you. He knows where you have been and what you have been up to. You are not a surprise to our Heavenly Father. He doesn't care what you have done in the past nor will he ever bring it up to you. Our Heavenly Father's wish is that all His gay, lesbian, and transgender children will hear Him calling and come home to Him.

Do just as the son in this story did. Embrace God by calling His name. Tell Him you are sorry for all of your sins. Tell Him you love Him. Ask Him for forgiveness through His Son Jesus Christ. Embrace all the love waiting for you in His warm loving arms and go in peace rejoicing.

God is calling you!
God's call to His Lgbt children is loud!
Do you hear God calling?

Luke 15:7
I say unto you, that likewise joy shall be in heaven over <u>one</u> sinner that repenteth, more than over ninety and nine just persons, which need no repentance.

Additional Reference

(1Co.7:1-40)(Mt.9:13)(Ac.22:12-16)(Neh.1:9-11)(Mt.13:30)
(Isa.65:13-25, 35:3-10)(Ro.10:4-14)(Lu.5:32)

WHO HAS LIED ABOUT

LGBT PEOPLE?

You cannot believe in God or the truth of the Bible without also believing in Satan. After all it is the scriptures (God's Word) that have taught us about Satan. Many people today say they believe in God but not in Satan. Satan would like nothing more than that. He would love for you to think he doesn't exist or that he is some kind of ugly monster. In reality he is much more crafty and misleading than that. Let's look at what God has said about Satan in the book of Revelation:

Revelation 12:9
*12:9 And the **great dragon** was cast out, **that old serpent**, called the **Devil**, and **Satan,** which **deceiveth** the whole world: **he was cast out into the earth**, and **his angels were cast out** with him.*

Revelation 12:12
*12:12 Therefore rejoice, ye Heavens, and ye that dwell in them. **Woe to the inhabiters of the earth** and of the sea! for **the devil** is **come down unto you,** having great wrath, because **he knoweth that he hath but a short time.***

Notice the words, "Woe to the inhabiters of the earth." The earth is where we live! Satan has come down with great anger. Angry at who? Angry at God. Angry at God's angels, and angry at God's children.

John 8:44

*8:44 Ye are of your Father the devil, and the lusts of your Father ye will do. He was a murderer **from the beginning,** and abode **not in the truth,** because **there is no truth in him. When he speaketh a lie, he speaketh of his own: for he is a liar, and the Father of it.***

These scriptural events are past tense. Satan and his demons have been here on earth for quite some time. Satan and his demons are angry. Who are they coming to destroy all of God's children through false teachers and their followers? These false Bible teachers spread Satan's anger by twisting scripture, spreading lies, and using God's Word to conjure up violence against God's children. Let's be realistic: who would Satan come after first? <u>God's children with a name in Heaven greater than son or daughter, those with a monument in Heaven.</u> Keep in mind Satan and his demons have seen this monument in Heaven with their own eyes. We are already a living testimony to that.

Notice Satan is misleading the entire inhabited earth.
Notice who came down with him.
This explains today's view of Lgbt people.
As well as many other problems in today's world.
The scriptures tell us Satan is the original liar,
the lover of the lie.

Remember brothers and sisters,
Satan and his demons have known about this name,
they have seen this monument in Heaven
with their own eyes.
They will be very unhappy to see this revelation released.
You will see them on the news,
and on talk shows, and standing on the street corners,
with their lies and blasphemy
scrawled across their picket signs.
There Bible in hand, with their Jesus pins and bumper
stickers, in their endless pursuit to oppress
God's Lgbt children.

Additional Reference
(Ez.22:25-31)(Job13:1-5)(Jer.5:21-26)(Ac.20:25-30)(2Co.11:12-15)
(2Th.2:6-12)(Ro.1:21-28)(2Pe.2:19-21)(Ps.7:14-16)

Satan and his followers are out to hurt God's gay, lesbian, and transgender children. Satan has deceived generations of Bible teachers and Christians. Satan has motivated these false teachers and their followers to attack and oppress God's children for generations. These false Bible teachers and their followers have driven over 20 percent of God's gay, lesbian, and transgender children to commit suicide. They have lead a multitude of God's Lgbt children to hate themselves and come to believe they are not worthy of life. In spite of all their hatred and oppression, they continue to press on, in their evil desire to hate and oppress those less fortunate and weaker than themselves.

Lgbt brothers and sisters in my 52 years of life I have seen terrible atrocities against our people. As a result of the false Bible teachers and so called Christians and their lies against us. Lies perpetrated in the name of God, so they have said.

I was able to verbalize that I was gay at the age of fourteen. I told my family and friends I was a homosexual, because the slang term "gay" wasn't in wide use yet. My family was very loving about it. My mother told me, when I was 4 years old my grandfather told our family I was going to be one of those homosexuals. He instructed the family to accept me and not to judge me about it. The majority of my family could not have been more loving or accepting of me.

However, the world I was embracing was hateful, ignorant, and violent against me. Every single friend I had turned against me for not keeping the lie sacred. After two years of the abusive hatred towards me for not living the lie and not loving the lie I grew to hate myself. By the time I turned 16 I tried to kill myself but was unsuccessful. The hostility and opinions of our pastor, our church, the children at school, my neighbors, my entire environment, finally lead me to believe that I was such a horrible person for being openly gay that I didn't deserve to live.

Yet, I knew I could not have peace with God and hold the lie sacred. The only person who ever knew about this was my best friend Sharon. My parents and siblings had gone to six flags for the weekend. I opted to stay home knowing full well what I was going to do. I went to a drug store and purchased a bottle of over the counter sleeping pills. I took every one of them and went to bed.

Considering my best friend Sharon knew my family was going to be away she had big plans for us. Sharon could not reach me by phone for two days. She came to my house and knocked on the door a few times and of course I did not answer. I was in a deep sleep.

By the third day Sharon became worried. She tried to look into my bedroom window to see through a crack in the curtains. When she saw me sleeping she thought it was strange. She started to knock on the bedroom window. The more she knocked the more hysterical she became. Finally, Sharon was hitting the window as hard as she could and crying. She thought I was dead.

I awoke to her pounding and screaming my name and crying hysterically. I walked over to the window and opened it and said, "What's wrong Sharon?" She shouted! "What did you do? Let me in!" When Sharon found me and came to realize what I had done she set up an appointment for me at a local mental health center without my knowledge.

At the time of the appointment she arranged for us to be across the street from the center. She announced what she had done and said my appointment was in 15 minutes. I told her I could never tell anyone that I had tried to kill myself. I told her I wasn't going in that place. Sharon suddenly became this mad woman. Sharon grabbed hold of my coat and dragged me through three feet of snow, over snow banks, between cars, across the street, in front of traffic, across the lawn of the center, straight up to the front door, slamming my body against it. Standing in front of me huffing and puffing, because I was kicking and fighting her all the way. She said, "Your not getting past me Rickie! Now, if you want everyone in this place to see us kicking, fighting, and pushing all the way up to the reception desk, then so be it, but your going in!" I took a deep breath turned around and walked in. She walked me up to the reception desk smiled and said, "Hi, this is Rickie Bartlett he has an appointment in five minutes."

I now realize this angel was directing her actions at that time. He used that sweet loving little girl to save my life. I wondered where she had suddenly obtained all that strength to manhandle me like she did. I felt like a rag doll. Needless to say if not for the intervention of the angel and Sharon, I would not be writing this revelation to the world now. I would not have had the blessed life that I have had. God bless Sharon! I hope her life has been a blessed one. About 20 years later I searched for her by phone. Upon reaching her, she said, "I have been searching for you for 20 years." She said she had been searching every area of California. She said, "I needed to know if you were saved." When I told her I was, she was happy. I asked her if we could stay in touch, but she said, "She was a Christian, and could never socialize with a gay person." I told her that was okay. I have never held that against her. How could I? After all, she and an angel saved my life, when I was just a boy.

The years of therapy that followed changed me forever. I can't count the number of times I have thanked God for Sandy my therapist. Sandy taught me as a young boy how to love myself again in spite of my imperfection and how to cope and face a world that hated me for it. It took Sandy two appointments a week for two years to undo all that society and my home environment had done to lead me to believe I was not worthy of living. God bless this angel and Sandy for watching over me for so long. I hope God has blessed Sandy's life for all that she did for me. The self love and coping skills Sandy taught me have always been with me. She comes to my mind often.

My gratitude and thankfulness for Sharon and Sandy has always been overwhelming. If not for God, the angel, Sharon and Sandy, I would not have lived to have the blessed, joy filled life that I have had. By the looks of it the blessings and joys of life are about to start flowing like a flood, a flood of God's blessings. I am so grateful.

Homophobic Straight People

Heavenly Father,
Please forgive them, for they know not what they do.

I hope you weren't thinking this angel had forgotten or forsaken you.

What would Jesus say if He had to cover this subject?

Matthew 17:17
Then Jesus answered and said,
O you faithless and perverse generation,
how long shall I be with you?
How long shall I suffer you?

1 John 4:20 +21
If a man say, I love God, and hateth his brother,
he is a liar:
for he that loveth not his brother
whom he hath seen,
how can he love God whom he hath not seen?

And this commandment have we from him,
That he who loveth God love his brother also.

Before I begin this chapter I'd like to define the term straight people. When I use the term straight people I am referring to heterosexual women and straight men. I think we all understand what a heterosexual women is. A heterosexual women is attracted to men. Most women world wide are heterosexual.

A straight guy is a male who sleeps with both male and female but keeps their same gender activity secret. I do realize not all men who identify themselves as straight are sleeping with men. However, most straight guys do have sex with other men. In my lifetime I have rarely met a heterosexual male. Heterosexual men are rare in today's world. Most men who have sex with other men and date and marry women label themselves as straight. I think it is proper to identify people with the label that they themselves use as their social identity.

I do realize many straight women will read this and say, "That's not true I know many heterosexual men." Let me say now that I'm not even going there with straight women. People see what they want to see. This is my definition of straight people. Let's just move forward into this chapter.

Homophobic straight brothers and sisters, what I'm about to say, I say out of tremendous love for you. This nation that we live in, this great and beautiful America, has been dominated by a straight majority from the beginning. This majority has never been accepting or loving of open Lgbt people. As a matter of fact the last few generations of straight people have exhausted themselves in an attempt to oppress open gay, lesbian, and transgender people. Depriving them of every basic civil and human right. For generations open Lgbt people have had to fight for every single civil and human right that they have. From the beginning of this modern world all the civil and human rights have been written for the benefit of straight people.

I know many of you are gasping right now. Many of you are thinking what is he talking about. Your thinking I'm wrong, there are open Lgbt people on television, what more do they want? Allow me to give you a reality check. Television is make believe. It is a media of entertainment. In the real world over 60 percent of Americans vote against Lgbt rights and openly admit they disapprove of Lgbt rights and Lgbt people all together.

Your stone cold hearts have created a brutal environment for open Lgbt people world wide. The suicide rate in America among open gay, lesbian, and transgender children is currently at 20 percent, higher than ever before in history. The suicide rate among Lgbt teens is higher than ever before in history. Congratulations, your efforts have been productive and successful. You must be so proud of yourselves. All the while our Heavenly Father has observed your hatred with disgust.

If you have ever voted against a bill benefiting Lgbt people, if you have ever rejected the hiring of Lgbt people, if a derogatory statement or cruel word of any kind has ever passed your lips in regard to Lgbt people, you are homophobic. You are the people I am speaking to here.

2 Timothy 4:4
*4:4 And **they shall turn away their ears from the truth**, and shall be turned unto fables*

Many of you are religious, avid, active church goers, busy in what you perceive as God's work. Some of you are not spiritual at all. Many of you never think of God, know nothing about God and never mention God, until the subject of homosexuality comes up. Then suddenly you become religious and start quoting scripture and remember a God whom you have never had anything to do with. A God whom you have never known.

Matthew 7:22+23
*7:22 **Many will say** to me **in that day,** Lord, **Lord,** have we not prophesied **in thy name?** and **in thy name** have cast out devils? and **in thy name** done many wonderful works?*

*7:23 And then will I profess unto them, **I never knew you:** depart from me, **ye that work iniquity.***

Some of you believe there is a God of some sort, and pick and choose what you want to believe, depending on what you want at any particular moment in time.

James 1:6
But let him ask in faith, nothing wavering.
For he that wavereth is like a wave of the sea driven
with the wind and tossed.

1:7 For let not that man think that he shall receive
any thing of the Lord.

1:8 A double minded man is unstable in all his ways.

Isaiah 6:9
And he said, Go, and tell this people, Hear ye indeed,
but understand not; and see ye indeed, but perceive not.

6:10 Make the heart of this people fat, and make their ears heavy,
and shut their eyes; lest they see with their eyes, and hear with
their ears, and understand with their heart,
and convert, and be healed.

Some of you walked away from God years ago. The reality of it is many of you have never known God. Not for one moment. You blow back and forth like the wind in a constant wavering. The majority of you follow trends and adapt opinions depending on what the latest trend of hateful thinking happens to be.

When the subject of "a same gender attraction" comes up you are suddenly quoting scripture. When your lifestyles are anything but Godly or righteous. Your love is for yourself and no one else. You see gay marriage and all Lgbt rights as a threat to your way of life. The last thing you want to see is someone who's not going to be attracted to you get any rights or privileges at all. You are so arrogant and so full of yourselves. The last thing you want is more competition. The last thing you want to see is your competition get one more privilege or a better way of life. You live in fear that these Lgbt people may have more fun and joy out of life than you are having.

Don't think for one minute that Lgbt people do not see the look in your eyes when you come to realize we are not attracted to you. Don't think for one minute gay men don't know you take those feelings of arrogance, rejection, and anger, with you to the voting booth. Your hearts are not behind God. Your hearts are arrogant and self serving. You use God as a shield to try and hide what really motivates your corrupt hearts.

When I was in high school I saw the look in the eyes of heterosexual females when they saw the straight boys giving me more attention than they were getting. The look of jealousy, which grew into hurtful comments and hurtful behavior towards me later. Needless to say even in my 50's, I still see that look in the eyes of females. You straight men are the same as well. Don't think for one minute lesbian women don't know you take those feelings of arrogance, rejection and anger, with you to the voting booth. Your motives are no surprise to us and your true motives are no surprise to our Heavenly Father. He sees right through you all the way down to your kidneys.

Psalms 9:15-17
9:15 **The heathen are sunk down in the pit that they made**: In the net which they hid is their own foot taken.

9:16 The LORD is known by the judgment which he executeth: **the wicked is snared in the work of his own hands**. Higgaion. Selah.

9:17 The **wicked** shall be turned **into hell**, and all the **nations** that **forget God.**

When it comes to the Lgbt issue you all band together united with your current trend of twisted oppressive religious thinking to stand against Lgbt people. You stand together with your, "Who can I hate next?" type of Christianity. The only thing that binds you together is your jealousy and desire to hate, and oppress those weaker, and those with less social and political power than yourselves.

Ephesians 4:18+19

*4:18 Having the **understanding darkened,** being alienated from the life of God through the **ignorance that is in them,** because of the **blindness of their heart:***

*4:19 Who being past feeling have given themselves over unto lasciviousness, **to work all uncleanness with greediness.***

Considering 60 percent of you homophobic straight people tend to band together. While united on the side of twisted oppressive religious thinking when it comes to Lgbt people and their rights. I am going to group you people together for the purpose of this chapter. Yes, I said,

"YOU PEOPLE!"

Considering you believe the heterosexual and perceived heterosexual way of life is the only acceptable and tolerable way of living.

You are puffed up with pride. Because you were born heterosexual. You are full of yourselves because you just happened to be born part of the majority.

As for you straight men the only lifestyle your trying to preserve is your own down low lifestyle. Your fear is that a day will come when the nations rest areas will be empty. The only people you are fooling are the heterosexual women. Our Heavenly Father see's what you are doing in the dark and He see's your true motives. He see's right through you all the way down to your kidneys.

Straight people have had a haughty and oppressive trend of thinking for generations in this nation. Let me remind you that the ancestors of today's Lgbt people in America shed their blood and gave their lives for the safety and the civil and human rights of their descendants just as yours did. America's Lgbt ancestors built this country with their sweat and tears. They struggled and made sacrifices for a better life in this country for themselves and for their Lgbt and straight descendants. Yet Lgbt people continue to fight for simple civil and human rights that you homophobic straight people have enjoyed and taken for granted for generations. Still you complain that enough is never enough. You are never satisfied or content with all the blessings God has bestowed upon you.

Lgbt people of America would just like to know:

- What is it like to be open about your sexual orientation, whenever and wherever you are?
- What is it like not to worry about loosing your job, or loosing everything you have worked for your entire life, including your children.
- What is it like to live with the luxury of that freedom each and every day of your lives?
- What is it like not having to worry about your family disowning you, and throwing you out of the house as a child, or out of the family for a lifetime?
- What is it like to be open about who you are, and not have to worry about someone physically abusing you on the streets, or killing you, for being open about your heterosexuality?

- What is it like to walk down the street or through a store holding the hand of the love of your life, and not have to worry about ugly stares, or being abused or killed for that simple pleasure?
- What is it like to know while growing up and as a young adult that you can have the blessings of a spouse and children with no problems?
- What is it like to gather with co-workers and not have to hide your orientation, or your lover from them?
- What is it like to introduce the love of your life to your family members without fear of how they will react
- What is it like growing up as a child knowing your going to have all of these luxuries and blessings without any problems from family and society?
- What is it like knowing you can go into any bar, restaurant or mall, and be treated with dignity and respect, instead of getting bad service and a snarl?
- What is it like to walk into any church of your choosing with your family and be automatically welcomed, and embraced, and accepted because you are the majority, confidently knowing no one is going to have a problem with your sexual orientation?
- What is it like going to any church of your choosing, and not be asked to leave, once the members find out your heterosexual?
- What is it like to go on a job interview and know your sexual orientation is not one more thing going against you to get that job?

- What is it like to send your children out to play with the neighbor children, and not have to worry about the other children or their parents, abusing your children in some way, because they do not approve of your sexual orientation?
- What is it like to watch your children fall in love for the first time and want to get married, and not have to worry if the in-laws will forbid the marriage, or reject your child because of your sexual orientation?
- What is it like to go to high school and through your adult life, and not have everyone thinking about what's going on in your bedroom, as soon as they come to discover your heterosexual?
- What's it like to see your children get their first boy-friend or girl-friend and see them welcomed, instead of torn apart, because the other parents do not approve of what goes on in your bedroom?
- What is it like to take a walk in your neighborhood and not have neighbors assume you are a child molester, and not have to watch them scurry their children together in fear as if you are out to hurt them?
- What is it like to take a walk in your neighborhood without teenagers and adults pointing at you and calling you a faggot?
- What is it like to have politicians cater to your every demand and wish, sending staff members ahead to research what your needs and wishes are, before arriving to win your votes?
- What is it like to have favor from national, state and civil court judges when it comes to laws pertaining to your basic human and civil rights?

- What is it like to wake up each and every morning and go through your day, your week, your year, your life, and not have to deal with the hateful environment you homophobic straight people have created for open Lgbt people in this nation?
- What is it like to walk into your work place, and say, "Hello!" to one of your male co-workers, where they do not cringe in fear and look around to see if any homophobic female co-workers will see you say, "Hello!" back?
- What is it like to be homophobic and live in fear of each other?
- Lgbt people want to know what it is like to have the luxuries that you have in this life?
- Lgbt people in America and world wide want to know, what is it like to have **so much to look forward to?**

You homophobic straight people have so many luxuries that Lgbt people do not have. Yet, all you do is complain that you want more out of life. You are never happy. This is what Lgbt people of the world would like to know. This is the environment you homophobic straight people have created for open Lgbt people in this great nation of America and world wide.

**Our Heavenly Father
is so heart broken and ashamed of you,
and so am I.**

From the birth of this nation your twisted religious oppressive trend of thinking has all but destroyed this country and all the people in it. The generations before you came to this country as immigrants. They fought in wars, went hungry, and poured out their sweat and tears in an attempt to make this country a beautiful place to live. A place with peace, dignity, and equality for **ALL** Americans.

The generations before you started out in life driving covered wagons and a team of horses, and before their lives were over they were driving brand new Cadillacs which they paid for with cash.

The generations before you provided a nation for you that was safe and prosperous. Not only did you know you were going to have good paying secure jobs, 401K's, health insurance, homes, cars, safe neighborhoods, extravagant vacations, retirement and wealth, you expected and demanded it. You expected this even at the expense of oppressing others.

You homophobic straight people have been the envy of the world. You are also the most hated generations in history. You are not hated for your wealth, don't fool yourself. You are hated for your lack of compassion and extreme arrogance. The generations before you saw to it that you were going to be well cared for and have all the things they did not. This has made all of you empty headed, spoiled, arrogant, selfish, demanding, and self centered, lacking empathy for anyone other than yourselves. The spoiled lives you have lived have made you hardhearted towards everyone and everything. This includes anyone different than yourselves in any shape, way, or form. The past few generations of you straight people have been hardhearted towards your own kind. So hardhearted that Americans can't even trust their own neighbors anymore. The generations before you looked out for and looked after their neighbors.

Your twisted religious, and oppressive hardhearted hearts have turned every fiber of this country into a den of demons. Your trend of thinking has corrupted this entire nation and all but brought it to ruin.

Our children can't even discuss or honor our Heavenly Father in school without being accused of committing a crime. Our University students can't discuss, or honor, our Heavenly Father in fear that they will be viewed as ignorant. I cannot count the number of scientists I have known who have said, If they ever mentioned the word "God" in their universities or in their professions, they would be viewed as ignorant and simple." You have made God taboo.

You refuse to support laws to protect Lgbt people or provide Lgbt people with all the civil and human rights that you possess and take for granted. You have arrogantly deceived yourselves into believing Lgbt people are horrible sinners, an abomination to God, and unworthy of God's blessings. Because we do not possess the same sexual orientation as you do. You are so arrogant you believe you are <u>without sin yourselves</u>.

James 5:16
5:16 **Confess your faults one to another,** *and* **pray one for another,** *that* **ye may be healed.** *The effectual fervent prayer of a righteous man availeth much.*

You blame and accuse Lgbt people of promiscuous and unseemly behavior. Let's take away your future, secure jobs, marriage, family, and children and make heterosexuality taboo for hundreds of years. Then we will see how long it is before your behavior is promiscuous and unseemly. Most of you have promiscuous and unseemly behavior as it is.

Many of you have deceived yourselves into believing Lgbt people aren't worthy or fit to be married and raise children. You are so arrogant you think, "How dare Lgbt people want to get married and have families with their sins." As if marriage and children were blessings God wanted only for homophobic straight people like yourselves. Telling yourselves only heterosexuals and perceived heterosexuals are fit to have marriage and raise children. Believing only straight people like yourselves are worthy of God's blessings in this life. What arrogance!

1 Timothy 4:1-3

4:1 ***Now the Spirit speaketh expressly***, *that in the latter times some shall depart from the faith, giving heed to seducing spirits,* ***and doctrines of devils;***

4:2 ***Speaking lies in hypocrisy;*** *having their conscience seared with a hot iron;*

4:3 ***Forbidding to marry,*** *and commanding to abstain from meats,* ***which God hath created to be received with thanksgiving*** *of them which believe and know the truth.*

To add insult to injury you arrogant homophobic straight people have passed laws to make killing your unborn children legal and acceptable. While in the same breath declare, Lgbt people are not fit to marry and raise children of their own. What monsters you have proved yourselves to be. What nerve you have to even open your mouths on any subject concerning anyone regarding anything. You straight people lost your credibility before the world at large years ago. Yet you continue to make fools of yourselves before God and the world with your ignorance and hatred.

2 Timothy 3:1-7

3:1 This know also, that in the last days perilous times shall come.

3:2 ***For men shall be lovers of their own selves, covetous, boasters, proud, blasphemers, disobedient to parents, unthankful, unholy,***

3:3 ***Without natural affection,*** *trucebreakers,* ***false accusers,*** *incontinent, fierce,* ***despisers of those that are good,***

3:4 Traitors, ***heady, highminded,*** *lovers of pleasures more than lovers of God;*

*3:5 **Having a form of godliness, but denying the power thereof:** from such turn away.*

*3:6 **For of this sort are they which creep into houses,** and lead captive silly women laden with sins, led away with divers lusts,*

*3:7 **Ever learning, and never able to come to the knowledge of the truth.***

The number one cause of death for pregnant women in America is murder by the men who got them pregnant. You homophobic straight people have kicked out your own Lgbt children and disowned them for life. Leaving them to fend for themselves in the dangers of the streets and elements. Many of whom did not survive on their own. Wild animals have more protective natural affection for their offspring than you have displayed.

Your wrath against Lgbt people has been so severe that your own children have lived lives of misery and secrecy. They live in fear of what kind of cruelty you might bestow upon them should you discover they are not heterosexual or straight. Again, wild animals have more natural affection for their offspring than you do.

In the face of your deplorable example as human beings you still have the nerve to call yourselves lovers of God. You have the audacity to suggest Lgbt people are unfit to marry and have children. You deceive yourselves into believing Lgbt people are not worthy because they have a particular sin that you do not possess or display openly.

**If any group of today's society is unfit
for marriage and raising children it is you!
You homophobic straight people are
a living and breathing testimony
of bad marriages and unfit parents.**

You claim this thinking is from God and the Bible. You have been deceived! You did not learn any of this barbaric, hateful, oppressive behavior from God or God's Word. In your brain dead state of mind you have blamed Lgbt people for the spread of AIDS. Let me remind you, Lgbt people are not the only people having sex on this planet.

In the last 25 years married women have been diagnosed with aids at the highest rate of all other groups. I can assure you not one heterosexual women got aids from an openly gay man. Yet, these are the very men that you despise and oppress.

Your twisted religious oppressive trend of hardhearted thinking has broken the heart of our Heavenly Father. You have wounded the hearts of His angels, and His gay, lesbian, and transgender children, with your every thought and expression. Your twisted religious oppressive trend of thinking has produced a world of despair. You have turned God's Word into the **UTTERANCES OF DEMONS.**

You twist God's truth to fit your own arrogant selfish desires. You hate and oppress all those different than yourselves. All the while living your sorted promiscuous lifestyle in secret. All the while shoving your promiscuous lifestyle and filthy behavior down the throats of every living human being on the planet. All the while exhausting yourselves in your attempt to oppress others.

1 Peter 2:13-17

*2:13 Submit yourselves to **every ordinance** of man for the Lord's sake: whether it be to the king, as supreme;*

*2:14 Or unto governors, as unto them that are sent by him for the **punishment of evildoers**, and for the praise of them that do well.*

*2:15 For so is the will of God, that with well doing ye may put to **silence the ignorance of foolish men:***

*2:16 As free, and **not using your liberty for a cloke of maliciousness,** but as the servants of God.*

*2:17 **Honour all men.** Love the brotherhood. Fear God. Honour the king.*

Here are just a few things you homophobic straight people have accomplished in the last generation. These statistics are at astronomical proportions. Never before in history has so much lawlessness been rampant in America and world wide.

- Over 50 million children murdered by their mothers
- Alcohol abuse
- Drug abuse
- Sexual harassment in the workplace
- Our streets are no longer safe to walk
- America and other nations are no longer safe to live in
- Death by hazing of our high school and college children
- Rape by hazing of high school and college children
- Harassment of school children
- Suicide rate among Lgbt children

- Suicide rate among Lgbt adults
- Suicide rate among heterosexual children
- Suicide rate among heterosexual adults
- Teen violence
- Violence by children
- Violence in sports
- Violence against Lgbt children and adults by police officers
- Death of Lgbt children by violence of other children
- Death of Lgbt adults by violence
- Child molestation by men
- Child molestation by women
- Children killed by fathers
- Children killed by mothers
- Child molestation by mother's boy friends
- Children murdered by mothers boyfriends
- Rape is rampant everywhere
- Men are gang raped
- Women are gang raped
- Cereal killers
- Death by shootings
- Car jackings
- Elderly abused
- Elderly raped
- Wrongful death by police
- Abuse by police
- Neighbors committing crimes against neighbors
- Money scams in the billions
- The majority of the earths populations living in poverty
- Prison populations ever increasing
- American jobs going to other nations

- Poverty is sky rocketing world wide
- American unemployment rate higher than ever before

This is just a small taste of the world you homophobic
straight people have created for all of us.
**Yet...you have the nerve to boast that you
are the righteous ones!
You are deceiving yourselves!**

Your hateful and twisted view of God's Word and
oppressive religious trend of thinking is not working for any
nation. It is not working for your descendents heterosexual or
homosexual. God has heard the cries of His open gay, lesbian,
and transgender children and His patience with you
homophobes is coming to a close.

Need I remind you what our Heavenly Father did the
last time He heard the cries of His children, such as the cries
from Sodom and Gomorrah? YES! For once someone is
showing you homophobes the real picture of Sodom and
Gomorrah.

Ephesians 4:20
*4:20 **But ye have not so learned Christ;***

*4:21 If so be that ye have heard him, and have been taught by him,
as the truth is in Jesus:*

*4:22 That **ye put off concerning** the former conversation the old
man, **which is corrupt according to the deceitful lusts;***

4:23 And be renewed in the spirit of your mind;

*4:24 And that ye **put on the new man**, which after God is created in
righteousness and true holiness.*

*4:25 Wherefore **putting away lying**, speak every man truth with his neighbour: **for we are members one of another.***

*4:26 Be ye angry, and sin not: **let not the sun go down upon your wrath:***

*4:27 **Neither give place to the devil.***

      Homophobic brothers and sisters over the years I have heard many of you state: "All Lgbt people should be put on their own island if they want to be that way and live that kind of life style. We don't want those kind of people around us." Let me set you straight on this matter.

      My great grandfather was Dutch and came to America from Amsterdam. The love of his life his wife, my great grandmother, was full blooded Cherokee. My great grandmother lost her parents when she was small in the Oklahoma territory. She was raised in an orphanage after the cruel murder of her parents and her people. She later married my great grandfather. My great, great, grandparents were likely members of the Trail of Tears in 1838, considering all Cherokees were forced to move. My ancestors including my great grandfather, and my great grandmother, paid a horrific price for their freedom and prosperity in this nation

and for mine.
As did their descendents.

      My ancestors have fought and given their lives, in World War I, World War II, Pearl Harbor, the Korean War, the Vietnam War, and the Gulf War.

This nation does not belong exclusively to you homophobic straight people nor should it. This great nation encompasses many different kinds of people. As a nation you homophobes need to stop hating everyone who is different than ourselves. You need to embrace all people, whether or not you agree with them, share the same religion, or same skin color, or same sexual orientation. History has taught us that accepting and feeling love and compassion for **only** those who are like ourselves, is not only against God, it also leads to destroying nations and societies.

My ancestors have lived on this soil for thousands of years.
This is my homeland, this is my nation,
this is my America.
I have a right to all of God's blessings,
and all the civil and human rights everyone else has.
Our Heavenly Father says it is so.
I am speaking for all the Lgbt people
in this great nation of ours.

This is Our America.

This is our America. This is our land and it is going to be left to our descendents. I love this great nation and all the beautiful people in it. These are American people, my people, we are all one in this country. Whether all Americans realize that or not. No, we are not all the same, nor do we all think the same, nor should we all be the same, that was not God's plan. God's plan was for us to have intense love for one another.

Have you forgotten Jesus last words to mankind?

1Peter 4:8
Above all things,
have intense love for one another,
because love covers a multitude of sins.

This is America, Americans should embrace each other in spite of their differences. Our ancestors have paid an enormous price for us, for our benefit.

Romans 15:1-7
*15:1 We then that are strong ought to **bear the infirmities of the weak**, and not to please ourselves.*

*15:2 Let every one of us **please his neighbour** for his good to edification.*

*15:3 For even Christ pleased not himself; but, as it is written, **The reproaches of them that reproached thee fell on me.***

*15:4 For whatsoever things were **written aforetime were written for our learning,** that we through patience and comfort of the scriptures might have hope.*

*15:5 Now the God of patience and consolation grant you to be **likeminded one toward another** according to Christ Jesus:*

*15:6 That ye may **with one mind and one mouth** glorify God, even the Father of our Lord Jesus Christ.*

*15:7 **Wherefore receive ye one another, as Christ also received us to the glory of God.***

It is a good thing to hate sin or imperfection. God hates sin or imperfection. The problem with you homophobes in today's world is that most of you people do not have a clear understanding of sin. We need to have a clear understanding of sin (or imperfection). God knows we are imperfect. He knows this better than we do. God is not struggling and fretting over our sins or imperfections. God knows this is inherited from Adam. It is something all mankind must deal with. God knows we are all imperfect from birth.

Romans 3:23
For all have sinned, and come short of the glory of God;

THIS DOES INCLUDE YOU HOMOPHOBES HELLO!

What God wants to see is how mankind is going to handle their own sins as well as the sins of others. Remember, God only judges mankind by their individual hearts. How could our Heavenly Father ever judge us if He doesn't put us to the test? I hate to tell you but God is putting all of us to the test continuously throughout our lives. It is never ending. What many people don't realize is that we are always under test even when we least expect it.

- Are you going to pretend you don't have any sin of our own?
- Are you going to deceive yourselves into thinking you don't have any bad sins, just a few little ones, nothing to worry about?
- Are you only going to notice sin in others?

- Are you going to hurt and oppress those with certain various sins?
- Are you going to make one sin worse than another, depending on what your particular sins are, or are not?
- Are you going to forgive others for their imperfections or sins, and embrace others with love and compassion, regardless of whatever sins any one particular person may be burdened with?
- Are you going to pray for others, asking our Heavenly Father to help others to overcome their sins, through God's undeserved kindness, as our Heavenly Father has instructed you?
- What have you done all of your life?
- Most importantly what will you do after reading this revelation.
- What will you do for the remainder of your life?

God tells us quite clearly in the scriptures, if we are guilty of one sin, which we all are, then we are guilty of all sin. According to our Heavenly Father we are all guilty of each and every sin listed in the Bible.

EVERY ONE OF THEM!
THIS DOES
INCLUDE YOU HOMOPHOBES!

It is okay to be against all sins?
Let me just list a few for example;

- against homosexuality
- against adultery
- against fornication
- against lying
- against stealing
- against drunkenness
- against gossip
- against smoking
- against drug abuse
- against murder

God is against all sin and so am I. God has said we are all guilty of all the sins in the Bible. Whether one person has gone their entire life never gossiping, never fornicating, never stealing, etc. God says we all have sin even if sins vary in each individual. God says we are guilty of all these sins whether we have partaken directly in them or not and this does include homosexuality.

Yes, you homophobic people are just as guilty of homosexuality as any open Lgbt person. **Yes,** according to our Heavenly Father this is true. If you do not believe that, then you do not believe the scriptures, you do not believe God, and you are calling God a liar.

This modern Christian belief that people have today about one sin being better or worse than another, and one person being better or worse than another, is an absolute lie! A lie taught to today's Christians by false teachers. They are God's enemies. These corporate preachers are concerned foremost with money, and not concerned with God's truth and mankind's salvation. Use the reasoning powers God gave you; just how much does a man, a Preacher, love God if he puts money and wealth before your salvation and ever lasting life, and the salvation of your children and families.

THINK ABOUT IT!

Everyone has a right to be loved. God created mankind to be loving towards each other. God created mankind to be sexual, and to enjoy the pleasures of sex, or to abstain from sex, if a person so chooses. As you can see, God created sexuality in various forms and created people with different sexual orientations. Regardless of the sexual orientation God blessed each one of us with, God created love and sex for all of mankind. Not just for you homophobic heterosexuals and perceived heterosexuals.

Matthew 11:24-30
*11:24 But I say unto you, That **it shall be more tolerable for the land of Sodom in the day of judgment, than for thee.***

*11:25 At that time Jesus answered and said, I thank thee, O Father, Lord of Heaven and earth, **because thou hast hid these things from the wise and prudent, and hast revealed them unto babes.***

11:26 Even so, Father: for so it seemed good in thy sight.

*11:27 All things are delivered unto me of my Father: and no man knoweth the Son, but the Father; neither knoweth any man the Father, save the Son, **and he to whomsoever the Son will reveal him.***

*11:28 Come unto me, **all ye that labour and are heavy laden**, and I will give you rest.*

11:29 Take my yoke upon you, and learn of me; for I am meek and lowly in heart: and ye shall find rest unto your souls.

11:30 For my yoke is easy, and my burden is light.

Everyone wants to be heard and validated. Everyone is important and worth while. Everyone deserves to be loved just as you homophobic straight people. Those with a same gender attraction deserve validation and are worthy of love, tolerance and acceptance, regardless of their sins and imperfections. Lgbt people do not look at you homophobic straight people in judgment, hatred, and unworthiness when it comes to your sins, or imperfections, or your right for salvation.

1 Peter 4:7+8
*4:7 But **the end of all things is at hand:** be ye therefore sober, and watch unto prayer.*

*4:8 **And above all things have fervent charity among yourselves: for charity shall cover the multitude of sins.***

1 Peter 2:17
*2:17 **Honour all men.** Love the brotherhood. Fear God. Honour the king.*

1 Peter 1:11+12
1:11 Searching what, or what manner of time the Spirit of Christ

which was in them did signify, when it testified beforehand the sufferings of Christ, and the glory that should follow.

1:12 **Unto whom it was revealed, that not unto themselves, but unto us they did minister the things, which are now reported unto you by them that have preached the gospel unto you with the Holy Ghost sent down from Heaven; which things the angels desire to look into.**

James 4:8-11

4:8 *Draw nigh to God, and he will draw nigh to you.* **Cleanse your hands, ye sinners; and purify your hearts, ye double minded.**

4:9 *Be afflicted, and mourn, and weep: let your laughter be turned to mourning, and your joy to heaviness.*

4:10 *Humble yourselves in the sight of the Lord, and he shall lift you up.*

4:11 *Speak not evil one of another, brethren. He that speaketh evil of his brother, and judgeth his brother, speaketh evil of the law, and judgeth the law:* **but if thou judge the law, thou art not a doer of the law, but a judge.**

Matthew 6:14

6:14 **For if ye forgive men their trespasses, your Heavenly Father will also forgive you:**

6:15 **But if ye forgive not men their trespasses, neither will your Father forgive your trespasses.**

Homophobic heterosexual and perceived heterosexual brothers and sisters it is you who are keeping God's blessings from Lgbt people. You are the majority. You have the power to change this terrible oppression against Lgbt people in this great nation. These ancient Bible secrets, this revelation, is a liberation for you as well as it is for God's gay, lesbian, and transgender children. Our Heavenly Father is making a call to you as well, a call to repent and change your hateful, jealous, oppressive thinking and actions.

Homophobic brothers and sisters your "saved or damned" Christian mentality is so hurtful to so many of God's children. A multitude of God's Lgbt children have already gone to their graves believing you and God hated them. The suicide rate among God's Lgbt children is over 20 percent, higher than ever in history, and the highest suicide rate in the world. Do you really want to continue to press on with your "saved or damned" Christian mentality? Really?

Your "saved or damned" Christian mentality closes the doors to God's love and salvation for so many. Your "saved or damned" Christian mentality prevents God's Lgbt children from getting to know our Heavenly Father and ultimately losing out on God's love and salvation. Is this what your hearts find joy, peace, and pleasure in? Really?

Of course not all straight men and heterosexual women are guilty for all the issues I have mentioned in this chapter. However, most of you are.

This angel's purpose was to shake you up.

This chapter is an attempt to make you think, to bring you to your senses.

THINK ABOUT IT

The angels purpose in this chapter was to give you homophobic straight people a taste of what you have given to Lgbt people for generations. How does it feel taking a good look in the mirror. How does it feel to be blamed and accused of things you have never had anything to do with. How does it feel to be innocent of horrible behaviors and be accused and held responsible for behavior you wouldn't participate in if your life depended on it? How did that feel? This is what Lgbt people deal with in every aspect of their daily lives everywhere they go and in everything they do.

You are not obligated to date or marry open Lgbt people. You are not obligated to wine, dine, dance with, or socialize with open Lgbt people. However, our Heavenly Father has made it quite clear that oppressing, depriving civil and human rights, standing against, or harming God's Lgbt people is an abomination in His eyes. An abomination that will not go ignored and unpunished.

One of the main problems in the last few generations and today is that people have become afraid and have lost trust in one another. To many people today have seen to much ugly, vicious, sexually demented behavior. This has made everyone paranoid and fearful of one another. Just for the record Lgbt people possess those same fears as you do. The world population today looks just as scary and untrustworthy to us. Perhaps even more so considering all of us have been accused and targeted for the ugly and vicious behavior committed by so others.

Take all of the latter topics and insights I have mentioned in this chapter and throw them before a multitude of simple small minded people and what do you get? What you get is a world full of fearful people ready to devour anything that moves. This is the behavior of a roaring lion. Anything that moves before them they will chase and devour. This is how lions were created, this is their instinct. Mankind was not created by God to be this way. We were created with love, compassion, and an intellect and power of reason.

Unfortunately the majority of the world's population is small and simple minded, not to bright. This is the same mentality that breeds their offspring to believe such things as:

- All white people are good.
- All black people are bad.
- All straight people are good.
- All Lgbt people are bad.
- All Americans are good.
- All people from other nations are bad.

I could go on and on for pages with these types of examples. The world is full of simple minded people. People who either choose to be lazy and weak and not use their intellect and power of reason, and those whom are simply without intellect and the power of reason altogether.

Our Heavenly Father did not create mankind to be simple minded in this way. God expects all of us world wide to use our power of love, power of compassion, power of intellect, and power of reason with each and every individual person we come across all throughout our lives. We are to look at each person individually. We are instructed by God to approach each person with open hearts and open minds. Our first instinct should be to love and accept others until our intellect and power of reason tells us to do otherwise.

One of the many things I have learned from the scriptures over the years is to put myself in the shoes of others. Or should I say in the shoes of those whom have sins that I do not possess.

I pose the following questions to you homophobes:
If you were gay, lesbian or transgender how would you want to be dealt with?

- How would you want to be treated?
- How would you want to be judged?
- How would you want to be punished?
- Would you want to be punished at all for something you never had any choice about?

PLEASE GIVE THIS SOME THOUGHT.

At the completion of this revelation, if these Bible secrets from our Heavenly Father have not changed and moved your hearts, I for one forgive you. God has proved that He does love people with a same gender attraction. We have a name in Heaven greater than son or daughter, there is a monument in Heaven in our honor. Your opinions and majority rule have no power over us. We are with God. Who could ask for more out of this life than what our Heavenly Father has already given us? Homophobic straight people I wrote this chapter for you, for your benefit. The Lgbt community already knows these things.

HOMOPHOBIC STRAIGHT PEOPLE, CHANGE YOUR HEARTS. GO TO OUR HEAVENLY FATHER AND REPENT, AND GO IN PEACE REJOICING!

Now I know there are many Lgbt people reading this right now who are thinking, "Boy, Rickie sure told those straight people a thing or two." So let me be the one to say these words: If the majority of the population were open Lgbt people the world would not be one bit different. Lgbt people are just as sinful, just as corrupt, and just as dishonest as straight people. The majority of the world's population today is far removed from our Heavenly Father and His wisdom and are a mess in general.

Heavenly Father,
Please forgive them, for they know not what they do.

Homophobia: The End Result

Heavenly Father,
Please forgive them, for they know not what they do.

What would Jesus say if He had to cover this subject?

My mother and father divorced when I was five years old. One year earlier we left Chicago and moved to a small town in the Illinois River Valley. It was a very homophobic place as was most of the world at that time. We moved into a brand new house. It was just about the only house in the neighborhood. There was new development all around us. The neighborhood was full of new young families. Everyone was living the American dream.

Within the first three years that we lived there I had been rapped by eight different men. Six different men within one block of my house. I witnessed the brutal rape of my best friend who was seven years old. To this day I can still hear the haunting cries of my precious little innocent friend.

Witnessing that rape was more traumatizing than all of the rapes I had experienced combined. None of us ever talked about any of the rapes. Not even to this day. That was just the first three years that I lived in my new house. I could go on and on but it would be to brutal to relive. I am trying to teach a point about the effects of oppressing gay men not write an autobiography. Some will say you cannot combine pedophilia and oppressed gay men. But I say you cannot ignore the similarities of a same gender attraction whether with children or adults. These events took place in the early sixties and were rampant then. Now it is 2009 and these events are dominating the news each and every day.

When I was ten years old my grandmother asked me to go to the drug store which was about six blocks away from her home to pick up her medication. On my way back to her home I had to walk through the city park. There was a public restroom near the children's play area and I went into the restroom to urinate. There was a police officer at the urinal when I walked in. He asked me what my name was and what I was up to that day. I told him that I was coming from the drug store for my grandmother. He proceeded to ask who my grandparents and parents were and I answered all of his questions. Of course I felt very safe because he was a police officer. After answering all of his questions about my family and where they lived he backed me up against the wall and raped me. The police station was across the street from the park. A few years later I came to learn that he was married and had children that were my age.

Again at age twelve he saw me in a restaurant near my home and he tried his best to lure me into the restroom of that restaurant.

I couldn't begin to count the number of straight and openly gay men whom have told me that they were rapped by their fathers and other men in their childhoods.

When I was in 5th grade my history teacher taught us about slavery in the United States. As he taught this subject he used the word "Nigger" every time he referred to the slaves or to any black people. As I sat in my history class my childhood friend and classmate all through school who we will call Betty sat next to me. Betty was black. What a hateful and hardhearted man that history teacher was in my eyes then and now. God bless Betty I hope her life has been full of God's blessings. There were very few black people in town at that time. Only three that I can remember prior to high school. I think there were maybe six black kids in my high school.

One black classmate who we will call Big Joe was my classmate throughout my entire childhood. He had a very hard time. Most of the kids made fun of him. Let me say for the record I was never one of them. As a matter of fact I stood up for him on many occasions and made the other kids leave him alone. I was very popular in school and as we all know children listen to the popular kids in their desperate desire to fit in.

For entertainment the children would convince Big Joe to do stupid and embarrassing things. Often getting him in trouble with teachers and the principal. Big Joe was so desperate for their attention. He was always happy to oblige them knowing he would regret it later. He didn't have any friends and was an outcast and desperate for any attention that he could get. Big Joe endured that brutally heartbreaking reality even through high school.

Every year our town held an annual carnival in the city park. When I was sixteen one of my best friends a lesbian girl and I went to the city park to enjoy the festivities of the annual carnival. I was in high school at that time and had been openly gay for two years. As she and I were walking about we started to notice four closeted gay boys from school following us calling me a "F---ing Fagot" and her a "F---ing Lesbian." Others started to join them in their hatred and violence against us. The violent crowd escalated into about 100 teenagers and adults very quickly.

Suddenly Big Joe passed by and the kids called him into their hatred and violence. They were pushing him to the front of the crowd encouraging him to "beat my ass" and so on. In just a matter of a few minutes there were over a hundred teenagers and adults following us in a mob. All of them encouraging Big Joe to kick my ass. My friend and I were trying to leave the carnival when we realized we were cornered. We were surrounded by people shouting "Kill that f---ing Faggot," and so on.

When I realized I was cornered and knew there was no way out I turned and found Big Joe standing in front of me. The crowd was egging Big Joe on and pushing him towards me. All of them were screaming, hollering, smiling, and laughing with excitement over the hatred and violence they had created against me. I looked Big Joe right in the eyes knowing I was dead if he hit me. Because I was no match to him. Big Joe and I stood there looking into each others eyes. I was thinking of all the times I had protected him from the abuse of those very same people over the years. I knew he was standing there thinking the very same thing. Big Joe said, "Look at you, you f---ing Faggot, you're a disgrace!" He pulled his arm back putting his entire body into a punch. His fist coming at me seemed bigger than my entire head. He hit me on the side of my face. The crowd went into a roaring cheer, screaming, "Beat his ass, Big Joe, beat that f---ing Faggots ass good!" All the while continuing to push Big Joe at me. Big Joe said, "No, that's enough!" and walked away from me and the mob.

Big Joe was a high school student at the time and probably the strongest man in the town. After Big Joe and the crowd walked away I felt my cheek and face wondering how much damage had been done. I wondered how much blood was streaming down my face. As I felt my face I noticed there wasn't any damage or pain for that matter. No pain at all. At that point I realized Big Joe only made it look like he was hitting me a good one to please the crowd. An attempt to prove his heterosexuality and gain momentary popularity once again. Let's not forget he did not want to harm me and saw to it that he didn't. A fact I was very grateful for.
The carnival packed up and left that night a day early.

Two days later I was sitting on a park bench in the very same spot where Big Joe, and the mob had cornered me. I felt I needed to return to that park and to the very same spot to regain my courage. I felt if I could return to the scene of the violence without fear I could go on with the rest of my life. With courage to face the violence and hatred that lay ahead for me. I was confirmed that I would never come to love the sacred lie, known as the down low, the closet condition as so many other males did.

As I sat on that peaceful park bench, in that beautiful park, enjoying the quiet and tranquility, an elderly man about seventy years old sat down next to me. He said, "You're Rickie Bartlett, aren't you?" I said, "Yes." He said, "I want you to know I was in this very spot sitting on this bench when you were attacked by that mob the other night. I couldn't believe my eyes as to what I was witnessing. I've never seen anything like it in my life. I want you to know I went to the police station and filed a police complaint over what I saw."

I said, "Thank you." He said, "I'm very surprised to see you here. Are you looking for more trouble?" I said, "No, I'm looking for the courage to go on with my life. A life of honesty true to myself and true before God." The man said. "Perhaps you should move to L.A. or New York." I said, "I'm only sixteen, how could I possibly do that?" The man said, "Rickie I'm going to be praying for you and your safety." I said, "That makes two of us." The elderly man and I spoke about the weather and what a beautiful day it was and then we parted.

I saw Big Joe standing on a street corner about ten years ago. As I passed by he turned to the man next to him and started to brag about that night. Big Joe said and I quot; " I beat his ass good at the carnival and I would do it again!" How tragic and heart breaking for all those homophobic heterosexual young women, straight guys, and for Big Joe and myself. How sad for all of us.

A few months after the park incident I went to my principal and told him between the abuse at home by my mother and stepfather and the abuse at school I didn't think I could take much more abuse. I asked him if their might be some other options for me. I told him I had many dreams and plans for my life and one of them was to be highly educated and I feared my circumstances were getting the best of me.

I asked him if I could go to the local community college and finish high school through a GED program and he said that would be impossible. Because back then you had to be 19 years old to enter a GED class or to take the test and I was only 16 at the time. After my proposal he sat there and pondered about it and said he would look into it but not to get my hopes up. He said it would take a lot of phone calls and red tape and it would still be highly unlikely.

My principal had much compassion for me in those days. Whenever fellow students came into his office to complain about me slapping them upside the head he said he always fired them out of his office. Because he knew if I slapped anyone upside the head it was in self defense. A few days later he called me into his office and said he pulled strings, jumped over one hoop after another, and made my wish come true. I started attending the community college a few days later. My world changed over night. It was so much fun.

All the students knew me by name. Groups of them would come up to me and ask me if I was a student their and ask my age. After responding they were amazed. They would ask me if I was gay and I would tell them I was. I was known as "That little gay genus kid." They were all very friendly and saw me as a novelty. My world changed over night thanks to my principal, my mother and God.

When I was 16 I was raped by my family doctor who I had known my entire childhood. I went into his office for a routine physical. The waiting room was packed and I mean packed. People had been waiting for a long time to see the doctor. For some odd reason I was let right in ahead of all the others who had been waiting. There was one thin wall between the examining room and the waiting room.

The doctor told me he needed to check my rectum. I told him I was against it but he convinced me it was absolutely necessary. He told me to drop my pants and lay face down on the examination table. He started with his fingers. The next thing I knew I was being sodomized by his penis and asked if I liked it. He asked over and over if it felt good. I gripped the table in total shock trying not to scream and cry because there were about 30 women and children just a few feet and a thin wall away. As I laid there all I could think about was that I had known this man all of my life and how his son and I had always been close friends. Of course I never reported it. I was a male. He was my much respected doctor. His son had been a good friend of mine ever sense I could remember. I never went to that doctor again and I avoided his son as best I could from that day forward. I had loved his son as a friend all of my childhood and I knew for his sake I needed to keep my distance. I thought it would be better to break his heart by avoiding him for life without explanation what had happened, than to tell him I couldn't be his friend anymore because his father had rapped me.

When I was 18 years old I had been openly gay for four years and lived outside of the Chicago area. I had a good paying job and a nice home that I rented. I had a openly gay boyfriend named Dave who not only lived in the city of Chicago but he owned a huge part of the real estate in the city. Dave was a self made 27 year old drop dead gorgeous millionaire.

He had the looks of a model and he was very sophisticated, very kind, and very generous. Most importantly he was so fun to be with. Not only did he have a great personality but he had millions of dollars. The combination of personality and wealth provided much fun and took me places that most people would never experience in a lifetime. I was very happy with Dave and all the blessing our Heavenly Father had provided for me.

During this time I had a friend who we will call Kyle. Kyle and I had been good friends for two years. Kyle was 26 years old, brilliant, successful, kind, loving, insightful, and your all around normal straight guy. He had a wife that he meet in high school and a daughter both of whom he loved very much. His family was his life and his heart. Kyle was so brilliant that six months before he graduated from University one of Americas richest and most prestigious companies offered him a job. He graduated at the top of his class.

Kyle and I lived about two minutes from each other and we saw each other often. His family and our friends and I did picnics, shows, dinners, and just hung out together often. I also came to know his entire family mother, father, sisters, brothers etc. I saw Kyle about twice a week on average.

One summer evening he called me and said that he had a surprise for me. He told me he would arrive at my house in about two minutes. I kept asking him what the surprise was and where he wanted to take me. But he kept insisting he had a surprise and he couldn't tell me anything about it. He was filled with excitement upon arriving. I couldn't imagine what he was up to or where we were going. I jumped into his car and off we went. Once Kyle hit the highway and we started heading out of town I became more and more curious and annoying with questions. He just kept saying he couldn't tell me where we were going. Insisting it was a big surprise.

Suddenly he pulled into a rest area and found a very specific place to park in the rear of the parking lot. I though he had to use the restroom. He shut off the car and asked me to get out. He sat down on the trunk of his car and invited me to do the same. As we sat there watching the sun go down very quickly he proceeded to tell me that he felt that I was missing out on a lot of fun in life. He proceeded to say that the open gay lifestyle that I was living and remaining monogamous to Dave was a boring and empty life.

Kyle went on to tell me that he had brought me to the rest area so I could find sex with multiple men. He told me I could have all the sex with all the men I wanted at any time. I told Kyle I was very happy with my life and made it very clear to him that I was not having sex with anyone at the rest area that night or any other night. I had heard that men gathered at rest areas after dark all over the U.S. for that very purpose but I always found such behavior disturbing and very dangerous.

As night feel the rest area began to boom. It was like a rush hour of semi's, pick ups, and cars. Straight men from every walk of life.

Kyle insisted that we stay so he could introduce me to some new friends. As we sat on the trunk of his car men of every age passed coming and going from the rest rooms and vehicles. He knew all of their names and where they lived and what they did for a living. He introduced me to many. These males ranged from ages 14-90. High school boys, truck driver's, doctor's, attorney's, politician's, priest's, pastors, factory workers, farmers, etc. Most of these men had wives and children at home. As the night progressed the atmosphere became more dramatic. Men were having arguments and near fist fights because men were having sex with other men's regular tricks. Trick is what they called a sexual encounter.

As the night continued men began to become more violent. Men were breaking into fights everywhere. Men were having sex everywhere. In the restrooms, in semi's, in cars, in pick ups, behind semi's and cars, and trucks. All the while America's families where pouring into the rest area. Mom's and dad's sending their small children into the restrooms alone. Men were having sex in the stalls next to the children. There is no telling what was on the stall walls and toilet seats.

Two men began to fight violently right next to our car. It was a very bloody fight and it became very loud. After the two men decided to stop fighting the one went into the rest room to clean the blood off his face and body and clean himself up. While the man was in the rest room the other man walked over to his car which was parked next to us and slashed all his tires. He jumped into his pickup at left.

Immediately after that I noticed men were gang raping someone in the tall grass area. I pointed it out to Kyle and told him I had had enough. He said these things happened from time to time and assured me that we were safe. I told him if he didn't get me out of there I was going to start walking down the highway and hitch hike home. At that point we left.

Once we hit the road I didn't say a word. I was doing all that I could do to keep from crying. My heart was just breaking for Kyle. I asked Kyle how long he had been a part of the straight rest area community and he said about a year. Explaining that a straight friend of his had introduced him to the lifestyle. After a period of silence Kyle asked me what I was thinking and I began to sob. I began to plead and beg Kyle to give up that lifestyle. I told him I feared for his safety and his life. It was common for men to be found dead up and down that highway for miles and in the nearby state parks. The newspapers would always say the police had no idea or leads regarding to the deaths. But every male from 14 years old up knew why those men were killed as well as the state troopers. Everyone man in that county knew what had happened to those men.

Kyle insisted that he loved his life and what his wife didn't know wouldn't hurt her as he laughed. He told me I was too conservative and he was just trying to add some fun to my life. He went on and on about how young and attractive I was and how I could get any guy at the rest areas that I wanted. Insisting that the men would go crazy for me. I made it very clear to Kyle that 100 of those men did not measure up to one Dave. I enlightened Kyle on the fact that I had a man who loved me. I had a man that I loved. I had a man who wanted to share his life with me. I had a man who took me to expensive places and spend endless amounts of money on me. I had a man who wanted quiet nights holding me in front of the fireplace. I tried my best to make him understand I not only had a life but I had a life that every openly gay and straight man dreams of. My attempts to reach Kyle's intellect and heart was unsuccessful. I must say I found it quit odd that Kyle was involved in the rest area community. I thought it was so completely out of Kyle's character.

As the months went by we rarely spoke of his lifestyle. Every time he brought it up I pleaded with him to give it up. I tried to suggest that he return to the monogamous life he once had with his wife or to just divorce her and live a open gay lifestyle. He made it quit clear that his family and bosses would never tolerate or accept that. He made it quit clear that he could kiss his entire family, wife and daughter, and his job goodbye if any of them knew that he was gay. My heart just broke for him and his situation.

Whenever I think of that night in that rest area I am reminded of the daily lives of straight men and my heart just breaks. All the innocent and fragile straight men in America putting their lives at risk are probably in the same situation as Kyle was. Desperate to be themselves. Desperate to be loved and to love in return someone of their same gender. All the while the best they can hope for is a few minutes of physical sex in dirty restrooms, back of pick ups and cars and in the tall grass with complete strangers. Putting their lives at risk on a regular basis because our society doesn't allow masculine men to be together openly.

A few months later about three weeks had gone by and I had not heard from or seen Kyle. Which was unusual. I assumed he had been busy or I was busy and we were just missing each other. On one bright and beautiful summer morning I was making a cup of tea in my kitchen and Kyle walked in. Kyle was all smiles and bright eyed. I told him I had been wondering what had happened to him. He said he had been very busy with work and family. I offered him a cup of tea and breakfast he said he just wanted tea. As I stood at the stove preparing the tea Kyle burst into tears and laid his head on my kitchen table and cried his heart out. I thought something just terrible had happened to one of his family members. Men rarely cry.

Kyle proceeded to tell me that he had just lied to me. He said he had just spend the last 48 hours at the local rest areas. He said in the last 48 hours he had had sex with 29 different men as he sobbed uncontrollably. Needless to say my heart began to break. He told me that he had been trying for months to give up the behavior and had come to realize that he had become addicted to the behavior and the lifestyle.

I had just turned 18 years old I didn't know what to do or say. I suggested that he see a therapist. He said he had already done that and it was not helping. He said he went out and got a second job so he wouldn't have time for it and he said that wasn't working. He said he was miserable and was thinking of killing himself. With each word I began to panic more and more. Of course I tried to make him think about everyone who loved him and how his suicide would hurt so many people that he loved.

He said he wished he could be like me. He said my life was so perfect and so together. I told him he could live the very same life that I was living. He said, "I can't be open like you and where an I going to meet a millionaire." I tried to tell him Dave was only temporary and a millionaire boyfriend was not a good goal or desire for happiness. I told him how it wasn't easy to have a rich drop dread gorgeous boyfriend. I told him how male and female models threw themselves at Dave all the time even with me at his side. I also mentioned some other hardships about having a rich boyfriend. But he couldn't see anything but dollar signs.

I told Kyle to stay close and contact me often because I would be worried about him. I told him to call or come over any time day or night if he needed a hug, an ear, or whatever. He was just miserable.

A few months later Dave and I ended our relationship on one brutally harsh and hurtful night. He wanted me to move into his house and become his wife. I told him I had places to go and dreams to fulfill and becoming anyone's wife at 18 was not one of my goals. Dave knew that from the beginning. But God bless him he feel madly in love with me and rather than watch me fly he wanted to hold me down.

I moved to LA six weeks later. Three years later I ran into a mutual friend and he told me that Dave and Kyle had died from what people were calling at that time, "That gay disease." Brothers and sisters I am having the hardest time writing this chapter my heart is just breaking. Let's just keep moving forward.

When I was 21 years old I moved back to my home town. I ran into a childhood friend and he asked me to stop by his home sometime to caught up with our lives. I saw him out in his yard a few days later so I parked my car in my driveway and walked over to his house. We sat and chatted for a short time and I began to feel very tired. He told me he had given me some kind of drug and that's why I was feeling so tired. To make a long story short I was drugged and gang rapped by six men. Three of them I had grown up with and the other three I had gone to high school with.

These six young men were all married and had children at the time of the gang rape. I awoke to my childhood friend slapping me across the face as I was surrounded by all the other men laughing. I was laid across the bed completely nude on my stomach. He told me to put my clothes on and that I had better go home. I was looking around wondering what I was doing in the bedroom and what the hell had happened. The last thing I remembered was sitting in my childhood friends living room and talking. As I walked away from the house of who I thought was my friend semen began to soak my pants and I had a hard time walking. As I walked away from his house towards my own house the men all stood out in the front yard and pointed and laughed and asked me if my butt hurt.

That rape absolutely broke my heart. I knew I was not the first person they had raped and I knew I would not be the last. I wondered if they had grown up in an environment where they could have been open about who they were, and able to date, and fall in love as heterosexual people were afforded, perhaps they would not have become what they had become.

When I arrived home I knelt in my bath tube and cried my heart out for myself and for them.

About a year later I witnessed another similar gang rape in a straight bar by a much larger group of straight men. They were raping a young man about 18 years old. Keep in mind "Straight" was the label they went by. They dated and married women and had children. They were known in the community as straight men and still are today. The straight men who were committing the rape saw me, observing what they were doing, and were hell bent at preventing me from leaving the bar. The leader of the group knew me and had had a crush on me for years. Because of his lust for me he assured the men it would be safe to let me leave in peace.

I felt I had only one choice and that was to report it to the authorities. I felt if I didn't report it that every rape those men committed from that day forward would be on my head. I felt I had to do something to stop the cycle of rape. Out of general distrust of the police and legal system in America I decided I had better let someone know what I was about to do. So I contacted three acquaintances in nearby Chicago. One: A pastor of one of Chicago's largest churches. Two: Another pastor of one of Chicago's largest churches. Three: The owner of one of Chicago's most prestigious security companies.

I called each of them and gave them all the details. They all three begged me not to go to the police. Only now as I write this do I realize how odd it was that I knew these three powerful men well enough to call them and say, "This is Rickie and I need your help." How I knew these men is a long story that is not worth explaining.

I called the chief of police and told him what I had witnessed and that I feared for my safety. He suggested that I come down to the police station and speak with him in person. When I arrived the chief of police said the best way to protect me was to put me in jail for disorderly conduct which I agreed to. He asked me if I had told anyone about what I had seen and I told him, "No." I was afraid to tell him who I had told. After being put into the cell they took my shoes and shirt and cranked up the air conditioning. I was so cold I had to ripe open the lining of the thin mattress to try and stay warm. They kept me there for three days no food no water. During my stay I heard a few conversations from another room. They spoke of killing me and leaving my body somewhere.

After three days in that cold cell, hungry, and thirsty the door opened. I was greeted by the Chief of Police and the District Attorney. The Chief of Police said and I quote: "You think your a real smart ass don't you! You little son of a bitch! You told me that you didn't tell anyone about what you saw! Your damn lucky to be getting out of here you little son of a bitch! Our phones have been ringing off the hook around here! People from all over the state have been calling here demanding that we let you the hell out of here! How many f---ing people did you tell about this you little son of a bitch! Your damn lucky you know the people that you do! I'm going to give you some good advise you little son of a bitch! You better leave this town or your going to find yourself dead in a ditch somewhere! Now get the f--k out of here and we better not ever see you again!"

I went to my home that I was renting packed my bags and left never to return. I walked away from my home, furniture, pictures, all of my belongings, my good paying job and friends without any notice or explanation. I started my life over again in the city of Chicago.

When I arrived in Chicago the recession was becoming worse and jobs were becoming scarce. I was having a hard time finding a job so I thought I had better find something just to try to bring in some kind of income. I went to the local fast food restaurant and got a job working in the kitchen. The restaurant was managed by a husband and wife team in their late thirties. Almost all of the employees were of high school age.

On my second day on the job one of the teenage male employees walked in the back door all chipper and happy and walked up to the time clock and punched out. One of the other employees said, "Why were you punched in? You haven't been here all day." He proceeded to tell the other teen co-worker that he had been at the bosses house having sex with him all day and getting paid for it. The other boy and he shared their similar experiences they had had with the boss. Days of endless sex with the boss while on the clock.

After listening to their conversation for about thirty minutes the boss walked in the back door. I immediately walked up to him and told him of the events that I had just become aware of and told him I was going to report him. He asked me to step out the back door and into the ally. There he told me that the last Asst. Manager had the same problem that I did and he was found dead in an ally a few weeks earlier. He said if I didn't want the same thing to happen to me I had better keep my mouth shut. When he was through with his threats I turned and walked home. Upon arriving home I called the police and the fast food headquarters and made my report. A few months later I was walking by the restaurant only to see that the same manager was still working there.

Day after day the news reports high school sports teams all across America gang rapping players as a part of hazing. In one school the principal canceled a football game for such hazing and the entire school and the parents protested until the principal changed his decision and allowed the football game to proceed. The students and the parents felt canceling a football game was to severe a punishment for the mere gang rapping of a child by their sons. The parents were quoted saying, "Boy's will be boy's."

Day after day the news reports coaches rapping child athletes that they are intrusted to teach, coach, and mentor. Unfortunately we are always finding that the rapists have abused hundreds of children for many years before they are caught or prosecuted.

In my twenties I belonged to a church where the pastors son asked me if I'd like to get together and play basketball on a Saturday afternoon. I told him that would be great. I hadn't had time to play basketball in many years. As the pastors son asked me to join him I noticed his best friend standing behind him glaring at me with an evil eye. To make this event as clear as possible we will call the pastors son Brother Big Guy and we will call his best friend Brother Princess. I had known that these two young straight men were involved sexually for years. This was basic knowledge among the men in the congregation. Of course the women didn't have a clue.

My wife and I had both of these young men over to our house on many occasions. Although never together. Brother Princess came to our house for a Bible study every Saturday morning for years. I noticed Brother Princess had a strange look on his face when I was talking to Brother Big Guy but I didn't pay much attention. There were many people around us and a lot of activity.

A few days later during church service I needed to use the restroom so I took my son down to the restroom with me. Which gave him a chance to stretch his legs. He was four years old and as you know giving a four year old a chance to stretch their legs during church service is often needed. I was in the stall while my son was getting a drink from the fountain just outside the restroom door.

Suddenly he came running into the bathroom calling my name terrified and ran into the stall. I asked him what was wrong and noticed a hand print across his face. He proceeded to tell me that Brother Princess had slapped him across the face while he was getting a drink. He must have hit my son very hard because the hand print was very red and distinctive. Needless to say I had to spend the remainder of the service pacing back and forth with my little son in my arms downstairs by the coatroom to prevent myself from causing a scene in the middle of church. While I paced with great anger like I have never felt in my life I could not imagine why Brother Princess would do such a terrible thing to my son and ultimately me. Then I started to remember the look on his face when Brother Big Guy asked me to play basketball a few days earlier and everything started to fall into place.

I paced downstairs until the sermon was over knowing Brother Princess would be making a bee line for the door in an attempt to save himself from bodily harm. I meet him outside around the corner of the church. Brother Princess was moving at a very fast pace as you can imagine. Needless to say I stopped him dead in his tracks. I will not repeat everything that I said to Brother Princess that morning but for the record every other word started with an F. I made it very clear to him that I knew why he did what he had done to my son. I told him if he ever so much as gave one of my children a dirty look in the future I was going to beat his ass to a pulp right then and there. The congregation members that didn't pass by and hear my rage were soon told of it through church gossip.

A few days later the church officials called me to the church for a meeting. I was informed that I could not go around church threatening people. Certainly not the pastors sons best friend for goodness sake. They informed me that if any harm came to Brother Princess they would file charges against me. The truth of the matter was they could have cared less about Brother Princess's well being. Their biggest concern was that I was going to out the pastors son with the entire event. However I never intended to do that. But I must admit coming into that church every Sunday and keeping my fists off of brother Princess's face was going to be next to impossible. I left the church a few weeks later. To this day my only regret is that I didn't beat his ass good right there in the middle of church.

I saw Brother Princess a few years later coming out of a drug store and I found myself waiting for him to come out to take care of some much unfinished business. It took all that I had in me to get back into my car and go home unsatisfied.

Eight years later a friend of mine was giving a sermon at that church and I attended. Right behind me sat Brother Big Guy who couldn't take his eyes off of me as he sat next to his wife. Right behind Brother Big Guy sat Brother Princess and his wife as he glared at me with a face full of hatred. A few days later I received a call from Brother Big Guy. He said he had heard that my wife and I had divorced and wanted to talk. All the while using a very soft low voice. I told him he was not welcome to call me again and I hung up the phone.

Little did Brother Princess know but nothing would have ever happened between Brother Big Guy and myself. Because I was happy and faithful to my wife. But I think what Brother Princess feared more than anything was the fact that Brother Big Guy was in love with me and sex or no sex didn't really matter. For Brother Princess that was a fact to heartbreaking for him to deal with. It is not uncommon for men to be attracted to each other, or to love each other in friendships, or for only one to love the other. Most men including myself don't let things like that get in the way of such things as basketball, football, and all around fun in general. However as you can see depending on the intensity of love and the personality of the men it can be hurtful and even deadly at times.

My wife once said shortly before we split up. "It's so hard to be married to you. You get so much attention from so many women and men. I feel like I always need to watch my back and I am constantly living in fear of competition." I must say that has always been true and still is to this day. Sometimes it's a blessing and sometimes it's a curse from hell. I have always hoped that old age would cause this type of thing to diminish. However I am now old and gray, fat, and have lost my physical attractiveness and it has not even slowed down. What's with that??? I have never understood it and I still don't understand it. It is as if people become obsessed. Here's a thought. Perhaps they are obsessed before I meet them.

Over the years I have watched heterosexual men enter the work place and refuse to be sexually active with the straight male co workers and get dogged and sabotaged until they are gone. Either they are fired or they quit. Even the women join in with the harassment. Because the women know the way to get the approval of men is to back the behavior of the men they are seeking the approval and attention from.

Often times the men will set a stage for women and stand back entertained with the power of their manipulation. The women are just as bad if not worse to these openly gay and heterosexual men. Most woman are not bright enough to realize what they are doing. Most men depend on that. A woman's need for the attention of men has cost many of them their salvation and everlasting life.

They have been treacherous towards God's heterosexual and open gay men and they don't have a clue what they have done. All the while the straight men stand back and choreograph and direct the future for all men who enter the work place. I have seen this over and over all of my life. But God forbid don't hire an openly gay person. No one wants those kinds of people around. Not those kinds of sinners working along side decent straight men and women. Satan really is a manipulating genius.

I have seen parents throw their young children out on the streets for being openly gay. Disowning them for life. Never giving them a second thought. I have seen parents and their doctors put their children into electroshock treatments. Medicating them until they didn't even know their own names much less their sexual orientation. I have seen parents take their young gay children to church seminars lasting eight hours. As they listen to talks teaching how much God hates open Lgbt people. I've watched these young brothers and sisters come in all bright eyed and smiling. While leaving with heavy hearts, heavy eyes, looking down to the floor, with broken hearts, and shattered spirits crying. All at the hands of the people who should have had love and compassion for them. People who should have had unconditional love for them. What a world. What a bunch of cruel misguided idiots.

When the general public sees and hears of all the sexual promiscuity, alcohol abuse, drug abuse, domestic abuse, and high rates of suicide in the open Lgbt community they write us off as just being unhealthy people. Just people with many problems because we are gay of course. I've watched people in the work place treat openly gay people like dirt. After all, they believed an open gay person was lucky to have a job at all. I've seen unions do the same. I've seen open Lgbt people murdered on the streets. Because the people who committed the murders believed their Lgbt victims didn't mean anything to anyone anyway. They believed they were worthless and deserved to die.

I've seen police officers abuse our open Lgbt brothers and sisters just because they could. As if we deserved it for being openly gay. Many of the people guilty of these atrocities are like us but in the closet. They cower on the down low living in fear terrified they might be discovered. The down low or closeted community are willing to hurt, maim, or kill anyone necessary to keep their sexual behavior secret.

I have seen gay pastors of Lgbt churches deliberately insult members and gay visitors because they themselves are full of treachery. Pastors lacking natural affection for their own open gay, lesbian, and transgender brothers and sisters. The self hatred and self loathing in our community is rampant. There is no love between us and far to much treachery.

Lgbt people have come to believe the lies against them. They go through their lives full of hatred and contempt for themselves and their own kind. I have been to Lgbt churches where not one person shook my hand. Not one person smiled at me or made any effort to say hello. I have listened to God's Lgbt children label each other with terrible derogatory names such as: Hag, Bitch, Whore, Slut, Gym Bunny, Queer, Faggot. The list of self loathing labels goes on and on. God's Lgbt children have come to believe the lies spoken about them for generations. I am hoping this revelation will end all the self loathing in our community.

I have seen huge churches with thousands of members send the open Lgbt Christians who wanted to attend their church to tiny store front churches that only seat a few people. After all the sight of openly proud Lgbt people walking in the front doors of their big beautiful church might offend the lovers of lies.

I have sat in a church with my small children beside me as we listened to a church member scream and yell, "What the hell is this? Are we letting gay people like that in to our church now? What the hell is the world coming to? Jesus Christ! They never should have let him come through the front door!" Not one church leader, not one usher, not one member asked him to leave or even to restrain himself. After all there was an open gay person in the church. God forbid.

Nine years ago I applied for a job that I was more than qualified to do. The Human Resource Manager called me back for a second and final interview. After the final interview he announced the job was mine. He handed me a pile of paper work and sent me down the hall to another office to fill them out. As I was filling out my forms the receptionist came out from behind her desk. She walked across the lobby, and entered his office saying, "You're not going to hire that guy, are you?" Both of them knew full well that I could hear them perfectly. The Human Resource Manager said, "Yes, is there a problem?" She said "You can't hire that guy. He's gay!" His response was, "Is he? How do you know?" She said, "You couldn't tell that guy was gay? How could you not have noticed he was gay?" He said, "I couldn't tell. What makes you think he's gay?" She said, "It's obvious he's gay. We can't have a gay person working here." The Human Resource Manager walked back to the office I was in, pulled the forms out of my hands as I was filling them out and said, "I'm afraid I made a mistake. I guess I have already filled this position, so you can leave now." and then he walked out.

As I passed the receptionist she had a mean and angry look on her face, with nostrils flaring and eyes rolling. The Human Resource Manager knew I was gay from the first interview. I am certain that he knew without a doubt. That 6' 5" Human Resource Manager feared a woman's scorn. The scorn of a receptionist who was 4' 4" so much so, he trashed his grace before God and his eternal life over it. What a disgrace in the eyes of our Heavenly Father that must have been. Who is really responsible for all the gang rapes? Who is really responsible for this world where the only way a man can have sexual intimacy with another man is through an organized secret gang rapping? A world where America's grandfathers, fathers, and sons resort to sex with strangers in public restrooms. Think about that the next time you feel hatred or discriminate against another openly Lgbt person.

I left the company and went home and shaved off my beautiful long hair that was down to my waist. I had two children depending on me and bills to pay and food to provide. I went to their competitor and was hired immediately. Never in my life have I ever meet or worked with people like these. They were the most depraved and unprofessional bunch of people I have ever worked with in my entire life. At that job I was treated worse than a dog. Never in my entire life have I ever been treated so badly in the work place. Not only did I have the nerve to be openly gay, but I had the nerve to make a complaint about a man in the mechanic's department for referring to people as Niggers and Half Breeds. My not loving the lie, and not hating blacks, was more than they could tolerate.

After making my complaint not one of my co-workers spoke to me not even to offer a greeting for years. The men hated me for not loving the lie and some hated me for not hating blacks. Many were afraid that if they were found speaking to me they would receive some of the same harassment that I was receiving. Over the course of nine years I watched many open gay and heterosexual men come into that company. I watched the supervisors and managers abuse and harass them until they were gone. Most didn't last four months. My company and the Union totally ignored my 15 page complaint.

I had to provide a roof over our heads, a car, and keep food in the house and the very basic necessities for my children and myself. I was an openly gay parent in America what more could I ask for. I was happy and thankful to have a job of any kind. The unemployment rate was sky rocketing and I was getting up in years. I thanked my Heavenly Father for all he had provided for us every single day and I still do. In spite of the ugly environment I have been forced to deal with.

One night around midnight in our upper middle class neighborhood, as my two small children lay in their beds asleep, I awoke to hear a woman screaming at the end of our driveway.

She screamed, "Go up there! You heard me! Go up there and bust his f---ing door down and drag that f---ing Faggot out here and beat that f---ing Faggots ass!"

She continued, "What's the matter! Why won't you guys do it! Are all of you guys f---ing Faggots too! If you're not a bunch of f---ing Faggots, then why won't you do it!"

I jumped out of bed terrified. Terrified they would wake my small children and terrify them as well. I looked out the window to see one woman and about twelve men standing at the end of my driveway. The woman's rage and banter continued towards the men as half of them shouted,

"Yeah, Lets do it! Lets teach that f---ing Faggot a lesson that he will never forget!" As laughter rang out among them.

The other half were saying, "I'm not doing that. Do you realize we could go to jail for that? I'm not going to jail over some f---ing Faggot!"

The woman continued screaming in her rage relentlessly insisting and accusing them. By this time I was standing in the dark where they couldn't see me. Holding a phone in one hand and a baseball bat in the other. Calling on my Heavenly Father for protection. I was praying my children would not wake up to the horror that was going on around them. The men finally persuaded the woman to leave with them.

This event lasted about one half hour after I awoke. Every one of those people were my neighbors. They knew full well I had a seven and eight year old in the house sleeping. Imagine the fear I lived with after that event. Try to imagine being at work knowing your children are walking to school in the morning and home in the afternoon after an event like that. Sending them outside to play. Allowing them to go to a friends house to play or to play in the park across the street. I was terrified for my children's safety. Because I knew some of my neighbor's felt so much hatred for me. I endlessly prayed to our Heavenly Father to keep me and my children safe.

I bought the house I am living in now eight years ago. A few days after I moved in, I noticed about 10 neighbors congregated on the corner. I overheard them saying, "What's his name? Rickie? He's a what? A what? A Fag?" They were congregated out on the corner for quite some time. I have never, not anywhere that I have ever lived, shared or discussed my sexual orientation or sex life with any of my neighbors. I am not a transgender person. Their opinions and speculations are only that: opinions and speculations. The area that I live in is your normal everyday very straight community. Heterosexual women and straight men dominate this area as they do most all of America and the world. In spite of the conversation that I overheard my neighbors were somewhat friendly. The men came over to my house to chit chat whenever they saw me in the yard or out in the garage.

About five months later I stepped out of my back door one night to smoke a cigarette. As I sat there I could hear a group of my immediate male neighbors congregated next door in the gazebo. Suddenly one of the guys asked the group if any of them had ever seen me at any of the local rest areas. They all exclaimed that they had not. There was a lull of silence.

Then the men began to state to each other that they didn't like me. Each one giving one bogus excuse after another to support their dislike. One said I was unfriendly. One said I was stuck up. One said I was a prick. Let me state for the record; I have never been anything but friendly and kind to all of my neighbors. When I first moved in I was busy making changes to my new home and working extra days to pay for all the changes I was making. I didn't have much time to socialize. I gave two bedrooms full of children's furniture to one neighbor. Because my children had grown up and moved out. Just as a friendly gesture I bought 50.00 worth of chicken for another neighbor. I gave a huge expensive freezer that I didn't want to another neighbor. The point is I have always been very kind to all of my neighbors. The reason they were conjuring up reasons to hate me is because they did not see me at the rest areas after dark and that pricked their consciences.

As the days, months, and years have passed my neighbors have tried to set my house on fire while I was sleeping. They have damaged my cars, and property into the tens of thousands.

I have had neighbors that I have never meet give me the finger. Neighbors have walked by my house screaming, "Faggot!" and "Pervert!", etc. I live in a private lake community and women have walked by my house saying such things as, "I hope he doesn't go into the lake."

I walked down to the lake one lovely sunny day just to enjoy the beauty of **my lake** and enjoy the day. There were four children playing on the shore line and swimming. These were my neighbors children. Suddenly my neighbor came running out of the house screaming at his children to get out of the water. They were shocked, startled, and bewildered as to why they had to get out of what was basically their back yard. Their father was screaming and insisting that they could return to swimming after I left. Explaining that he didn't want them out there as long as I was out there.

On numerous occasions nails have been spread over my driveway. Some were arranged to stick straight up so I would walk on them as I walked down my sidewalk. Neighbors have driven their cars way up into my lawn damaging much landscape and grass. Neighbors have uprooted and damaged over 300 trees. They have thrown beer bottles and garbage at my house and into my lawn. They have destroyed thousands of dollars worth of flowers, shrubs and trees. And for what reason? Because they do not see me at the local rest areas after dark.

For many years I left for work at 4:00 A.M. It is dark and few are on the road at that time. One morning at about 4:20 A.M. I saw my neighbor at the gas station. He left the gas station a few minutes before I did. When I left the station and took the exit ramp for the freeway, there was a metal chair lying in the middle of the ramp. It was dark and I barely missed hitting it. The legs of the chair would have gone straight threw my radiator and who knows what else.

A few days later I saw the same neighbor at the gas station again at the same time. Again he left about the same time I arrived. After I got on the road, moving at about 75 mph. in the complete darkness I noticed directly ahead of me my neighbor's car sitting on the road in the middle of my lane. The lights off, no emergency lights flashing, in total darkness. My neighbor must have been standing off the road in the grass because no one was in the car. In total darkness I missed hitting his car by inches. As I proceeded slowly I saw the dome light come on and then his head lights came on. Eventually he passed me giving me the finger.

I had a bonfire one night. It was a gathering for my son's 21st birthday and about 30 people came all friends of his. My neighbors called the police on me for having a bonfire. I was wise to them and had obtained a permit days before. Let me add that my neighbors have bonfires every night without permits and the police are never called on them. Bonfires are part of the culture in this part of the country where people own such large properties. About an hour later into our gathering my neighbors came out of their homes and shot off their shot guns at the same time. Just to let me, my children, and our guests know we were not welcome.

I am afraid to have my children and friends over for dinner or for any other reason in fear my neighbors may try to hurt them. Since the night I overheard them ask one another if any of them had ever seen me at the local rest areas to this day the terrorism has not stopped.

My straight male neighbors hate me because I am not on the down low and the way that I live my life pricks their conscience. The women hate me because the men hate me. Women will do whatever they need to do without rime or reason to have the approval of their husbands and other men.

Some of the local police have gone to my neighbors and threatened to arrest them for the crimes they have committed against me over the years. Some have just smiled at me and done nothing. Sarcastically smiling and telling me to feel free to call them any time. All the while making it clear they intend to do nothing. Nothing but protect their own kind that is.

Welcome to modern Sodom and Gomorrah.

Is it the open Lgbt people who have created this environment or is it the heterosexual women and straight men? I'll let you answer that for yourselves.

The neighborhood I lived in for 18 years before this one was not much different. We had our problems there as well. My state and my neighborhood are no different than the rest of America and the world. The heart of mankind is treacherous just as our Heavenly Father has foretold.

I have been treated with hostility and unfairness in many jobs because of my open orientation. I have never once considered living the lie. I have always loved righteousness and our Heavenly Father more than the world.

Unfortunately all the laws, equal rights, and open Lgbt acceptance in the world will not change the horrid condition of mankind that has already been put into motion. These sexual terroristic mind sets are only continuing to grow and grow world wide. This Sodom and Gomorrah mind set began before I was born and now it is the majority. Not one man, woman, boy, or girl is safe from these evil straight people in these last days.

Yet, these homophobic straight people have the nerve to accuse openly gay and lesbian people of "Sodom and Gomorrah" type behavior. Sodom and Gomorrah is what homophobic straight people have created for all of us today. How completely hateful and violent are these homophobic terroristic people.

The majority of straight women spend their evenings reading romance novels and entertaining themselves with battery operated toys keeping themselves in a constant state of arousal. While trolling their work places and neighborhoods seeking all the attention from men they can in their attempt to violate them. While the majority of straight men spend their evenings watching one television show after another full of gruesome violence and sexual violations against women for entertainment. While trolling their work places and neighborhoods for men to sexually violate.

The majority of America's law enforcement spend the majority of their work day breaking up violence between men and women costing tax payers a fortune. And all the while women sit back and say men are no good anymore and men sit back and say women are no good anymore. What a world straight people have created for the Lgbt community and for themselves. It is so sad and heartbreaking for all of mankind.

Yet straight people who have the nerve to call openly Lgbt people sinners and an abomination to our Heavenly Father. They do not have the slightest clue how revolted our Heavenly Father is with them. As they raise their fists to us and shake their picket signs before us. Their preachers have tickled their ears with hatred and violence against openly gay and lesbian people. Ultimately resulting in this environment that is the "ugly reality" for all of us today.

I once saw on the Oprah Show, one of God's gay children with aids had entered a public pool in Williamson, West Virginia. The young man had returned to his home town to die near his family and loved ones but was greeted with hatred and violence because of his sexual orientation. His entire family became objects of hatred. These lovers of hatred and violence came out of the wood work to proudly display their hatred for open Lgbt people. Of course claiming all the while to be straight God loving Christians.

They used the Word of God to mean things other than what God had intended. They made statements on behalf of God when God did not say such things. How heartbreaking it was to watch this young child of God go to his death knowing he was hated by so many for something he never chose and could not change. Yet so many of these people were so proud of themselves for their hatred and violence against him. God bless Oprah Winfrey for having love and compassion for this precious child of God. For bringing this hatred and violence against him and all openly gay, lesbian, and transgender people to the worlds attention. Oprah is one example that one person has the power to make the world a better place. Love her!

I cannot mention this Christian brother of Williamson, West Virginia, without speaking on behalf of the ignorant people of that region. Before I make this statement let me mention that this kind of ignorance is world wide. It is not exclusive to West Virginia. I feel nothing but love for all straight and Lgbt people, including the brother who appeared on Oprah. However, I feel he made a mistake by entering that pool that day. But his mistake by no means warranted the hatred and violence that erupted against him. I cannot speak about this subject without speaking in defense of the parents of Williamson. These parents felt their children were in danger of getting aids. These parents were only trying to get their children out of harms way. We cannot hold that against any parent. God bless this Christian brother and his family, and the people of Williamson, West Virginia. God used all of them for the stage they presented as an example of brutally harmful ignorance for all the world to witness.

That event was a witness of just how fragile, fearful, and ignorant we all really are. That event was a witness of just how far removed so many people are from God's Word, God's plan and God's purpose. Most people are clueless about our Heavenly Father's way of thinking and His ability to love. Mankind has completely forgotten that we are all brothers and sisters. We are all truly blood relation. Most people today are without a doubt absolutely afraid of each other. People are so afraid that most keep an attitude of defensive hatred on one shoulder and a gun over the other shoulder. Everyone world wide lives in a constant state of fear. Fear of what? Fear of each other.

Brothers and sisters from every community and every walk of life I am bringing this chapter to a close with these words: You did not get to choose your same gender attraction. Our Heavenly Father will not hold that against you. However, how you manage your same gender attraction is a conscience deliberate choice. Our Heavenly Father is watching your every thought and action your every move and decision. I highly advise you to live responsibly and walk in the ways of righteousness.

Brothers and sisters I as well as you have seen it all! Who is responsible for all we have seen? Satan is of course. Satan's churches and his followers. Those lovers of lies and violence. Don't let that big smile, bumper sticker, Jesus pin, and Bible in hand fool you for one minute. It is absolutely amazing to me that Satan has convinced the majority that God's openly gay, lesbian, and transgender children have no value. He has convinced them our hearts and lives are worthless. They stole God's blessings and promises from us once. They will not get a chance to do it again! God will see to that!

God's Word and this revelation are here for eternity. It is my wish that never again will a openly gay, lesbian, or transgender child of God walk this earth believing God hates them. The fools who deny the Words and promises in this revelation from our Heavenly Father will look ever more foolish as they try to make their life's work of hatred, violence and oppression credible and worth while from this day forward.

Lgbt brothers and sisters walk through these last days with extreme caution. I cannot stress enough how important it is to walk as closely to our Heavenly Father and His Word as you possibly can. In these treacherous times one false move, one little tip toe over to the other side of sexual curiosity and disobedience could cost you your life. It is no longer safe to waver between good and evil. Because the evil has become so evil it will entrap you to become a part of it through addiction. Just as it did to the people of Sodom and Gomorrah.

The next time you hear the ugly words of homophobia or see homophobes in action I highly recommend you to move out of harms way. Because these people are most certainly harmful and dangerous.

Heavenly Father,
Please forgive them, for they know not what they do.

ENSNARED BY

CORPORATE PREACHERS

Unfortunately the majority of preachers past and present are Corporate Preachers. Everything they teach and do is motivated by mass appeal and profits. They have a Board of Directors who are calling all the shots. Often the preacher is the head of the Board. What to teach and how to teach it comes from the Board of Directors. Church Boards have profits as their number one priority. The vast majority of money that is donated to large churches does not go out of church bank accounts to help others. Large churches take the donation monies and reinvest it back into the church. For example they us donation money to build other churches and those churches ask for more donations. Then they take that money and build more churches. Through this process the church is becoming richer and richer. All the while the communities that gave that money does not see their donation monies returned to their community or any other community.

In order to have a license to accept tax deductible donations the state and federal guidelines and laws require the church or institution to return the vast majority of that money back into the community whether to the state community or the national community. The guidelines require that the monies donated at tax exempt status return to the public. That amount is about 90% of donations and that must be returned to the public within a certain time frame. That time frame in most states is a fairly short.

The way corporations (I mean) churches get around this loophole while staying within the law is by building a new church for a different community. Now we all know what these new churches do once they are built. They ask for more money, more money, and more money. All the while repeating the same process over and over. Becoming richer and richer. Additionally churches buy exclusive properties and let those properties just sit for many decades. All the while these properties become more valuable. The end result is these corporations (I mean) churches sit on vast amounts of wealth. Wealth that is never intended or used to help anyone in need in any way. These corporations (I mean) churches will continually ask for additional donations for various projects such as feeding a few children in Africa, buying a few shoes for children in South America, providing necessities for a family if their house burns down, etc. Only the monies donated for that specific project actually goes towards those causes. Of course after all expenses for the cause are deduced.

To make a very long and extensive revelation about how churches tip toe around ethical behavior and state and federal laws and guidelines short. Corporate churches today are not using your donation money ethically. Large churches today are out to get rich and stay that way. Even mediocre church pastors have many mansions around the world. Mediocre preachers live like kings with donation money that most think is going to help the poor and desperately needy.

Now that you have a bigger picture of how many churches operate and have operated for many generations you will better understand the reason why we have so many false teachings today. Most false teachings we hear today were designed to please the masses. The more followers the more donations. The more donations the more wealth for the church and the more lavish the preachers live. Many preachers are living in tremendous wealth at the cost of millions in need. When Our Heavenly Father and His son Jesus Christ said to take our excess money and feed the poor that's exactly what they meant. They have told us over and over to care for those in need.

Yes, preachers do work very hard for their money and they should be paid. Preachers should not be made to live in poverty to teach God's Word. But many mansions around the world and all this extravagant living? Absolutely not! This is excessive, greedy, selfish, and corrupt. I could go on and on. But I think I have made my point. Think twice before giving a donation to any church. Look at their yearly intake, year end profits, and what money went where. Be wise brothers and sisters mansions are listed under business or church expenses. Preachers salaries go under administrative cost etc. Be wise about who and where you put your excess cash. Ask yourself each time you give a donation, "Do I want my hard earned money going towards a pastors new mansion or do I actually want it to go towards feeding the poor and helping those in need, etc?"

The truth is many private people and corporations have vast amounts of money to unload each year and churches are tax deductible and these types of donations make them look generous on public reports.

The moral of this information is: Be wise when donating money. Be sure your donated money is going to a good and productive cause. Why on earth would anyone be so careless with their hard earned money? Why would anyone give their hard earned money to any organization to provide a preacher another lavish and obnoxious mansion and lifestyle? Yet, people do this every day and have for generations while millions are starving and struggling each and every day of their lives all over the world. If you take the time to look into the state and federal guidelines and laws and see what churches have been doing for generations you will be appalled.

In this chapter I will point out just a few false teachings because I want you to walk away from this revelation (book) with your feet firmly grounded as you walk with our Heavenly Father and His son Jesus Christ with your new found knowledge, understanding, and liberation.

Many of today's Bible teachers will tell you if you're not obedient you will go to Hell. Then they tell you Hell is a horrible place of eternal torture, eternal falling, eternal burning and eternal gnashing of teeth. A place of eternal torture and torment.

Brothers and sisters,
do you have an ear, are you listening?

- Hell, a place,
- of eternal torture?
- of eternal falling?
- of eternal burning?
- of eternal gnashing of teeth?
- of eternal torture and torment?

This simply is not true!

I'd love to meet the man who came up with that interpretation. What a demon he must have been. When I think of all the people today who believe that nonsense! The only way a person could believe such nonsense is through ignorance of God's loving Word, and God's loving heart and personality.

If you know God at all, you know He would never do such a horrible thing to one of His children, obedient or disobedient. What insanity! That description of Hell has Satan's personality all over it. But only those who know God and who know Satan would know the difference.

Only through generations of lazy mankind letting others do their thinking for them could bring us to today's magnitude of deception.

The English word "Hell" is derived from the Hebrew word "Shohl," and the Greek word "Haides," and the Greek word "Geenna." All of these words in translation mean:

"THE GRAVE."

At the time the scriptures were written men and women understood the illustrations explaining death used in the Bible. The Bible writers used descriptions and languages people of that day were familiar with. After thousands of generations, many different languages, slang, changes in world powers, and Satan's power and influence, many of the Bible's true meanings have become misunderstood.

If we had another seven thousand years before the millennium (second coming of Christ) which we don't, but if we did, how much true understanding would those people seven thousand years from now have about our understanding today? They would be in the same situation we are in today without a doubt.

**Brothers and sisters, do you have an ear, are you listening?
Here's what God says about death.**

Ecclesiastes 9:5+6, 10
*9:5 For the living know that they shall die: but **the dead know not
any thing**, neither have they **any more a reward;** for the
memory of them is forgotten.*

*9:6 Also **their love,** and **their hatred,** and **their envy,** is now
perished; neither have they any more a portion for ever in any
thing that is done under the sun.*

Ecclesiastes 9:10
*9:10 Whatsoever your hand finds to do, do it with your might; for
there is **no work, nor devise, nor knowledge, nor wisdom, in
the grave,** whither you go.*

Psalms 146:4
*164:4 His breath goes forth, he returns to his earth; **in that
veryday his thoughts perish.***

It is not possible for a dead unconscious person to feel
torture, falling, burning, or gnashing of teeth. They feel
nothing at all.

Our Heavenly Father has promised a millennium. A
resurrection of the righteous on earth. He has promised a new
Heaven and a new earth. All mankind will be full of peace
and joy, with no dying, or reason to cry anymore. How could
such peace, joy, and serenity be remotely possible for
mankind if they believed their disobedient parents, or
children, or any other loved ones were in such a place of
torture and torment for eternity?

Those men and women with the wrong hearts will be destroyed by God through death. They will have no thinking and no feeling for eternity. Disobedient mankind will cease to exist. They will no longer reside anywhere, not in a "torturous hell" or "purgatory" of any kind. Mankind with the right hearts will have salvation and eternal life in paradise on earth. After hundreds and thousands of years we will forget those disobedient people ever existed. Our hearts will no longer be heavy over their loss by death.

Hell is a place of death, unconsciousness, a place of no thinking, no feeling, a ceasing to exist.

**HELL IS NOTHING MORE
AND NOTHING LESS THAN THAT.
DEATH IS NOTHING MORE
AND NOTHING LESS THAN THAT.**

Let's face it the best way to get a multitude of people to follow your lies is to tell them if they don't adhere to your lies, there is an eternal torturous, eternal falling, eternal burning and eternal gnashing of teeth type death waiting for them.

Of course if you could not read and were dependent on others reading and interpreting the Word of God for you what else could you believe. For many years it was against the law and against the church to read the Bible. This is how these demonic beliefs got passed down for generations.

It was the Catholic church that came up with this interpretation and made it a law of the land for anyone except a priest to read the Bible. The Catholic church also influenced other nations to make reading the Bible illegal. Are Catholic priests living their lives as if there was an eternal torturous, eternal falling, eternal burning and eternal gnashing of teeth type death for those who are disobedient? I'll let you answer that question for yourselves.

The best way to deceive a multitude of people is through a church twisting God's Word. If Satan stood on a street corner with a flaming pitch fork not many would follow or listen to him. Satan knows that hatred, violence, and judgment is enticing to most people. He is like a salesman looking into the hearts of humanity to see how to entice them for the big sale.

Brothers and sisters there's an old saying that demons have used against us for years in their attempt to steal God's blessings from us and it goes as follows:

**"God created Adam and Eve,
not Adam and Steve."**

Let's clear up that viscous lie. God created gay, lesbian, and transgender people. God created Adam, and God created Steve. God created Eve, and God created the Ethiopian eunuch. We are all His creations.

Our Heavenly Father created all of His children to be sexual knowing many would have, "a same gender attraction." So yes, our Heavenly Father did indeed create Adam and Steve. He created them to have a same gender attraction. He created Adam and Steve to fall in love, to marry and have sex and build a life together. Our Heavenly Father created millions of people to have a same gender attraction, and God said He was pleased with all of His creations.

If some eunuchs were born eunuchs, as Jesus has said, and some were made that way by other men, as Jesus has said, and some of us choose it for the kingdom of Heaven, as Jesus has said, it appears that this was God's plan. Scripture shows that God intended happy and full lives for gay, lesbian, and transgender people, in the beginning with spouses and children, family love and respect, and all the joys of life heterosexual people have always had.

**It has been Satan through man
who has distorted and destroyed
God's original plan and purpose
for gay, lesbian, and transgender children.**

It has been mankind under Satan's influence who has deprived generations of gay people from God's blessings. Lgbt people have not been deprived of these things by God. The blessings that God once established for us in the beginning have been stripped away from us as a result of Satan's influence over mankind. God did create eunuchs just the way he intended eunuchs to be, just as they are, attracted to the same gender.

He is still pleased with His eunuchs of past and proud of His Lgbt children today. God knew what Satan and his followers would do to us. Now our Heavenly Father has come to deliver His precious Lgbt children. God's day of reckoning has arrived. Gay, lesbian, and transgender people are those with a name in Heaven greater than son or daughter, with a monument in their honor in Heaven. We are the chosen whom God has boasted about in Heaven and now on earth for all mankind to hear.

TEN WORDS

Moses saw a burning bush up on a mountain 3600 years ago. Moses was a man who loved God and God loved him. He was the leader of the Hebrew nation of God's people and he delivered them from bondage and oppression. Moses was a Bible teacher, judge, commander, historian and writer. Let's take a look at what God had to say about Moses.

Exodus 3:2
*3:2 And the **angel of the LORD appeared unto him** in a flame of fire out of the midst of a bush: and he looked, and, behold, the bush burned with fire, and the bush was not consumed.*

Exodus 34:27+28
*34:27 And the LORD said unto Moses, **Write thou these words:** for **after the tenor** of these words I have made a covenant with thee and with Israel.*

*34:28 And he was there with the LORD forty days and forty nights; he did neither eat bread, nor drink water. And **he wrote upon the tables** the words of the covenant, **the ten commandments.***

Notice the words at Exodus 34:27, "after the tenor," which means to: "conclude." The word "conclude," means: to shut up, bring to a close, end something, finish something, settle something, determine something, come to an agreement and to deduce.

The word "deduce" means: infer by logical reasoning, reason out, or conclude from known facts or general principles." Ultimately meaning: "God's final Words."

Notice the words at Exodus 34:28, "ten commandments."

Moses came down a mountain 3600 years ago with 10 concluding commandments from God, now thousands of years later we have over 2200 laws and commandments among the scriptures.

Let's take a look at the 10 original commandments from our Heavenly Father. "God's final concluding Words."

1. *Thou shalt have no other god's before me.*
2. *Thou shalt not make unto thee any graven image, or any likeness of anything.*
3. *Thou shalt not take the name of the Lord, thy God in vain.*
4. *Remember the sabbath day to keep it holy.*
5. *Honour thy father and thy mother.*
6. *Thou shalt not kill.*
7. *Thy shalt not commit adultery.*
8. *Thou shalt not steal.*
9. *Thou shalt not bear false witness against thy neighbor*
10. *Thou shalt not covet.*

Three thousand six hundred years ago, Moses came down Mount Sinai carrying two tablets on which he had recorded 10 commandments from God. By the time Jesus arrived 2009 years ago there were over 2200 commandments and written laws.

**Gay, lesbian, and transgender
brothers and sisters,
do you have an ear, are you listening?**

Don't let your walk with God to salvation become difficult or complicated with legalism, the over 2200 laws, traditions, and rituals as Satan's followers have said it should be. Don't let those false teachers trick you into juggling all those laws and regulations. It will cause you to loose your joy and happiness and slow down your walk with God. Satan's hope is that it will cause you to stumble and stumble others, and cause you to become discouraged all together.

The law does nothing but minister death. No man or woman can live up to all of them. Therefore, I want you to be light in heart, and calm in spirit, and happy in your walk with God. God does not want to see you struggling over thousands of laws. The law is there to show us we are all imperfect and therefore sinners, to show us we need Jesus as our savior.

Jesus died for our sins. Our Heavenly Father and Jesus wants to see us live in obedience because our hearts are motivating us out of love for them.

- **We are not sinners because we break the laws.**
- **We break the laws because we are sinners.**
- **We are sinners from birth because we inherit sin from Adam, the first man.**

However, you can not go through your life running a muck either. God's laws are here for our benefit and protection.

The laws are for us, not for God.

TEACHINGS HANDED DOWN FROM BABYLON

Babylonia was an ancient empire and is mentioned often in the Bible. Not once does the Bible make a positive statement when referring to Babylonia. Babylon was the capital of Babylonia. Babylon was known for it's wealth, luxury and wickedness. What Babylon was most renowned for was it's false religion, and false religious practices. Our Heavenly Father pointed out this fact to His children over and over throughout the scriptures. He repeatedly warned that there would be "A Babylon the great" in the last days.

Let's dispel one of Babylons popular false teachings.

Dispelling the Trinity:
The belief that God is three God's in one.

- Our Heavenly Father, is one person (person one)
- Jesus is the son of God, another person (person two)
- The spirit, is a myriad of God's angels, separate spirit people (many persons)

The Father, and the Son, and a myriad of angels known as the holy spirit are not all one person. This three God's in one practice known today as the trinity was at the root of the Babylonian religion. They had poles placed all over Babylonia, that had carvings of three heads representing three God's at the top of the poles, representing the three God's in one type religion.

Our Heavenly Father, His son Jesus Christ, and the holy spirits are not all one person. This teaching comes from false ancient religions. The first nation to have this type of teaching and worship was Babylonia, and this type of, "three God's in one" worship is still practiced today. Our Heavenly Father warns mankind of a "Babylon the great" in the last days. This is a very large scale false religion. That very large and powerful religion is here now. "Babylon the great" looks like the Babylon of ancient times, "three God's in one, and molesting little boys in the temple." The generations on this earth today have had enough proof, and way too much historical documentation to be deceived by Satan's nonsense.

Beware of churches that:

- tell you how to dress
- tell you how to wear your hair
- tell you how to wear your makeup, or not wear make up
- tell you what to eat
- tell you what you should not eat
- tell you to live in one specific area
- tell you to live in a group
- tell you to live in a commune

- tell you to live in a remote village
- tell you to live in a compound
- tell you to mark and shun others
- frown on the fact that you question everything
- frown on the fact that you question anything
- frown on learning scripture for yourself
- encourage blind faith
- suppress individual people and individual groups
- campaign against civil and human rights for anyone
- tell you only certain people have a right to human and civil rights
- let a group of Bible scholars do your reading, thinking and feeling for you
- that masquerade as God's children, when in reality they are adult sex cults
- are sex cults that solicit, hide and protect child rapist and pose as God's churches
- band together to oppress gays in an attempt to create media diversions away from their own immoral behavior

Just to name a few. Beware and keep yourself out of harm's way. Keep in mind these cults or should I say churches are using God's Word to back up their immoral perverted behavior and beliefs. Beware, because some of these churches I have just described are among the wealthiest and largest and therefore the most powerful churches on the planet. Many of which have been campaigning against open gay, lesbian, and transgender people for generations. As the masses begin to abandon this hatred for gays the churches will change their format on the gay issue. More members more money.

In case you did not notice I just condemned many religions here. Many of them have false teachings and practices to some degree. I advise you to get to know God. Look into a church's beliefs and practices. Make a personal decision as to what you are comfortable with in truth. Most importantly do your own thinking using the power of reason that God created in each one of us.

Beware their churches and their members are so beautiful, FROM A DISTANCE!

Don't be seduced by Satan's beauty. These church's appear to speak the Word of God so eloquently. When all the while you are being seduced and deceived for everlasting destruction. Our Heavenly Father doesn't want to see you involved in Satan's nonsense in these last days.

Our Heavenly Father doesn't want to see you:

- fasting
- wearing ashes on your face
- hanging crystals
- abstaining from meat on Fridays
- speaking mindless gibberish (in "tongues")
- rolling around on the floor
- raping and molesting little boys in the temple
- raping children in any fashion
- giving money to protect child rapists

or any other such nonsense in this day and age with the wealth of Bible understanding that He has blessed us with.

All of these types of ancient rituals are Satan's nonsense, church nonsense, man made church dogma, and way outdated. Some churches will teach anything to distract you from God's real truth. Anything to distract you from what they are up to behind closed doors. These Bible teachers will do anything to bring church goers back to church and to the offering plate again. Remember more members, more money, more personal gain.

These silly ancient ritualistic customs are designed to fill your head with more things to distract you from God's real Word and truth. This is all more of Satan's nonsense to lead you further from God's truth and blessings. Be sober minded. Be realistic in your thinking. Be mature using your reasoning power, using the gifts of intellect and the sound heart and mind God has given each of you.

When you are listening to a churches teachings stay alert and mature in your thinking. If it sounds ridiculous, looks ridiculous, feels ridiculous, then it is ridiculous. If it looks and sounds hateful and judgmental, and feels unloving or harsh then more than likely it is.

Don't let a Bible teacher or church worshiper or anyone for that matter teach you to ignore or suppress your instincts, your gut feelings, your power of reason, or your power of love and compassion.

Over the years I have watched churches manipulate the minds of millions of kind loving innocent people. People whom entered a church with the type of heart God is drawing to Him for salvation. I have seen church leaders and members slowly deplete every ounce of God's love and compassion right out of God loving people. They teach them to hate, suppress, and campaign, against God's poor and less fortunate children. They will even teach innocent children to hate.

They teach them to attack like a pack of wolves hardhearted and insensitive towards those different or less fortunate than themselves. They lead these people to believe they are pleasing our Heavenly Father with their hateful hearts and behavior They twist the understandings of God's heart making them believe God is pleased with them only when they hate. Yet, our Heavenly Father did not say these things and does not feel this way about others.

Unfortunately too often we see non Christian people, so called heathens, with more love and compassion and human decency than so called Christians have. Satan must be so pleased with himself. This fact alone has stumbled millions of God's children. Many have seen how hateful and viscous "so called Christians," display themselves and want nothing to do with Christianity or the Christian God.

God says to be obedient, reasonable, and moderate and balanced in all things. You need to be as disciplined and obedient as you can be, **but not legalistic,** or lead by Satan's distracting nonsense. This is religion.

Religion is man's ideas and opinions, not God's.

This is the type of thing the Pharisees were known for. The Pharisees made the Jews miserable in their walk with God and they took every bit of joy out of their lives. The Pharisees were corrupt and abused God's Word and people. Jesus was angry at the Pharisees for all the harm they had done to God's people. Jesus said the people of Sodom and Gomorrah stood a better chance of salvation than they did. Today's world is full of modern day Pharisees, doing the same kind of things, and using God's Word to do it.

Beware brothers and sisters! Our Heavenly Father has not given you this loving revelation to see you walk away and get ensnared or entangled in Satan's manipulations and lies again. Walk, learn, and grow ever so cautiously because these are the last days. Satan has created a million stumbling blocks to prevent all of us from attaining and keeping salvation. Do not underestimate his power and influence over the entire world population. Satan did not come to earth to undermine the trees, grass, or rivers. He came here to undermine and destroy God's precious children.

Romans 4:1-5

4:1 What shall we say then that Abraham our Father, as pertaining to the flesh, hath found?

*4:2 For if Abraham were **justified by works,** he hath whereof to glory; **but not before God.***

*4:3 For **what saith the scripture?** Abraham believed God, and it was **counted unto him for righteousness.***

*4:4 Now to **him that worketh** is the reward **not reckoned of grace, but of debt.***

*4:5 **But to him that worketh not, but believeth on him that*** *justifieth the ungodly, his faith is counted for righteousness.*

Abraham was imperfect. Abraham was a sinner. Yet through his faith and only by his faith he was declared righteous by God. It's the same blessing for us today. We are all sinners, all imperfect, and only through faith in our Heavenly Father's forgiveness and His Son Jesus Christ, are we seen as righteous in God's eyes.

Romans 3:19-23
*3:19 Now we know that what things soever **the law saith, it saith to them who are under the law:** that every mouth may be stopped, and all the world may become guilty before God.*

*3:20 **Therefore by the deeds of the law there shall no flesh be justified in his sight: for by the law is the knowledge of sin.***

*3:21 But now the righteousness of God **without the law** is manifested, being witnessed by the **law and the prophets;***

*3:22 Even the **righteousness of God which is by faith of Jesus Christ** unto all and upon all them that believe: for there is no difference:*

*3:23 **For all have sinned, and come short of the glory of God;***

The law is there
to show us our imperfections,
(or sin) and remind
us why we need Jesus.

You cannot obtain or earn righteousness or salvation before God through laws and regulations.

- **We are not sinners because we break the laws.**
- **We break the laws because we are sinners.**
- **We are sinners from birth because we inherit sin from Adam the first man.**

We will always be sinners but keep in mind all obedient people are still sinners. Be as obedient as you can and God will be able to praise His gay, lesbian, and transgender children before the angels in Heaven and man on earth. However, all the obedience in the world will not make you perfect. At this time in history you will not be able to escape sin. We are only righteous through God's undeserved kindness by way of His Son Jesus Christ.

Brothers and sisters, the pit of legalism has been a snare for many of God's children for generations. Please do not let anyone persuade or seduce you with legalistic thinking. It has stumbled and taken joy and happiness away from many of God's children for thousands of generations.

Let me give you an example of legalism.

The Bible says, "divorce is a sin." So is it a sin to divorce? Yes it is, but Moses went to God, and God allowed a concession (or pardon) for it, because so many of His children were unhappy in their marriages. Is divorce still a sin today? Yes. Divorce was not part of God's original plan, or state of perfection, therefore making it a sin or imperfection. Will divorced people still be able to obtain salvation. Yes, through God's undeserved kindness and forgiveness of all our sins through the sacrifice of Jesus Christ.

Let me give you another example of legalism.

The Bible says, "a same gender attraction is a sin." So is a same gender attraction a sin today? Yes it is. But Jesus reveals a concession or pardon for it when He included the eunuchs in the discussion of the marriage arrangement. He mentions this concession or pardon before the Pharisees, his disciples, and a large crowd. This pardon was common knowledge long before Jesus earthly ministry. Everyone who was born or those whom died prior to the coming of Christ knew they were doomed for all of their sins if not for the Crucifixion of Christ as their sacrifice. Is a same gender attraction still a sin today? Yes. A same gender attraction was not part of God's original plan, or original state of perfection, therefore making it a sin or imperfection. Will people with a same gender attraction still be able to obtain salvation. Yes, through God's undeserved kindness and forgiveness of all our sins through Jesus Christ. Moses through God made this same type of concession in regard to divorce.

Legalistic people are no longer casting stones and judging those who are divorced.
Are legalistic people still casting stones and judging those with a same gender attraction?
"YES"

This is legalism.

God has exposed these false preachers through this revelation. These false preachers will try to use scripture by twisting it and lying to steal this glorious revelation away from us again. Be literate in God's Word and firm in what you know to be truth. If you cannot back up your beliefs with scripture, all you have is an opinion, a theory, not faith, not God's truth. At some point in time all scripture passages were directed for a particular purpose; that purpose may belong to the past rather than the present so you need to learn the difference.

For example one scripture says to stone people who sin but obviously today we do not need to do that. That scripture was for different generations a different time in history. In a storm of demons, or misguided humans who have been taught lies about God, you will need to be firm in what you know is God's truth for mankind today.

God has exposed these false preachers through this revelation. These false Bible teachers are fat with riches bought by the lives of so many of God's open Lgbt children. They have gained great wealth selling their lies, hatred and violence. Their financial empires based on lies have made them arrogant and vicious in their successful attempt to please the masses. It is not likely they will be humble enough to repent for their treachery against God's open gay, lesbian, and transgender children and the world. This revelation will expose them and one day their financial empires will crumble before our very eyes. These false preachers will go down kicking and screaming and seeking revenge. Their followers will be confused and angry as well, because they have lost the reason they became Christians in the first place; to have an organized venue in which to hate and create violence against God's precious open Lgbt children. They lay their heads down at night puffed up with pride, thinking they are God's gift, above reproach and believing they are without sin themselves. They wear smiles on their faces as they commit atrocities against God's precious open Lgbt children with a name in Heaven. They boast among themselves for their evil deeds for the day.

When this revelation is released they will become angry, confused, and lost, desperately trying to find some way to feed their lust for hatred, violence and oppression. God help their next victims, because they will find a new agenda, another less fortunate group to target with their hateful teachings. Which feed their violent and hateful appetites. As you come to embrace our Heavenly Father be diligent at making sure your not a part of such behavior. Remember, I have seen churches and the twisting of scripture change the most loving hearts.

Beware brothers and sisters, these false teachers and their followers come as wolves dressed in sheep's clothing. With smiles on their faces, bumper stickers on their cars, Jesus pins and Bibles in hand. They are fully prepared to steal God's blessings and promises away from you again.

Let me say these words: Not all of today's preachers are working for and deceived by Satan. Many are doing God's work. Many are pleasing in God's eyes and are preachers with the right hearts. These false teachers I have spoken of have already exposed themselves. We all know who they are. It is to late for them to run and hide. God gave them plenty of time to reveal their hearts and motives before releasing this revelation to all of mankind. Their destiny has already been written. God's day of reckoning has arrived.

Do not be deceived into believing God is only with one church or denomination as so many preachers have told you. Remember most of them are corporate preachers, business men greedy for wealth and riches. They tell you that to keep you and your families in **THEIR** churches. More members means more money, more clout, more prestige and more power. These corporate preachers are interested in your money not your salvation. God's Word in the Bible makes it perfectly clear that obedient children from all nations, languages, and walks of life, will be in Heaven on earth, and in Heaven with our Heavenly Father. God says He judges a man by **HIS HEART, and by his heart only, not by:**

- his <u>religion,</u>
- his <u>language,</u>
- his <u>place of origin,</u>
- his <u>skin color,</u>
- his <u>intelligence,</u> or
- his <u>lack of intelligence,</u> etc.

Heaven is a place on earth.

The scriptures speak of two Heavens. One Heaven up above earth where God, Jesus, and the angels live and a Heaven on earth for mankind.

The Heaven above was created for spirit people. Most of mankind has never seen that Heaven. However, a few have seen it according to the scriptures. This is the home of spirit people. This is where spirit people spend most of their time. Yet, spirit people do have the power to cover the entire universe including earth. I think most of you have a pretty clear idea of the Heaven up above and I'm not going to elaborate much on that. For most of you it is the only Heaven that you are aware of.

The Heaven above was not created for mankind. It was not created for us to live in, or visit, or to dwell in. The Heaven created for mankind is right here on earth. You are looking at it. You see it every day of your lives.

The earth was created for us to dwell upon forever. Our bodies were designed to renew itself and live forever. The earth was designed with the perfect vegetation and environment to sustain humans. The vegetation was designed to keep replenishing as well as the sunlight, water and everything needed to keep mankind alive, healthy, and happy for eternity. Let's look at Isaiah 45:18

Isaiah 45:18

45:18 *For so saith the LORD; that created the heavens; God himself that formed the earth and made it; he has established it, he created it not in vain, **he formed it to be inhabited:** I am the LORD; and there is none else.*

Psalms 37:29

37:29 The righteous shall inherit the land, and dwell therin for ever.

Psalms 104:5

*104:5 Who laid the foundations of the earth, that **it should not be removed forever.***

Revelation 21:1-4

*21:1 And I saw a new heaven and a new earth: for the first heaven and the first earth were passed away; and there was **no more sea.***

21:2 And I John saw the holy city, new Jerusalem, coming down from God out of heaven, prepared as a bride adorned for her husband.

*21:3 And I heard a great voice out of heaven saying, Behold **the tabernacle of God is with men, and he will dwell with them,** and they shall be his people, and God himself shall be with them, and be their God.*

21:4 And God shall wipe away all tears from their eyes; and there shall be no more death, neither sorrow, nor crying, neither shall there be any more pain: for the former things are passed away.

Matthew 25:31-34

*25:31 When the Son of man shall come in his glory, **and all the holy angels with him,** then shall he sit upon the throne of his glory:*

*25:32 And before him shall be gathered **all nations**: and he shall **separate them one from another**, as a shepherd divideth his sheep from the goats:*

*25:33 And he shall set the **sheep on his right** hand, but the **goats on the left.***

*25:34 Then shall the King say unto them on **his right hand,** Come, ye blessed of my Father, **inherit the kingdom prepared for you from the foundation of the world:***

Before mankind sees Heaven on earth we will live through the millennium which is a 1000 year period after Armageddon. During this millennium the dead will be resurrected and past generations of mankind will heal from the lifetime of living under Satan's brutal earthly influence. This healing process will take many years for most to return to a state of wellness that our Heavenly Father originally intended for all mankind.

CAN YOU PRAY THE GAY AWAY?

Having a same gender attraction is not a choice.

Whether you act on that desire or not is a choice. Now some of you may be thinking, "Oh my God it is a choice." You may be thinking you will go throughout your entire lives without sex considering acting on a same gender attraction is a choice. My response to that is, "Good luck with that." Now I'm going to pose an equal scenario.

Having an opposite gender attraction is not a choice. Whether you act on that desire or not is a choice. Now some of you may be thinking, "Oh my God it is a choice." You may be thinking you will go throughout your entire lives without sex considering acting on a opposite gender attraction is a choice. My response to that is "Good luck with that."

Many gay people have had this philosophy beat into their heads for generations. This kind of thinking is so unfair for gay people. Not once have I ever heard of a heterosexual person ever being told to live a lifetime of celibacy.

For generations gay people have been told to pray the gay away. When that philosophy fails they are told they do not love God enough, they do not have enough faith, they are not trying hard enough, if they really wanted to be straight they would have turned straight by now etc.

This philosophy simply isn't Biblical or logical. This philosophy has driven millions of Lgbt people to suicide and deep into the down low lifestyle. This philosophy has documented proof that it is destructive in every way. Whenever you see this kind of destruction it has Satan's name all over it. That's a guarantee. Mankind was created to be sexual for procreation and pleasure. This is a blessing from our Heavenly Father to all of mankind. This is not something to deprive ourselves of or to be ashamed about.

Personally I never wanted to be gay. Yet, I have never asked our Heavenly Father to take away my same gender attraction. Only upon contemplating covering this issue did I realize this fact. There have been a few times that I did tell our Heavenly Father I was sorry for being gay and asked Him to forgive me for my same gender attraction. The last time I said this to our Heavenly Father was on October 30, 1996 the first time the angel came to me.

I think the reason that I never asked God to change me is because I have known so many people who did ask God to change them and saw the anguish and disappointment and brutal struggle they lived with. Many of those people tried to commit suicide, many were successful, because they became so frustrated and disappointed in themselves. They were also told that they were a disappointment to God.

I do not believe that a person can pray the gay away. I believe a same gender attraction is such a deep and inner part of a persons soul that it is meant to be a part of them for a reason.

Now our Heavenly Father does tell us to ask Him for all of our needs as we walk through this life. He says He will care for our needs and answer our prayers. Through my experience observing the attempts by others trying to pray the gay away God has answered those prayers for a multitude of people. A multitude of people have asked God to change their same gender attraction and God HAS answered their prayers. They are still gay. Unfortunately many of those people are still waiting for God's reply. Many are still waiting for God to turn them heterosexual. God has answered their prayers. God's answer was NO.

Often when people ask God for something they become frustrated because they did not get what they asked for. People often forget that God is not going to give them something He does not want them to have. Millions of gay people for generations have asked God to change their same gender attraction and they are still gay. When this happens many become frustrated and just keep asking God over and over and just become more and more frustrated. What most people do not realize is that God did answer their pray and His answer was NO.

Who has taught so many people to make their walk and relationship with God so stubborn and frustrating? Modern day preachers and their followers. It is modern religion that teaches people to refuse to listen to God and demand from God what they want instead of accepting God's wishes above their own.

Brothers and sisters don't make your walk with God so difficult. God did not create us to go through our lives living in constant frustration over who and what he created us to be. However, you are the masters of your own lives. If you want to live a heterosexual looking lifestyle that is an option. Many people have visions of the life they want to live. Whether they fit into that vision or not is another question. I have often found that people who create a lifestyle that does not remotely resemble who they truly are live in terrible frustration and unhappiness.

When a person creates a superficial life everything looks real good, looks real together, and looks real healthy from a distance. Once you get up close you find very unhappy and sexually frustrated people. Far to often you also find spouses and their children wondering what they have done to make their father or mother so unhappy. Because these are the people who bear the brunt of a parent who is living a life that does not remotely resemble who they truly are.

When a person lives a false life they loose track of who they were from the beginning. When you loose who you are you forget how to feel, how to nurture, how to love, how to be happy. People choose superficial lifestyles each and every day all across the world. Many feel pressured to please every one around them instead of believing they have a right to please themselves first. Satan has convinced many that a superficial life is more valuable than a real life that nurtures their hearts and souls ultimately bring real joy and happiness.

Most children and young people are taught that when it comes to a same gender attraction they are required to please their parents, family, and society before themselves. What is the end result of this philosophy? The end result is a suicide rate among the Lgbt community that is higher than ever before in history. The highest suicide rate in the world. A world full of brutally unloving marriages where everyone is just going through the motions of life hurting every step of the way. God created this life for us to embrace and enjoy with zeal, enthusiasm, and extreme happiness. God did not put us on this earth to live in utter emotional and sexual Hell loathing ourselves over our same gender attraction.

I do believe it is possible for a gay person to live a heterosexual life and be happy. I have known many people who have done just that. Our Heavenly Father has provided many choices for us in this life. Your life belongs to you and you only. Live the life that your heart is longing for whether gay or heterosexual if that is an option for you.

There are many gay people who can not make such a choice. Because they are totally gay and the thought of being with the opposite gender repulses them. For these types of people I highly recommend an exclusive gay lifestyle. Or a celibate lifestyle if that pleases you. You are the masters of your own lives.

I highly recommend that you make wise choices as you create a life for yourselves.

One last time:
You are the master of your life
in regard to sex and sexual behavior.

Rich or poor, many opportunities or no opportunities, whether you live in the U.S. or Russia YOU will always be the master of your sex life. With that being said you still do not get to choose your sexual attraction so make wise choices when building a life for yourselves. If you do not listen to your spirit and you make wrong choices as a result do not blame your parents or society. You have no one to blame but yourself. If you have found that you have already made such mistakes with your life I recommend that you correct those mistakes as best you can and move on with your new happy life.

Our Heavenly Father created us to be simple and to live simple lives and for our walk with Him to be simple. All of this complication and banging our heads and souls against God's instruction is Satan's nonsense. Satan is never ending in his attempts to keep us frustrated in every aspect of our lives.

The next time someone walks up to you and tries to feed you with their nonsense about being the person they want you to be, I want you to remember who sent them, and who taught them to believe their interests are more important than your true sexual orientation. The next time someone walks up to you with this philosophy send them running!

It is kind and loving to be considerate of the feelings and desires of others but not when it comes to your true sexual orientation. That belongs to YOU and YOU have every right to totally embrace your true authentic sexual orientation.

**Don't ever let anyone take your true
authentic sexual orientation away from you.**

I will wrap this subject up with
God's loving and liberating Words.

Heb. 13:18

> *Pray for us: for we trust we have a good* **conscience**, *in all things* <u>*willing to live honestly.*</u>

1Corth. 10:29+30

> **Conscience**, *I say, not your own, but of the other: for why is my* **liberty** *judged of another man's conscience? For if I by grace be a partaker, why am I evil spoken of for that for which* <u>*I give thanks?*</u>

Coll. 3.9

> <u>*Lie not to one another*</u>, *seeing that you have put off the old man with his deeds.*

1Peter 3:16

> <u>*Having a good conscience;*</u> *that, whereas they speak evil of you, as of evildoers, they may be ashamed that falsely accuse your good conversation in Christ.*

John 4:23+24

> *But the hour comes, and now is,* **when** <u>**the true worshipers**</u> <u>**shall worship the Father in spirit and in truth:**</u> *for the Father seeks such to worship him. God is a spirit: and they that worship him must worship him in spirit and in* <u>**truth.**</u>

BE SOBER MINDED AND REALISTIC

There are so many different types of gay people in our culture and I don't want any of you to be left out. As for you transsexuals, you may be concerned about Deuteronomy 23:1, because it states castration is a sin. Let your heart be light brothers and sisters. Go to our Heavenly Father, tell Him you love Him, ask Him to forgive you for all your sins through His Son Jesus Christ, get baptized, and go in peace rejoicing.

If any of you are thinking about having a sex change, I don't recommend it. God gave you your mind and your body and your identity, and God was pleased. God created you to be this way. You are not a mistake. God doesn't make mistakes. I advise you to learn to love yourself as God loves you. God made Lgbt people for a reason. He has a plan and purpose for us never doubt that. If sex changes were possible in ancient times I'm sure they would have had them. If a sex change is something you feel is written in your heart and you can't shake it, then it is between you and God.

There is no such thing as a man trapped in a woman's body or a woman trapped in a man's body. The brain of a woman and man are the same. You can not look at a person's personality or temperament and conclude it is a man's or a woman's. Men and women sometimes identify with the opposite gender more than their own gender. This is normal and common. These characteristics are formed at conception and at a very young age through social conditioning. Please don't try to distort what I just said. These characteristics are God's will and pleasure.

Our Heavenly Father has designed our brain with built in coping and survival skills that kick in when needed. For example if our environment has taught us to hate ourselves, our brains will take over and put us in a survival mode.

Hating ones self is very overwhelming for the brain and our emotions. Whatever the brain needs to do to make us love ourselves again it will do. For example little boys grow up believing "boys go with girls." Little girls grow up believing little "girls go with boys." If a person grows up feeling attracted to their same gender the brain becomes confused and stressed. That young child begins to rationalize that they must be a different gender on the inside. Because they grew up believing that opposite genders go together. As the brain tries to make sense of this confusion and stress, the coping and survival skills kick in. Bringing the person to a state of peace in believing they should have been born a different gender. Therefore believing there is a defect inside of them somewhere. The person clings to this rationale for survival purposes and in time becomes obsessed with changing their body, feeling happiness will only be attained when the physical defect is fixed. It is perfectly okay with God to be gay or lesbian. God created you to turn out this way and He loves you just as you are. He loves you the same whether you keep your body as He gave it to you or whether you change it. God has a deeply tremendous love for you whatever you feel you need to do. What God wants from you foremost is your love and devotion, everything else is details, details, details.

I do not recommend plastic surgery unless it is medically needed for heath reasons. Learn to accept and love what God has blessed you with. Basically a sex change is much like a plastic surgery. I do not want to see pharmaceutical companies and doctors coming up with medications, or "antidotes," or surgeries to change what God has created. This goes for you in the genetics field as well.

**Leave what belongs to God,
to God!**

**Remember,
do your own thinking
and feeling.
A sex change is between you and God.**

Our Heavenly Father instructs us to be true to our hearts.

Matthew 5:3
*5:3 Blessed are the **poor in spirit:** for theirs is the kingdom of Heaven.*

Matthew 5:8
*5:8 Blessed are the **pure in heart**: for they shall see God.*

Matthew 5:10+11
*5:10 Blessed are they **which are persecuted for righteousness' sake:** for theirs is the kingdom of Heaven.*

*5:11 Blessed are ye, when men shall revile you, and persecute you, **and shall say all manner of evil against you falsely**, for my sake.*

Psalms 51:6
*51:6 Behold, **thou desires truth in the inward parts:** and in the hidden part **thou shalt make me to know wisdom.***

Zechariah 8:16+17
*8:16 These are the things that ye shall do; **Speak ye every man the truth** to his neighbour; execute the judgment of truth and peace in your gates:*

*8:17 And **let none of you imagine evil in your hearts** against his neighbour; and love no false oath: for all these are things that I hate, saith the LORD.*

If it is written in your heart to dress like the opposite gender then be true to your heart and know that you are God's creation. Our Heavenly Father loves honesty and truthfulness and He hates a liar. How frustrating it must be for God to write something in our hearts and minds and watch us grow up to deny all that God intended for us, because we let "empty headed" mankind dictate our thinking. Remember we were created to please God and honor His wisdom, not to please mankind and honor man's opinions. God created you the way He intended, your body and your mind, and He was pleased. Love all of yourself as completely as God loves all of you.

If you do not live an authentic life, true to your own spirit, you will loose yourself in time. Not one thought or emotion will be your true authentic thoughts and emotions. How sad is that? What a waste of a life. What a waste of a gift from our Heavenly Father.

After all – if we all had the same orientation, the same mind, the same personality, the same temperament, the same body, the same face, and the same skin color, how would God ever be able to see our hearts. Remember it is within our hearts that God judges us, our hearts are what grant us salvation and everlasting life. Keep in mind it is our hearts that deprive us of God's blessings as well.

Additional Reference
(1Sam.16:5-7)(Jer.17:9-12)(Rom.10:4-14)

GAY PARADES

Leviticus 18:22
Thou shalt not lie with mankind,
as with womankind: it is abomination.

Lgbt brothers and sisters, I want to talk to you about gay parades. A same gender attraction is an imperfection and therefore a sin. Partaking in an event that celebrates any sin is wrong in the eyes of our Heavenly Father. Having a parade to celebrate being gay is no different than having a parade celebrating a group of gossipers, liar's, adulterers or revilers, etc. All sin holds the same weight with God, whether you were born with it or not. A murderer in the eyes of God is equal to a reviler, gossiper, etc. Sin is not something to celebrate or to be proud of.

**God does not boast about us in Heaven and on earth,
because we are gay or lesbian.
God is not proud of us because we are gay or lesbian.
God boasts about us,
and is proud of us,
because we are obedient in spite of our sin or imperfection.**

Don't think I am not aware of the struggles, hard work, and many efforts it took our people to get a gay parade and the gay pride celebration. Be advised I am very grateful for those accomplishments. I entered the gay scene two years after the Stonewall uprising occurred in Greenwich Village, New York. I experienced raids in bars by police in person as a child of 14 years old. I was in the middle of the gay fight in California in the 1970's when brother Harvey Milk was murdered after winning his election in San Francisco. Back in those days it didn't matter whether you were in San Francisco, Chicago, Dallas, Peoria or wherever you lived in America. If you were openly gay you were in the middle of the gay fight. Between the churches, Anita Bryant, and all the other followers of demons, tirelessly working against us there was no escape from their wrath and oppression.

Back then if you were in a restaurant, work place, department store, walking down the street, etc. and someone saw that you were openly gay, people were excited to share their views and opinions about every gay issue, as well as how they felt about you. Don't misunderstand me they were not nice about it. Often their views came along with violence and threats. In America in the 1970's, police officers would rush into gay bars and start beating our brothers and sisters, just because we had the nerve to live and breathe and have a little fun. Those raids were directed by the city councils and people of the neighborhood because they didn't want our kind coming into their neighborhood. They believed we were child molesters and perverts, as they were taught to believe in their churches. Oftentimes, the only difference between us and the people of those neighborhoods was our honesty about who we were. Thank God for the Gay Pride celebration and parades, because our people needed all the safety and support we could get. However, things are different now. Our Heavenly Father has lifted us to a higher ground with this revelation.

The point is;
I know full well the struggles our people have faced and the struggles we still face.

Now things have changed.

We are no longer generations of lost eunuchs. Our Heavenly Father has claimed His eunuch children by giving this revelation about us to the world. Our Heavenly Father has now lifted us up to a higher ground through this revelation. A higher ground with a place in His plan and a purpose in life, with the same blessings that heterosexuals have always had and taken for granted. We were taught or should I say lied to that only heterosexuals were worthy of these blessings.

Lgbt brothers and sisters, we are all a product of generations of lost and oppressed eunuchs.

However we are not lost anymore.

I advise you to change our Gay Pride celebration and parade to "A name in Heaven" celebration and parade. Consider that statement my approval and permission to use the title

A NAME IN HEAVEN
on our banner.

At no cost you may use this title for our Gay Pride celebration and parade. Our Heavenly Father gave this title to me for free, and I give it to you for free, for the pride celebration and parade only. A name in Heaven originates with God and belongs to Him and all gay, lesbian, and transgender people. The use of the title A Name In Heaven is forbidden in any other use without my written permission.

**Show the world that God loves you,
be proud of your name in Heaven greater
than son or daughter
and the monument in Heaven in your honor.
This is something to be proud of,
this is something to celebrate,
before God and man.**

Show the world you are representing one of God's eunuch children. Behave yourselves, not only display obedience but live in obedience. This means women will need to keep their shirts on, no nudity. Most Americans find nudity offensive. This means gay men and women need to avoid the use of vulgar speech and vulgar comedy shows. Also practice soberness and do not wear vulgar or offensive attire. Your days of holding onto an attitude that the world hates you and thinks you're disgusting, and reacting with a frame of mind such as: "I will show them disgusting," are over. This means Lgbt brothers and sisters will need to keep sexual activity off the streets and in the privacy of your bedrooms as the rest of the world has managed to do.

Brothers and sisters disown the rude personalities you are known for and proud of. Vulgarity, insulting attitudes and speech are pleasing to Satan and his people, not to God and His people. I know many of you macho and masculine Lgbt brothers and sisters are reading this and thinking I'm referring to the effeminate men. You would be wrong. I am talking to you as well because you are just as bad as the queens. Many of you are thinking, "Well, my mother always said I was pissy and rude, even as a small child. Everyone on my mothers side of the family are pissy and rude, or its genetic, etc." The "time of the end" that the Bible alerts us to is too close to nurture your excuses. There simply isn't enough time left to nurture your bad behavior.

You need to grow up. Be a mature adult and think like a mature adult. Be mature in your speech, in your dealings with others, in your attitudes and behavior. Not only are our Heavenly Father, Jesus, and His Heavenly angels watching us, but our heterosexual brothers and sisters are watching us as well. Remember God has made His Lgbt children to be an example for them. Now that God has reclaimed us before the world we would not want to do anything to stumble one of them. Heterosexual people are our brothers and sisters as well. We should love them as we love each other and be concerned about their salvation as much as our own.

Millions of heterosexual brothers and sisters left the churches years ago over gay oppression, out of love and compassion for us. Now it is time for us to be an encouragement for their sakes. I would hate to see one heterosexual person get left behind during this great harvest (return to God). This also includes our brothers and sisters in hiding. As you embrace God and church again, grab the hand of a heterosexual or straight friend and bring them back to God and church with you.

Our Heavenly Father has lifted us up to a higher ground through this revelation. There is a responsibility that comes with that. A responsibility to each other and God.

As for Satan and his followers, how pleased are they to see you misbehave and make fools of yourselves in front of God and the world. If any event is not appropriate for young children then it is not appropriate for you. Remember, you are God's children as well. Gay and heterosexual families and their children, should be able to attend a gay event and not need to worry about what their children might see or hear. You should have this same protective attitude for yourselves. We are not a lost generation of Lgbt people anymore.

If you think God sent me with this revelation to tickle your ear and make you feel all warm and fuzzy you would be wrong. God sent me with this revelation to show you how much He loves you. To reveal His plans for you and to show you where you fit into His plan and purpose. God sent me with this revelation to put you in line with faith and obedience, and to ensure your salvation and everlasting life. The end is near. God is gathering His Lgbt children together for the final harvest. It is time for a complete makeover for most of you.

As a matter of fact we shouldn't have any specific gay or heterosexual places or activities. We are all God's children and He intended for us to live in harmony together. God created families with heterosexual and gay people in them. Our Heavenly Father intended for families to stay united in love and fellowship for a lifetime. That includes all the heterosexual and Lgbt children born into the family. Families torn apart over this Lgbt issue is Satan's delight, not God's delight.

I recommend we change the premise of the "gay pride celebration," to pride in "A Name In Heaven celebration," a name greater than son or daughter, a monument in Heaven in our honor." Show the world that God loves you and is proud of you and boasts about you to His angels in Heaven. That is something to be proud of, to celebrate and to march in parades about. Let the world know God loves us after all.

- **A Name In Heaven, Celebration**
- **A Name In Heaven, Parade**

This is something the world will marvel at and applaud. This is something the angels in Heaven will marvel at and applaud. Be proud of and celebrate our Heavenly Father's tremendous love for His gay, lesbian, and transgender children.

DON'T BE RELIGIOUS

M any people believe that anyone who believes in a God is religious. Many believe anyone who attends church, reads the Bible, mentions God in conversation, or teaches the Word of God is religious. Let's explore what religion and religious really means.

The definition of the word religion is as follows:

A system of a specific religious belief. People that bind together with a specific religious belief. Belief in a divine power to be obeyed and worshiped. To be preoccupied in mind with a specific conduct mixed with ritual. To be earnest, obsessive, and excessive, in ritual and belief.

The definition of the word religious is as follows:

A strict adherence to a specific religion. Devout without question. Belonging to a community of one mind. To be conscientiously exact, careful not to form your own understanding or opinion.

There have always been many religions and religious people in the world. Many people feel religion is necessary if their going to believe in God or have a relationship with God. Most people today do not realize that many religions and being religious is not pleasing to our Heavenly Father. Let's take a look at what our Heavenly Father has to say in regard to religious people.

Matthew 23:23,27-29

(23) Woe unto you, scribes and Pharisees, hypocrites! For you pay tithe of mint and anise and cumin, and have omitted the weightier matters of the law, judgment, mercy, and faith: these ought you to have done, and not to leave the other undone.

(27) Woe unto you, scribes and Pharisees, Hypocrites! For you are like unto whited sepulchres, which indeed appear beautiful outward, but are within full of dead men' s bones, and of all uncleanness.

(28) Even so you also outwardly appear righteous unto men, but within you are full of hypocrisy and iniquity.

(29) Woe unto you, scribes and Pharisees, hypocrites! Because you build the tombs of the prophets, and garnish the sepulchers of the righteous.

John 12:43

For they loved the praise of men more than the praise of God.

2 Timothy 3:5-7
(5) having a form of Godly devotion but proving false to it's
power, and from these turn away. (6) For from these arise
those men who slyly work their way into households and
lead as their captives weak women loaded down with sins,
led by various desires, (7) always learning and yet never able
to come to an accurate knowledge of truth.

What these scriptures tell us is that knowing God, walking with God, serving God, and obeying God has nothing to do with pomp and circumstance. These scriptures show us that money is more important to religious leaders than serving the spiritual needs of their flocks. Instead they should be teaching the flock about having faith and a relationship with our creator.

These scriptures show us religious people look beautiful on the outside but on the inside they are like filthy rages. These scriptures show us that religious people appear righteous but are full of sin and hypocrisy loving the praise of men more than the praise of God. These scriptures show us religious people are always learning and yet are never able to come to an accurate understanding of God's Word.

The best example of a religion is the Catholic religion. The best example of religious people are the Catholic's. It is documented that for generations the behavior of the Catholic Priests and Nuns have been abominable. For generations the Catholic Priests have raped and gang raped a multitude of God's precious children while the Nuns turn a blind eye.

It is documented that 20 years ago an old Catholic church was tore down and discovered beneath the basement floor were hundreds of new born baby remains. It is believed the Nuns and Priests were having sex together and the babies were those of the Nuns. It is documented that this practice had gone on for generations.

The Catholic church has taken their contribution monies and reinvested that money back into their church by buying land, building churches and taking more donation money and reinvesting that money back into the church again.

According to tax exempt law donation monies should go back into the community in which it came from. To benefit the people of the community. The Catholic church uses a tricky loop hole to remain within the law. The way that they use this loop hole is by reinvesting their donation monies in property and building more churches, venues to collect more contributions. This way the monies never leave the hand's of the Catholic church as the church just continues to get richer and richer. All the while billions on earth are living in poverty and starving as the Catholic Church sits on trillions of dollars that never leaves the Catholic Church bank accounts.

Not one government has ever challenged the Catholic church on this issue. All the while using these trillions of dollars to protect these child rapist and child gang rapist from the worlds legal systems. Each time the news reports another horrible atrocity committed by the catholic church and it's priests the church grounds are full of catholic supports raising their fists at the media and assuring the public that the church is handling the crimes. Banding together to raise more money to protect the monstrous priests from the legal system. As all of you know I could go on and on about these child rapists and the documented unethical behavior of the Catholic church. But one need only watch the five o'clock news to obtain that information.

How is it possible that for generations the corrupt Catholic church has not only gone untouched by the governments they reside in but continue to flourish?

It is because the Catholic's are religious. Catholic people love their religion more than they love God. More than they love God's Biblical truths, obeying the laws of the land, and their children. Nothing is more important to them than their religion. They love their rituals, pomp and circumstance more than God or their children. They continue to stand behind their religion whatever the horrendous crimes or cost to millions of young lives.

For years I have asked countless Catholic people why they still remain a part of the Catholic church after all the documented proof of their crimes against government and humanity. They always say those crimes were dealt with by the church. This is in fact false. The Catholic church sweeps one horrible atrocity after another under the rug. The Catholic church pays off one government official after another. The Catholic church are masters at manipulating the public. After all there are no better manipulators than child molesters. These men are masters at manipulating children, governments, and the public. The money that it takes to accomplish there manipulations world wide is endless.

Every day catholic parents hand their innocent children over to these monsters for education and worship. There heads held high with pride full of the warm fussy intoxication of religion. While each passing day the news is reporting documented proof that the Priests are committing horrendous crimes against their children, nature, humanity, and God. Catholic people love their rituals, pomp, and circumstance, and the fussy intoxication of religion more than their children. They have already proved that for many generations.

It is my firm absolute belief that if the Catholic church installed an alter of fire tomorrow in their churches Catholic parents would be lined up with their children in hand. Their heads would be held high with pride full of the warm fussy intoxication of religion. They would be ready and anxious to drop their innocent children into the fire, and the Nun's would be adding wood to the fire and directing traffic.

This is a living breathing example
of religion and religious people.

Let's look into the scriptures and see what our Heavenly Father has said about the Catholic church.

Revelation 17:5

17:5 *And upon her forehead was a name written, mystery,* **Babylon the great,** *the mother of harlots and* **abominations of the earth.**

Revelation 18:2

18:2 *And he cried mightily with a strong voice, saying,* **Babylon the great is fallen, is fallen,** *and is become the* **hubilation of devils**, *and the hold of every foul spirit, and a cage of every unclean and hateful bird.*

Revelation 18:4

18:4 *And I heard another voice from heaven, saying,* **Come out of her, my people,** *that you* **be not partakers of her sins,** *and that you receive not of her plagues.*

Revelation 18:7

18:7 *How much she has glorified herself,* **and lived deliciously,** *so much torment and sorrow give her: for she saith in her heart, I sit a queen, and am no widow, and shall see no sorrow.*

Revelation 18:8

18:8 **Therefore shall her plagues come in one day,** *death, and mourning, and famine; and* **she shall be utterly burned with fire: for strong is the Lord God who judges her.**

These scriptures tell us that the Catholic church will be destroyed in one day. Did you notice that the scriptures warn those who are part of the Catholic church to get out before it is to late. Notice the scripture said:

"Come out of her MY PEOPLE."

This tells us that there are some of God's people in the Catholic church today. It is possible to be a member of any church and be religious. If your religion means more to you than God's truth it's time for a wake up call and reality check. Consider yourselves awoke and checked.

Not once does our Heavenly Father tell His people to be religious or to follow religion. Not once does our Heavenly Father refer to His people as religious. However, God does instruct His people to be lovers of righteousness. In God's scriptures He refers to His people as lovers of righteousness over 300 times. Not once as religious. Our Heavenly Father instructs His people to be lovers of righteousness before all other things. This would mean loving righteousness over our religion or religious beliefs.

Okay brothers and sisters now you know the definition of religion and religious people. Don't get ensnared by the fussy intoxication of religion. Your love for God and God's truth should be above all things.

GOD'S LGBT CHILDREN
ARE NOT LOST ANYMORE

Lgbt brothers and sisters,
GOD IS CALLING US.

G od is gathering His generations

of lost and wounded eunuchs for the day of
salvation and everlasting life.

God's harvest has begun.
He is calling His Lgbt children
from all four corners of the planet with this revelation.
Every Lgbt person, from every nation, every religion,
every tongue, every color, every city
and primitive remote village
are being called by God for the final harvest.

We are God's beloved children. He loves us so much
and is so proud of us for how well we have endured these lost
years. We are not lost anymore! God has claimed us in this
revelation. The calling from God to gather us together is loud
and the time is now. Embrace God! Clean up your bad
behavior and go rejoicing.

Brothers and sisters we are living in the wealthiest nation on the planet. Americans are known to be the most sophisticated people on the planet. Many Americans live in half million dollar homes or better, these are the most luxurious homes in the world. Americans drive the most expensive cars known to man, these are the most luxurious cars in the world. Americans wear the most expensive and finest clothes and jewels available in the world. As Americans live in these luxurious homes, drive these luxurious cars, wear these luxurious clothes and jewels they are beautiful to look at.

However, when one observes many Americans sexual behavior, the most inner part of their souls as to who they are on the inside, they're behavior is straight out of the "wood shed." This "wood shed lovin" mentality is completely without boundaries, without morality, without dignity and without respect for yourselves and others. The expression "you can dress them up, but you can't take them out" applies to most American people whether heterosexual or Lgbt.

Our Heavenly Father created us to be above the instinct of wild animals. He did not create man or woman to live or act like the wildlife. They are a different species than we are and their purpose in life is different than ours. Need I remind you, it was Adam who named all the animals, and Adam had dominion over them, and so do we. Far to many Americans have embraced this "wood shed lovin" mentality when it comes to their sexual behavior. Any kind of sex, nothing is too kinky or too perverted, any old time, any old person, any number of persons, any old place, etc. I think we have already seen what this kind of sexual behavior can do to a nation. I think we have already seen what this kind of behavior can do to a world. This "wood shed lovin" mentality is not what our Heavenly Father created us for. Our Heavenly Father created us for a much higher standard of life. A much higher quality of sex than this "wood shed lovin" mentality offers and displays. The sad part of this is that many Americans are proud of this type of behavior.

Brothers and sisters, I say this with all the love in my heart, your "wood shed lovin" is not working for yourselves or others. This standard of lifestyle will bring you nothing but heartache and disappointment, nothing good will ever come out of it. As you come to embrace our Heavenly Father you will learn a more intelligent and spiritual sexual experience, one that is in harmony with God's standards. Our Heavenly Father will raise you up to a higher level of conscientiousness regarding sexual expression and intimacy. Our Heavenly Father will shape and mold you over time. In time one can "dress you up, and take you out."

As for you sadists and masochists, child molesters, rapists and those of you involved in public restrooms and rest area promiscuous behavior, and in other revolting activity, I advise you to remember Sodom and Gomorrah. As I have taught you those people heterosexual, straight, and eunuch, were destroyed for their extreme corruption, lawlessness, immoral sexual activity and sexual violence. Sodom and Gomorrah were destroyed as a warning for those of you who are involved in such corrupt and lawless activity today. A warning to all Lgbt and heterosexual people alike. These are sins. You make a conscious choice to do these types of things. Your family members, wives, and children may not see what you do in secret, but our Heavenly Father does see your every corrupt and demented transaction.

YOU WERE NOT BORN THAT WAY.

Gay, lesbian, and transgender brothers and sisters, over the years I have seen so much self disrespect, self abuse, self sexual abuse and self loathing among our people. It never ceases to break my heart.

When a child is taught and comes to believe they are not loved by God, they come to believe they are not loveable by anyone. Let's face it, if a child believes that the God in Heaven who created them doesn't love them, why would they believe anyone on earth could possibly love them. This kind of deception has lead God's gay, lesbian, and transgender children to get involved in all kinds of destructive behavior, sexual and otherwise.

I have tried every way possible to bring you to a place of conscientiousness regarding your precious hearts, your precious bodies, and your precious souls. I have used every Word of God, every thought and expression, I can think of, in an attempt to reach your hearts on this issue of self loathing. Your hearts, your bodies, and your souls are so precious to our Heavenly Father. He wants the best life for you and that is only possible if you learn to love and respect yourselves. Please don't abuse your minds, bodies, and hearts. These gifts should be valuable to you because you are so valuable to our Heavenly Father.

Many of you have been deceived into believing that a life that isn't promiscuous is a boring life. Many of you have come to believe a life of sexual obedience is a life deprived of fun, joy, and opportunities. Many of you have come to believe a life without promiscuity is a life without love and real meaning, intimacy, and substance. Many of you have come to believe a life of sexual obedience would cause you to miss out on love, something valuable, or important. Many of you have come to believe God is keeping something from you by asking you to be sexually obedient.

Who has taught you to think so little of yourselves?

Who has taught you that your heart is worthless?

Who has taught you that your body is worthless?

Who has taught you that your soul is worthless?

Who has taught you that God is keeping something from you?

Who has taught you that you have such little value?

Who deceived Eve into believing she was missing out on something?

Who has taught you all of these lies?

Stay away from pornography. It will pollute your mind and heart. Pornography is addictive. Pornography establishes additive sexual behaviors. If you are engaged in pornography of any kind you are contributing to the exploitation of many of God's children of all ages. If you are thinking that looking at a little porn never hurt anyone, let me remind you of King David and how he manipulated his power of reason to have Bathsheba. He tried to pull a fast one on himself and God in the process. Many people think because television characters and the internet make references to watching porn all the time means it is normal and acceptable. Coming to believe that it is safe and okay. One of the worst things any person can do is let the media of entertainment direct their moral compass.

Please, heed these words:
If you allow television
and the internet to be your moral guide
on your road to obedience you are doomed.

If you are that bored with sex I advise you to find a new hobby. Get involved in sports, expand your education, or help the needy. Take this revelation out to your dying brothers and sisters so they don't go to their deaths, like so many gay people and their loved ones have, believing God hates them.

Find something pleasing to our Heavenly Father to occupy your time. Find something other than sexual activities that are only going to put you out of God's protection and in harm's way. In the scriptures our Heavenly Father does mention these kinds of sexual activities. He warns us against getting involved in such activities. One of the ways our Heavenly Father protects His children is through His Word in the Bible. If God's children refuse to follow His direction and council they are putting themselves in harms way and out of God's protection.

For example a young Christian friend once called me all upset because she had been badly treated and insulted in a bar the night before. She was so upset her heart was breaking. She felt she and her lover should be able to go out to bars and have a good time without dealing with such rude and badly behaved people. I said, "Don't go to bars and get bent out of shape because people are not displaying good Christian behavior. Don't go into bars where alcohol and drugs are used to ALTER people's minds and expect to rub shoulders with good God loving people. Bars are Satan's domain, not God's."

This fine Christian sister put herself out of God's protection by going into a place were God does not dwell putting herself in harms way.

Another example a young Christian friend called me one night all upset because his girlfriend just told him she was pregnant. He wasn't that fond of his girlfriend. She was more of a good time than a lover to him. He said he couldn't understand why bad things happened to him all the time. I told him that he put himself outside of God's protection and in harms way. He knew what God's council was regarding sex outside of marriage and he made a conscious decision to disobey God's Word. I informed him that "nothing happened" to him, because he did this to himself. He put himself in harms way by disobeying God's Word. I would think it would be very difficult for God to protect His children when they disobey His instruction. God's council and direction is in the Bible to protect God's children. In order to keep us out of Satan's destructive nonsense.

I want your full attention here. Notice who Paul is writing to directly in the following scriptures.

Romans 1:18-21

*1:18 For the wrath of God is revealed from Heaven **against all ungodliness and unrighteousness** of men, who hold the truth in unrighteousness;*

*1:19 Because that which **may be known of God** is manifest in them; for **God hath shewed it unto them.***

*1:20 For **the invisible things of him from the creation of the world are clearly seen**, being understood by the things that are made, even his eternal power and Godhead; **so that they are without excuse:***

1:21 Because that, when they knew God, they glorified him not as

God, **neither were thankful;** but became vain in their imaginations, and **their foolish heart was darkened.**

Romans 1:24-28

1:24 **Wherefore God also gave them up to uncleanness through the lusts of their own hearts, to dishonour their own bodies between themselves:**

1:25 **Who changed the truth of God into a lie,** and worshipped and served the creature more than the Creator, who is blessed for ever. Amen.

1:26 For this cause **God gave them up unto vile affections:** for even their **women** did change the natural use into that which is **against nature:**

1:27 And likewise also the men, leaving the natural use of the woman, **burned in their lust one toward another;** men with men working that which is **unseemly,** and receiving in themselves that recompence of their error which was meet.

1:28 And even as **they did not like to retain God in their knowledge,** God gave them over to a reprobate mind, to do those things which are not convenient;

Did you notice in Romans 1:24,26,+27 the terms dishonor their bodies, vile, lust, and unseemly are used here? Now at this time eunuchs had been around for generations. Since the beginning of time really. Gay people were common in society and had been for generations. As you now know Lgbt people were honored and loved in all nations. Lgbt people of this time were marrying each other and had families and lived normal healthy righteous lives. Many held high ranking positions. Jesus had already made his love for Lgbt people evident and had already made his feelings about gay marriage clear to the disciples. With this in mind what was the Bible writer, Paul talking about here.

Paul's focus in these scriptures are people with a same gender attraction. The focus is that their sexual behavior was dishonorable, vile, lustful, and unseemly for gay people. Many have been taught through false teachers that these scriptures are referring to gay people in general. This is not the case here. These scriptures are talking about people with a same gender attraction but the scriptures go further in saying that their behavior was dishonorable even for gay people. Vile for gay people. Lustful for gay people. Unseemly for gay people.

At this time Paul knew that their were heterosexual people with these same problems with sexual disobedience and he does mention those heterosexual people in other areas. However here Paul is making a special point to make it perfectly clear that he is directing his message directly to the Lgbt population of Rome.

The point Paul was making to the Lgbt population of Rome was: Don't take for granted the alternatives and concessions that our Heavenly Father has provided for us. Our Heavenly Father made these provisions for His Lgbt children to show us how much He loved us. To show His desire to see His lgbt children attain salvation. He did not have to do that for us. He could have condemned us from the start for our same gender attraction without an ounce of compassion had He desired. Yet He did not. His compassion for us is heaping, overflowing, and overwhelming. Do we really appreciate His love and understanding, and compassion for us? Do you? Notice the severity of the terms Paul used here at the beginning of his writings to the Lgbt population of Rome.

ungodliness and unrighteousness

God hath shewed it unto them.

so that they are without excuse:

neither were thankful;

but became vain in their imaginations,

Paul was using these terms when writing directly to Lgbt people of Rome. That means he was writing these words directly to today's Lgbt people as well. I don't know how to make it any clearer to you Lgbt brothers and sisters than I have. Our Heavenly Father is telling His Lgbt children to live honorable, respectful, sexually clean, obedient lives. He is telling us that we better appreciate the love and compassion He has for us. If we don't, He will not ignore that.

Lgbt brothers and sisters, God created sex to be a tender expression of love between a husband (male) and a wife (female) for the purpose of pleasure and procreation, **in the beginning.** God intended sex to be a loving and tender expression between two married people. Anything that deviates from that original purpose, "established in the beginning" is an imperfection, a sin.

This is why God labeled us as eunuchs, because our sexual attraction is different from that of heterosexual people. Remember this is how our Heavenly Father created us to be. This is not something we ever chose for ourselves. And who would? God loves us, and He will bless us for being obedient in spite of our imperfection. Don't hate yourself for something you did not choose. Remember Jesus said, "We were born that way, or made that way by other men, or chose that way" in order to live a life of honesty and obedience for Heavens sake.

Do your best to build your faith by getting to know God. Be as obedient as you can, because your salvation and everlasting life depends on it. Our faith and obedience is one of the most important ways of showing God our hearts.

As for those of you who are angry at this instruction, or any other instruction you have read in this revelation, or any instructions you will hear from me in the future, let me say this with all the love in my heart: "Our Heavenly Father sent me with this revelation to the world to get you in line with obedience, for salvation, and everlasting life."

Don't ever forget what God said at: Isaiah 56:4
"For you eunuchs whom are obedient,
there is a name in Heaven greater than son or daughter,
and a monument in your honor."

**Don't ever let Satan and his demons
take God's Words and promises from you again.
Do not let your lustful desires come before your salvation.**

Keep in mind each person's level of obedience will be different because we are all different. I invite you to embrace God's love. God knows what your childhood and life have been like. He is waiting for you with open arms. Go to God and tell Him you love Him. Ask God to forgive you for your sins in the name of His Son Jesus Christ. Get baptized and sin no more. Go with a light heart because you have been forgiven and you will have a fresh start with God.

When the Bible says, "sin no more," that means: clean up the bad behavior that is in your control to overcome. God forgives you and doesn't hold your past sins against you. Go in peace, light in heart, rejoicing.

As for you gay people who are already married to people of the opposite gender: you are not alone; most gay people are married to people of the opposite gender. Due to social stigma against open gay people, open gay people's concerns over job security and social status, and people in general just wanting to have it all, this is today's situation for many gay people.

This revelation from God includes you as well every loving word of it. What I am about to teach you is very important.

Do you have an ear, are you listening?

Malachi 2:10

*2:10 Have we not all one Father? **hath not one God created us?** Why do we deal treacherously every man against his brother, by profaning the covenant of our Fathers?*

Malachi 2:13-16

*2:13 And this have ye done again, covering the altar of the LORD with tears, with weeping, and with crying out, **insomuch that he regardeth not the offering any more,** or receiveth it with good will at your hand.*

*2:14 Yet ye say, Wherefore? Because the LORD hath been witness between thee and the wife of thy youth, **against whom thou hast dealt treacherously:** yet is she thy companion, and the wife of thy covenant.*

*2:15 And did not he make one? Yet had he the residue of the spirit. And wherefore one? That he might seek a godly seed. Therefore take heed to your spirit, and **let none deal treacherously against the wife of his youth.***

*2:16 For the LORD, the God of Israel, saith that he hateth putting away: for one covereth violence with his garment, saith the LORD of hosts: **therefore take heed to your spirit, that ye deal not treacherously.***

Closeted brothers and sisters, no sex in the world is more important than the heart of your spouse. Your spouse loves you so much. He or she has given his or her entire life to you in marriage. Love and marriage between two people is a blessing from God. You are blessed if God has given it to you once. Sex is but a few minutes, and with age it becomes less and less important and desirable. Love is for an eternity, and your feelings of love for a spouse grows over the years and becomes stronger and stronger till death. This is not something you cast aside lightly.

Closeted brothers and sisters, no sex in the world is more important than the hearts of your children. Nothing is more painful for children than their parent's divorcing. Never should sex be more important than the tender, fragile hearts of your children.

Marriage is very important to God for all of the latter reasons. God did not create mankind to endure or inflict such treachery. However, if you are inflamed with lust and you can not remain faithful you should divorce.

In today's world inability to remain faithful in a marriage can be a death sentence for you and your spouse. Because of the prevalence of sexually transmitted diseases. If you can not remain faithful go to your spouse in total honesty and out of love end the marriage. In this situation divorce would be an act of love.

Lgbt brothers and sisters, keep in mind we are in every facet of society. Not all people live honest lives with regard to their sexual identity. I do not want you to expose closeted gay people to their families, socially, or in business settings. They have had different backgrounds than you. They have made different choices in their lives than you have. Most of them have spouses and children they are protecting. Quite simply their sins and personal lives are none of your business. Keep in mind they share the same name in Heaven as you do. God loves them just as much as He loves you. Do not think more of yourself, or less of them, because they are not honest about their same gender attraction.

I recommend you pay attention to the
board in your own eye,
before the splinter in your brothers eye.

I advise you to avoid dating and having sex with married closeted people whom choose to live in disobedience. They are married. They belong to someone else. Do not let them lead you down the road of sin with them. Now I know the gay community and closet community only too well. I know many of you are thinking, "Well they're married to someone of the opposite gender so who on earth will they have sex with?"

They will have sex with the spouse whom God has
united them in marriage,
NOT WITH YOU!

Your days of sleeping with married people are over.

I know many of you are married. You have sex buddies who are also married. You have been sex buddies for many years. I know you love him. Well, God has a question for you: "Do you love your sex buddy more than you love Him?" Go to your sex buddies and show them this revelation. Tell them you are no longer going to live in sin and disobedience. Send them back to their spouses to salvage the marriages that God has brought together. God has lifted you up to a higher ground.

Go to God and repent. Ask Him to forgive you for your sins in Jesus' name. Try to salvage your marriage and go in peace rejoicing and sin no more. Remember what Jesus said; "For those of you who are obedient, shall have a name in Heaven greater than son or daughter, and a monument in Heaven in your honor." Remember what God said about obedience. Obedience also applies to heterosexual husbands and wives.

Need I remind you, God sent me to share this revelation of love with you and the world, and to put you in line with obedience, for the purpose of salvation and everlasting life. God's blessings are for those who have faith and obedience.

Those with the right heart.

Our closeted brothers and sisters will come to God and walk with Him just as you will in their own way and in obedience. I want you to love and respect all people the way you want to be loved and respected.

Lgbt brothers and sisters, whether you are openly gay, obviously gay, transgender, closeted gay, bisexual gay, whatever: if you have a same gender attraction, you all fall under the label of eunuch described in the Bible. There is a name in Heaven greater than son or daughter, and a monument in Heaven in your honor for those of you who are obedient.

Again, God said,
"For those who are obedient."

Jesus advised all people of ancient times and all people of today to choose singleness as a first choice unless you are inflamed with lust. In this case you should marry to prevent yourself from getting involved in worse or further sexual sin. Yes, Jesus said to marry. He gave this instruction to the heterosexuals and eunuchs alike. Jesus knew eunuchs would marry someone of the same gender. He knew they were eunuch or gay, and had only a same gender attraction.

If Jesus expected all people to marry someone of the opposite gender he would not have brought the eunuch's into the discussion of marriage, or used the following illustrations.

"Let him that has ears listen"
"discern the sayings of understanding"
"that , that gives insight"
"things revealed belong to us"
" If anyone thinks he is behaving improperly toward his virginity, Let them marry"
"Let those with understanding have understanding"

Jesus did not need to use code words, or secret phrases, or parables, or say all that He did to the heterosexual people. The heterosexual people understood everything about marriage from the very beginning back with Adam and Eve and Moses covered the subject thoroughly. Jesus did not need to elaborate or give special code phrases to the heterosexual people about marriage. The Bible doesn't do so anywhere else when speaking to heterosexual people about marriage. Instead, He was trying to get the attention of the eunuchs. He was speaking to the eunuchs of ancient times and Lgbt people of today.

Brothers and sisters if you are attracted to both genders, and you are capable of living a heterosexual life without lusting for the same gender, I recommend you live a heterosexual life. Be as obedient as you can.

In regard to my situation, I was able to verbalize that I was gay at 14 years old. I lived an open gay life from that time to the present. At the age of 22, I meet a beautiful and intelligent young lady in the work place and fell madly in love with her. We were married 3 years later. We were married for 14 years and had two wonderful children. My ex-wife and I brought a lot of baggage with us into our marriage and our baggage got the best of us in the end.

God has blessed me with love and children among a myriad of blessings over my lifetime. I was never unfaithful to my wife nor did I ever consider such a treachery. The baggage in our marriage and the final ending of our marriage had nothing to do with my sexual orientation. From the first day I met her to the day our marriage ended my only sexual desire was for her. She is the only person I have ever been in love with to this day. Sex with someone you are not in love with, someone you do not respect or admire, is a totally different experience. An experience not worth having.

Yes, brothers and sisters gay men fall madly in love with women every day. Do I recommend it? It really doesn't matter whether I recommend it or not you can't fight human nature or love. Be true to your heart and spirit.

Would I marry again? I sure hope not. I have come to love the blessing of singleness too much to give it up for love, sex, or anything else. Keep in mind I am now 52 years old. I have experienced many years of an open gay life, many boy friends, and many years of marriage to a woman, as well as the blessing of raising my two children. I have had a blessed full life. All I want out of life now are new adventures, helping those in need, and some peace and quiet.

SHOULD STRAIGHT PEOPLE COME OUT OF THE CLOSET?

W hether you come out of the closet or stay in the
closet is between you and God. Of course our Heavenly Father
wants all of His children to live an honest life. He hates a lair.
Need I remind you who was the originator of the first lie and
who is the lover of lies and deception.
However, as long as:

- closeted gay men live in fear of a woman's scorn,
- closeted gay men and women lust for a household with
  two incomes,
- closeted men and women lust for the materialistic
  American dream,
- closeted men and women lust for job security,
- closeted men and women need a decoy,
- closeted men and women deceive others into becoming
  decoys,
- closeted men and women have the sexual appetite for
  promiscuity that only the closet can provide,
- the closet will always be a gay or lesbian person's first
  choice.

To make a long story short the majority of gay men and lesbian women will continue to be in the closet until Jesus returns. Satan created the closet and the majority will always follow Satan as the scriptures have foretold. Let's take a look at the life and events of Potiphar at Genesis 39:1-8

Genesis 39:1-8

39:1 And Joseph was brought down to Egypt; and Potiphar, an officer of Pharaoh, captain of the guard, an Egyptian, bough him of the hands of the Ishmeelites, which had brought him down thither.

39:2 And the LORD was with Joseph, and he was a prosperous man; and he was in the house of his master the Egyptian.

39:3 And his master saw that the LORD was with him, and that the LORD made all that he did to prosper in his hand.

39:4 And Joseph found grace in his sight, and he served him: and he made him overseer over his house, and all that he had he put into his hand.

39:5 And it came to pass from the time that he had made him overseer in his house, and over all that he had, that the LORD blessed the Egyptian's house for Joseph's sake; and the blessing of the LORD was upon all that he had in the house, and in the field.

39:6 And he left all that he had in Joseph's hand; and he knew not ought he had, save the bread which he did eat. And Joseph was a goodly person, and well favoured.

*39:7 And it came to pass after these things, **that his master's wife cast her eyes upon Joseph; and she said, Lie with me.***

*39:8 **But he refused,** and said unto his master's wife, Behold, my master wotteth not what is with me in the house, and he hath*

The original Hebrew manuscripts identify Potiphar as a eunuch yet not one Bible translation old or new identifies him as such. The Bible translators did not have a problem identifying many others as eunuchs. The reason the English translations do not identify Potiphar as a eunuch is because he was married to woman. The Bible translators could not understand why the original Hebrew manuscripts would identify Potiphar as a eunuch (or castrated they believed) when he had wives and therefore must have had a penis. Of course now we know eunuchs did have penises and where therefore sexually active.

In Biblical times a man's strength, power, and wealth, was measured by how many wives he had. Wives were a status symbol so the more wives a man had the more powerful and rich he was believed to be.   Most evident of men of Biblical times having many wives displayed a man's sexual ability and sexual prowess giving others the allusion of his greatness and power. Men were no different thousands of years ago than the men of today. Potiphar was obviously masculine to hold the position he had and would have wanted to measure up socially whether he was eunuch or not. Does this remind you of any men we see today?

Many eunuch men and women in Biblical times were married to the opposite gender. Often it was required for the purpose of keeping small villages populated therefore keeping them strong against their neighboring enemies. This was necessary in order to preserve the village. Even as recent as a few years ago remote villages required the same of gay men and lesbian women for the same reasons.

Was this arrangement fair to eunuchs in Biblical times? No! Is this arrangement fair to gays of today? No! Is this what God intended for eunuchs in Biblical times or for gays today? No! Is this part of God's plan? Absolutely not!

Our Heavenly Father is against the closet arrangement this is a sin of choice. This is treachery against both men and women. Any gay man or lesbian woman who goes against their spirit, and dates or marries a heterosexual, is treacherous against themselves and the heterosexual involved. Your same gender attraction is there for a reason. Any woman who tries to make a man love her when she sees he is gay is treacherous to herself. Any man who tries to make a women love him, when he sees she is a lesbian is treacherous to himself. Do not do things or make decisions that go against your spirit. It will cause you pain and heartache down the road every time. Our Heavenly Father did not give you the spirit that He gave you to see you spend your entire life ignoring and running away from it. This same gender attraction is part of you for a reason.

In regard to a persons spirit many people today are very treacherous towards themselves and others. Many don't even realize what they are doing. So go easy on casting blame on yourself and others when it comes to the closeted issues. Most gay people who date and marry heterosexual people do not realize how hurtful that is against their own spirit until it is to late to change the situation. Most people are just doing their best to be the best they can be. We are only imperfect humans. Now that our Heavenly Father has made you wiser you will live more wisely and make wiser choices.

Again, wise King Solomon said;
"There is nothing new under the sun."

I can't begin to count the number of people I've seen come out of the closet in my lifetime. Some have come out in an intelligent, tender, moderate, and balanced way, and some have come out by way of disaster.

A friend told me once that a man he went to high school with came out of the closet at his high school reunion. He said the reunion was held in a posh hotel. After dinner and drinks were served and all the protocol of statements and games were over the man stood up in the middle of the banquet room drunk raised his glass and announced that he was gay. He then proceeded to stand on a table while taking off his clothes and danced with a lampshade on his head until security personnel all but carried him out of the hotel.

Needless to say if you are planning on coming out of the closet I recommend you avoid coming out by way of high school reunions, alcohol, or lamp shades.

I have never been in the closet myself. That choice has never been easy for me. Nor has it been easy for my loved ones. From what I've heard and seen staying in the closet is just as hard. I have been told coming out of the closet is like being re-born a freedom to totally live an honest life for the first time. I've heard of and seen people's coming out experiences as a sense of exhilaration as a new opportunity to do everything right this time. I must say I have never meet anyone who said they regretted coming out.

However, if you are planning on coming out of the closet, I recommend you take all the time you need to do it in an intelligent, tender, moderate, and level headed way.

Although your new honesty, new beginning, and new found freedom, will be joyous and uplifting for you it may not be uplifting for the people in your life who love you. Your parents, siblings, aunts, uncles, grandparents, cousins, spouse, and children (if you have children) will be heart broken over your new found honesty.

Too often closeted people think when they first tell their loved ones that they are gay or lesbian everyone is going to jump up and down with the same excitement that they are feeling. The only people who will be filled with excitement over your coming out will be people who are also out of the closet and lusting for you and that will fade quickly.

The people who love you will oftentimes be devastated. As always the heterosexual and closeted people in your family and social circles are never happy to hear that you are gay or out of the closet. For the heterosexual people they are suddenly hearing for the first time you are gay. Notice I used the word suddenly. They have always assumed you were heterosexual. To hear that one of your loved ones is now gay is quite devastating for many. Your straight male loved ones will see it as a betrayal.

Walking in the door and telling most parents or spouses you are gay is equivalent to saying you have cancer. Most heterosexual people believe you are sick in the head and God is going to destroy you for it.

This is not good news for them. For them this is the worst news they have ever heard and their hearts will be breaking. Brothers and sisters this is no joke.

For the life of them they cannot comprehend why you are standing there looking all bright eyed with a big smile on your face and happier than they have ever seen you after dropping such horrible news in there lap.

If you are planning on coming out of the closet I advise you to put the hearts and feelings of your loved ones before yourself. Put yourself in their shoes and see it from their perspective before you tell them. However, you do need to tell them. If you are gay and you do not tell anyone, then no one really knows you, do they? If you are in the closet you are a stranger to everyone in your life.

I don't want you to forget that they have seen you from their heterosexual or closeted perspectives all of your life.

However, coming out and being in good standing with God is more important than your loved ones.

Keep in mind sophisticated or not, intelligent or not, spiritual or not, these are the people in your life who have always loved you.

Coming out will show whether they love the lie or you more. Regardless, should they love the lie more than they love you that is their problem. Regardless they deserve all the tenderness, patience, and understanding you can muster.

If you have children you really need to handle coming out carefully. If you don't take the hearts of your children into consideration you will live to regret it. If you are going to come out of the closet do not cast blame on your spouse. Accusing them of not being this enough or that enough is total treachery. If you are gay and have decided to end your marriage because you want to live an honest life with God and society accept your responsibility. It is unfair to blame a spouses past or current behavior as your reason for ending the marriage. The things you are finding fault with in your spouse you may accept in someone of your own gender with no problem because the problem is yours. You have a same gender attraction.

Our Heavenly Father tells us to live an honest life and to follow our true spirit. My advice is always to live in line with His direction.

Hebrews 13:18
*13:18 Pray for us: for we trust we **have a good conscience, in all things willing to live honestly.***

John 4:23+24
*4:23 But the hour cometh, and now is, when **the true worshippers shall worship the Father in spirit and in truth**: for the **Father seeketh** such to worship him.*

*4:24 God is a Spirit: and they that worship him must **worship him in spirit and in truth.***

Psalms 119:160
*119:160 **Thy word is true from the beginning:** and every one of thy righteous judgments endureth for ever.*

Psalms 119:163
*119:163 **I hate and abhor lying: but thy law do I love.***

Zechariah 8:16+17
*8:16 These are the things that ye shall do; **Speak ye every man the truth to his neighbour; execute the judgment of truth** and peace in your gates:*

*8:17 And let none of you imagine evil in your hearts against his neighbour; and **love no false oath: for all these are things that I hate, saith the LORD.***

Some people simply cannot come out of the closet for a variety of reasons. We should pray for them. Pray they will be able to walk with God and endure their hardship and obtain salvation. If you are in the closet you should pray for those of us who are living an honest life. Pray that our walk with God will be safe and that we will obtain salvation as well. There is not an **us** and **them** when it comes to being gay. Although the closeted community sees the open community as a threat to their way of life we are both gay and in this we struggle together. How happy is Satan that he can keep divisions between God's lgbt children?

Keep in mind brothers and sisters the reason the straight community works so diligently to keep you in the closet is because straight men can't have you if you are open and honest about your sexuality. They can only have you as long as you're in the closet and live the lie as they do. Closeted people don't even want to be seen with an open gay person for fear that it may blow their cover. While most straight women see you as a threat to children and a threat to their marriages. The hearts of these types are treacherous.

Should you come out of the closet?

Yes, for some, and No, for others,

it is between you and God, not between you and me.

LETTER TO THE PRESIDENT

Dear Mr. President,

I have much respect and love for you. I voted for you and hope to vote for you again. I have never prayed for any President, not ever, but I have prayed for you. I pray for your success and safety every night.

Back in Biblical times and in Israel's hey day eunuchs lived with many blessings as I have pointed out in this revelation. Ancient Israel was ruled by King David and later his son King Solomon. The scriptures mention these men over 1200 times in over 1200 different areas throughout the Bible. God loved these Kings and blessed the nation of Israel as never before because God felt these Kings were righteous. Israel had never been so blessed and prosperous and hasn't been since their rule.

2 Samuel 7:8-11

7:8 Now therefore so shalt thou say unto my servant David, Thus saith the LORD of hosts, I took thee from the sheepcote, from following the sheep, **to be ruler over my people, over Israel:**

7:9 And **I was with thee whithersoever thou wentest, and have cut off all thine enemies out of thy sight,** *and have made thee a great name, like unto the name of the great men that are in the earth.*

7:10 Moreover I will appoint a place for my people Israel, and will plant them, that they may dwell in a place of their own, and move no more; **neither shall the children of wickedness afflict them any more, as beforetime,**

7:11 And as since the time that I commanded judges to be over my people Israel, **and have caused thee to rest from all thine enemies.** *Also the LORD telleth thee that he will make thee an house.*

2 Samuel 8:15
8:15 **And David reigned over all Israel; and David executed judgment and justice unto all his people.**

1 Kings 10:23+24
10:23 **So king Solomon exceeded all the kings of the earth for riches and for wisdom.**

10:24 And all the earth sought to Solomon, to hear his wisdom, **which God had put in his heart.**

Mr. President, until this nation breaks it's historical practices of oppressing, categorizing, and casting aside God's gay, lesbian, and transgender children, people of color, and immigrants, this nation will not have God's blessings.

The suicide rate among God's Lgbt children in America has always been the highest suicide rate among all groups world wide. Now it is sky-rocketing. Currently well over 20 percent of Lgbt people commit suicide annually. This is shamcless.

In America the hostility and oppression our gay, lesbian, and transgender children live under is more than they can bear. The current suicide rate is more than enough proof of that. What a disgrace America has been in the eyes of God and the world over this issue. Other nations look at this situation in America with disgust and pity. Our Heavenly Father hears the cries of His precious gay, lesbian, and transgender children in America as well as world wide. The cries of God's Lgbt children are loud, loud enough that God, Jesus, and a myriad of angels can hear them in Heaven. The cries of America's Lgbt children are heard world wide.

My question for you is,

"Do you hear have an ear, are you listening?"

God is calling you.

Do you hear the cries of Americas LGBT children?

Mr. President, you are the leader of this great Christian nation and this Christian is asking you to be as wise as King David and King Solomon were. Do right by God and God's children. Give God's gay, lesbian, and transgender children with a name in Heaven greater than son or daughter, and a monument in Heaven in their honor, all the same rights and privileges that heterosexual people have. Equal rights from all four corners of this great Christian nation for everyone.

The 2000 census identifies approximately 10.5 million open LGBT people in America. Add to this immediate family and friends of open LGBT people, and the number of people invested in seeing LGBT Americans have equal rights, under the law grows quickly to approximately 153 million people in America alone. This number will change dramatically in the 2010 census. There are 300 million people in America. You cannot ignore 300 million voters who are living under unjust laws. I realize you are not the one who created this situation. However, I trust you are wise like King David and King Solomon and you will do right by God's children.

God has said many things to guide wise leaders.

Scripture Reference
(1Sa.16;12+13)(2Sa.7;15+16)(1Ki.4;24+25)(2Ch.9:22+23)(1Ki.3;16-28)(1Ki10:23)(1Ki.10:18-20)(2Ch.9:17-20)(1Ki.10:12)(2Ch.9:11)

America's Lgbt children are counting on you Mr. President

THANK GOD FOR THE RIGHTEOUS

I would like to start this chapter by speaking directly to the beautiful, loving, brave, and righteous open Lgbt generation before mine.

THANK YOU,
THANK YOU SO MUCH.

Thank you for your bravery, love, and concern for me and my generation when you were young and in your prime. In 1971 at the age of fourteen I started seeking out open gay people and gay bars. I was what people called back then a "street kid," and lied about my age of course. I still remember all of you as if you were my family members.

I remember the Stonewall uprising and the countless injustices all of you had to face. I remember how kind and loving and persistent you remained in a world that hated you and lied about you and your character. I remember your struggles and your strong relentless desire to create a better life and world for me and my generation. You were persistent with the cause even though you knew you were risking your lives and would be too far past your prime to reap the benefits of your courageous fight. Yet, you pressed on anyway.

Thank you for all your political efforts, for your blood, sweat and tears. Thank you for paving a safer journey for me and my generation. Because of **you** I have always had a job, car, nice home, and children that I was allowed to raise, safe streets and places of entertainment where I was welcomed, accepted, and loved. Thank you for creating an environment where I could be myself and be safe. Well safe for those days anyway. Not one of us were really safe anywhere back then and many are not safe today.

The types of sacrifices and the kinds of risks that gay people like yourselves made for me and my generation will be remembered forever. How does one pay back such a favor, such a gift, such a blessing? There are no words to express the appreciation and gratitude that my generation and I owe those of you for your courage and your love for equality and righteous. Thank you for paving the way for this Bible revelation titled: A Name In Heaven. I do believe our Heavenly Father has something glorious in store for you. I hope this revelation from God has brought your hearts joy, comfort and peace. You have been and will always be my hero's.

**Thank you,
thank you so much for everything,
you lovers of righteousness.**

I can't go any further until I point out that God judges a man by his heart. I want all Lgbt people to stop for a minute and think about the multitude of Christians, and general population, you have dealt with all of your lives. These people had nothing to stand behind when backing and supporting us other than the same lies and false teachings you have heard. They were not gay. They were heterosexual and straight men and women. They had been taught twisted versions of scripture by false teachers, these lovers of lies, hatred, violence, and death.

Yet, they stood in the face of all that opposition and felt love and compassion for us. They were kind to us. They gave us good service, hired us for jobs, gave us fairness in the workplace, and gave us raises and promotions. They voted "Yes" on ballots in an attempt to give us equal rights and welcomed us into their churches. They have not only let us live in their neighborhoods but many were good neighbors to us. Many left their churches for life because their consciences couldn't bear the hatred for gays their pastors spewed from their pulpits. I could go on and on. What kind of people stand in the face of all this opposition and say they don't care what they have heard from their preachers, parents, neighbors, and co-workers, but instead felt love and compassion for us? They followed their hearts and consciences instead of the majority.

Let's take a look at what God says about these kind and loving people we have known.

1 Samuel 16:7
*16:7 But the LORD said unto Samuel, Look not on his countenance, or on the height of his stature; because I have refused him: for the LORD seeth not as man seeth; for man looketh on the outward appearance, **but the LORD looketh on the heart.***

Proverbs 21:2

*21:2 Every way of a man is right in his own eyes: but **the LORD pondereth the hearts.***

Jeremiah 17:10

*17:10 I the LORD search the **heart,** I try the reins, even to give every man according to his ways, **and according to the fruit of his doings.***

Romans 10:10

*10:10 For with the **heart** man believeth unto righteousness; and with the mouth confession is made unto salvation.*

Additional reference
(1Sa.16:5-7)(Jer.17:9-12)(Ro.10:4-14)

Brothers and sisters I have been openly gay since I was 14 years old and today I am 52. I have encountered a multitude of people who fit these scriptures. May God bless all of them and they know who they are. As for the others who have acted treacherously against me I forgive them. Brothers and sisters I recommend you do the same.

GOD'S LGBT CHILDREN AND TEENS

Young gay, lesbian, and transgender brothers and sisters, today's world for Lgbt children and teens is just as difficult as it has always been. Years ago gay children had to remain in the closet. Those who were so feminine or so masculine that they couldn't hide it had a hard time. Today's society has become more sophisticated and savvy in regard to gay, lesbian, and transgender people. Fortunately that is a good thing. Unfortunately today's society has become brutally hostile, violent, and insensitive towards people of every kind gay or whatever.

It is not easy to be a child or teen in today's world. Lets explore why that is.

Isaiah 14:12
*14:12 How art thou fallen from heaven, **O Lucifer,** son of the morning! **how art thou cut down to the ground, which didst weaken the nations!***

1 John 5:19
*5:19 And we know that we are of God, **and the whole world lieth in wickedness.***

Revelation 12:12
*12:12 Therefore rejoice, ye heavens, and ye that dwell in them. **Woe to the inhabiters of the earth** and of the sea! **for the devil is come down unto you, having great wrath, because he knoweth that he hath but a short time.***

John 14:30
*14:30 Hereafter I will not talk much with you: **for the prince of this world cometh,** and hath nothing in me.*

Notice in these scriptures Satan has been cast out of Heaven and has no where else to go but earth. Notice he has come to destroy the nations of God's children and God's people in general with little time left because the end is near.

The only way Satan can destroy anyone is through humans, other people, Satan cannot touch us himself. Our Heavenly Father would never permit that. Satan is a spirit person with great power. So Satan knows he must influence people to do his dirty work for him. Many adults today are completely under Satan's influence and don't even know it. They have offspring and teach their offspring to follow Satan's influence as well.

When you get up in the morning and go to school you are surrounded by and interacting with other children who have been raised by homophobes. These children of homophobes are horrendously hateful and full of violence. In their demonic state of mind they find joy in hurting others. They use hurtful behavior and speech to break the hearts of others as a form of entertainment.

All of you children and teens today have a lot to deal with in today's world in your families, socially and at school. For example some children and teens are teased and harassed for many or should I say <u>any</u> reason. Let's look at just a few;

- heavy children
- extremely thin children
- children with big hair
- children with fine, thin hair
- children with heavy parents
- children with extremely thin parents
- children from low incomes
- children from high incomes
- children with speech impediments
- children who are loud
- children who are soft spoken and meek
- children who wear fashionable clothes
- children who do not wear fashionable clothes
- children with good grades
- children with poor grades
- children who have black skin
- children who have brown skin
- children who have olive skin
- children who have white skin
- children with loving attitudes, as you well know, I could go on and on forever.

The point is that all children have a hard time socially and in school in today's hurtful and violent world. What these children listed here have that you gay, lesbian, and transgender children do not have is a support group. There are many children who fit the descriptions listed here. When they are harassed and abused by others they seek out others like themselves for physical and emotional support so much so that they can hang out in groups.

Unfortunately many gay, lesbian, and transgender children and teens are totally alone in their environments. Most of you are totally isolated from others like yourselves or at least other children and teens who are out of the closet. This isolation is painfully difficult and heartbreaking for you honest children who are lovers of righteousness. Not only are you gay, lesbian, and transgender children misunderstood by the loved ones in your families but by adults and your peers as well. Your isolation makes you even bigger targets for the offspring of homophobes. The more they can hurt others the better it feels to them. Homophobic children cannot sleep at night unless they have done their evil for the day because their hearts are influenced by Satan and so corrupt.

If your school or your community has young gay teen support groups I recommend you seek them out. Unfortunately, most schools and communities do not.

Daniel 12:10
Many shall be purified, and made white, and tried; but the wicked shall do wickedly: and none of the wicked shall understand; but the wise shall understand.

Isaiah 57:20+21
20 But the wicked are like the troubled sea, when it cannot rest, whose waters cast up mire and dirt.

21 There is no peace, saith my God, to the wicked.

I recommend you take Ta-Kwan-Do or self defense classes. You would be amazed how that will build your confidence. It is a lot easier to be humble and turn the other check when you have the knowledge and power to drop a bully to the ground in one second.

When I was fourteen my older brother asked me if I was a queer. I said, "I was not a queer, I was gay." He begged me to go into the closet stating he feared people would try to beat me up. I told him I wasn't going to live a lie. He said, "Well if your not going to live a lie, I'm going to teach you Ta-Kwan-Do. So you can drop a man in one second. No one's going to beat up my little brother!" That is brotherly love. I love my brother to this day for teaching me how to defend myself. This angel must have been there directing him.

I must say the power and confidence went to my head. I went to school everyday hoping someone would mess with me; just to give me half a reason to keep my skills up to par. Don't think you are too much of a lady to learn self defense. No one could have been more of a lady than I was in high school. To go to school with the nails, hairdos, clothes, and the swish I went to school with in the early 1970's, in a small Midwestern town there were only two choices. Defend yourself or get beat up everyday.

I was not beat up one time yet many boys did try especially the closeted ones. Let me tell you after being beat down and left lying in the hall, trembling, whimpering, and crying, after getting your butt kicked royally by the biggest queen in town it was not easy to live that down. You know how boys like to tease.

God bless my older brother. "God forgive me for being so zealous about keeping my skills up to par and leaving those boys lying in the hall, trembling, whimpering, and crying in fear, totally humiliated." I have always been against violence but I am even more against someone getting violent with me.

If it were not for our Heavenly Father, my therapist, Ta-Kwan-Do, and the Supremes, I never would have made it through my teen years. For the grace of God I will not share anymore heart lifting stories from my teen years.

Of course not everyone has a loving brother. Many of you Lgbt children and teens could not bring yourselves to defend yourselves as I did. Unfortunately many of you Lgbt children are in situations you are finding unbearable. For those of you I recommend home schooling, or anything to get yourself out of your situation, even dropping out and completing school by G.E.D., if necessary.

Living under this kind of hostility day after day is brutal. As courageous as I was had I any other choices in the early 1970's, I would have used them to get out of that hostile environment. Whatever you're choices are keep yourself happy and productive and most of all sober and drug and alcohol free. You young people need to keep yourselves busy because you have an enormous amount of energy and creativity. Too often young people become bored and disappointed with the world they see around them. Out of their disappointment with life they use drugs and alcohol to suppress their brilliance. Please don't let that happen to you.

Remember our Heavenly Father, His Son Jesus Christ, and His angels are there for you at all times. Find healthy activities to keep your mind and body stimulated. No child makes it through adolescence or high school without some emotional scarring, not heterosexual children, nor homophobic children, nor open Lgbt children. Today's world is brutal for everyone of every age. But it does get better and it will continue to get better as you get older.

Don't let the negative experiences I have shared in this revelation discourage you or scare you. My life has been so full of God's blessings this revelation would be thousands of pages long if I shared all of them. These negative experiences I have shared have happened on the way to a blessing, or in the middle of another blessing, or coming back from a blessing. I have had enough blessings in my lifetime to amount to ten lifetimes. Your life will be just the same if not better.

Never forget our Heavenly Father loves **you**, Jesus loves **you**, a myriad of angels love **you,** and I love **you**. Keep up your spirits as best as you can let your heart be light and embrace God's tremendous love.

Adolescence is short lived and it goes by in the blink of an eye. If you are without friends and without love and support in your life find someone you can be a blessing to. Be a blessing for others. Bring joy to the life of someone in need.

- Mow the lawn of an elderly neighbor for free.
- Help out in a soup kitchen or homeless shelter.
- Volunteer your time to a food shelf.
- Gather coats, gloves, shoes, or clothing for a homeless shelter.
- Go to the internet and be an encouragement to other Lgbt children.
- Promote this book and revelation with others.
- You are brilliant you will find something to bring joy to those less fortunate than yourself.

Lifting the hearts of others is always more joyful than receiving. Bringing joy and being a blessing to one person can delight the heart of our Heavenly Father. It can delight the heart of Jesus, delight the hearts of myriads of angels, and delight your heart as well. As a gay, lesbian, or transgender child, teen, or adult, your brilliance and possibilities are endless.

Matthew 5:5,
Blessed are the meek:
for they shall inherit the earth.

Meek means; gentle, patient, and mild, not inclined to anger. It does not mean be a doormat for anyone looking for someone they think is weaker than they are to abuse or mistreat. This goes for adults as well. Those children of homophobes grow up and you are forced to interact with them in the work place. The same applies in your adult life. As an adult your power and confidence is not in Ta-Kwan-Do. Your power, and confidence, as an adult is in voting, and boycotting the companies, and their subsidiaries, products, unions, churches, and their subsidiaries world wide for life, of those who do not support gay equality, or treat gays fairly. I also recommend boycotting through websites and agencies that monitor these companies, their subsidiaries, products, unions and churches world wide. Become familiar with websites that monitor companies that violate and do not support the civil and human rights of Lgbt people.

Our Heavenly Father, Jesus, and His myriad of angels, are standing behind **you**. No child of homophobes can stand against them.

God wants **you** to always remember that He loves **you** just as **you** are just as He created **you** to be (Lgbt). Our Heavenly Father loves **you** so much that He has given **you** a name in heaven, a name greater than son or daughter and a monument in heaven in **your** honor. Our Heavenly Father has boasted about **you** to His angels in Heaven and man on earth. He is so proud of **you**.

Remember **you** are not alone out there. There are closeted and open gay, lesbian, and transgender children everywhere, in all rural areas, all small towns, all big cities and all remote villages all over the world. There has always been millions of us on this planet as I have revealed in the scriptures. There are still millions of us here today.

You are not alone in the world.
Our Heavenly Father is looking out for you.

****

****

When **you** find yourself among descendants of homophobes and in their line of fire or alone and feeling isolated, or sad, and feeling unlovable remember all the love **our** Heavenly Father has for **you**. Our Heavenly Father, Jesus, and His angels are always with **you** to protect **you** and keep **you** out of harms way. When you are feeling down pull out this revelation, **A Name In Heaven.** These uplifting Words from God will get **you** through **your** hard times. This book as well as the Bible are full of God's love and promises to **you**.

When **you** are feeling down and feeling like you can't take another day of **your** situation go to **our** Heavenly Father and tell Him how **you** are feeling. Ask God for anything you need to help **you** through **your** hour, **your** days, or **your** weeks of pain and anguish. Our Heavenly Father already knows how **you** are feeling He is just waiting for **you** to call on Him. Our Heavenly Father cannot help **you** if **you** do not call on Him. God is waiting for **you** to acknowledge Him as **your** Heavenly Father so He can show **you** His tremendous power and love. If God jumped to **your** rescue before **you** called on Him **you** would never know **your** rescue came from God.

CHEER UP

Our Heavenly Father
has such a tremendous overwhelming love for you.
He is watching over you at all times,
like a parent watches over a toddler in a park,
always alert to keep you out of harms way.

He is aware of your heartache and your troubles
and is always there to embrace you.
Be sure to keep these Words
and promises from God
in the forefront of your mind and heart,
at all times, as you walk through this life.

You are one of God's children.
You have a name in Heaven,
a name greater than son or daughter.
There is a monument in Heaven in your honor.
This is the Word of God.

You can trust God's Word.
God's Word is a promise to you.
Keep your spirits up. Things will get better.
Just trust in God and be patient.

Our Heavenly Father has provided a great example of faith and courage for you. This has always helped me in my time of need. This is a story about Elisha and his servant boy. Elisha was a great and powerful prophet. The love and obedience Elisha showed for God was like no other. God rewarded Elisha with great powers and used him to accomplish many things over the years. Elisha's accomplishments and miracles are so numerous I can't begin to tell you all of them in this revelation but I will share one with you. Elisha had a young servant boy. In the beginning of their relationship the servant lacked faith in Elisha and in God's power. In heated situations the young servant ran around whining and crying in a panic.

Notice the situation here in:

2 Kings 6:11-17 ,
6:11 Therefore the heart of the king of Syria was sore troubled for this thing; and he called his servants, and said unto them, Will ye not shew me which of us is for the king of Israel?

*6:12 And **one of his servants said,** None, my lord, O king: but **Elisha,** the prophet that is in Israel, telleth the king of Israel **the words that thou speakest in thy bedchamber.***

*6:13 And he said, **Go and spy where he is**, that I may send and fetch him. And it was told him, saying, Behold, he is in Dothan.*

*6:14 Therefore **sent he thither horses, and chariots, and a great host: and they came by night, and compassed the city about.***

*6:15 And when the servant of the man of God was risen early, and gone forth, behold, an host compassed the city both with horses and chariots. **And his servant said unto him, Alas, my master! how shall we do?***

*6:16 And he answered, **Fear not: for they that be with us are more than they that be with them.***

*6:17 And Elisha prayed, and said, LORD, I pray thee, open his eyes, that he may see. **And the LORD opened the eyes of the young man; and he saw: and, behold, the mountain was full of horses and chariots of fire round about Elisha.***

*6:18 And when they came down to him, **Elisha prayed** unto the LORD, and said, **Smite this people**, I pray thee, **with blindness.** And he smote them with blindness according to the word of Elisha.*

*6:19 And **Elisha** said unto them, **This is not the way, neither is this the city: follow me,** and I will bring you to the man whom ye seek. But he led them to Samaria.*

*6:20 And it came to pass, when they were come into Samaria, that Elisha said, LORD, **open the eyes of these men,** that they may see. And the LORD opened their eyes, and they saw; and, behold, **they were in the midst of Samaria.***

*6:21 And the **king of Israel said unto Elisha,** when he saw them, My Father, shall I smite them? shall I smite them?*

*6:22 And he answered, **Thou shalt not smite them:** wouldest thou smite those whom thou hast taken captive with thy sword and with thy bow? **set bread and water before them, that they may eat and drink, and go to their master.***

*6:23 And he prepared great provision for them: and when they had eaten and drunk, he sent them away, and they went to their master. **So the bands of Syria came no more into the land of Israel.***

To make a long story short, while Elisha and the young servant were sleeping, the King of Syria sent an enormous army with horses, artillery, and chariots, to kill Elisha. The Syrian army came in over night and surrounded the mountainous valley city where they were all alone and trapped. When the servant awoke and saw the terrifying spectacle all around him he again panicked. Elisha exasperated with the servants constant lack of faith called out to God to show the servant what was standing behind them. Our Heavenly Father answered Elisha's request.

When the young servant turned around he saw a myriad of angels in full armor, horses, and chariots with a glowing flame all around them. The Syrian army saw the myriad of angels as well and were terrified. The young servants faith and courage grew significantly over this event. Elisha asked God to blind the army of men and God granted his request. Elisha and the servant boy proceeded to lead them straight to the heart of the city of Samaria, right into the hands of their enemies. Elisha and his very young servant boy brought this huge army of men right into the middle of their enemies. The King of Samaria was so amazed by the power that God had given Elisha and his servant boy that the King fed the men and the nation of Israel was never bothered by Syria again. The young servant went on with his life with great courage and confidence in our Heavenly Father. He went on to do many powerful things. He performed many miracles and saw many miracles in his service with God during his lifetime.

The moral of the story is, God and His angels are always with you. All one needs to do is call on our Heavenly Father. The kind of miracles Elisha and his servant saw gave both of them great confidence and faith. Then this event was used to establish confidence and faith for the generations that followed. Our Heavenly Father had these events recorded in the Bible for you and for me. Remember God, Jesus, and His angels are always there for us. They have the power to do what ever they wish to protect us and keep us out of harms way.

Satan's number one focus is to stumble and destroy God's most cherished children, those with a name in Heaven, those who have a monument in Heaven in their honor. Remember, Satan and his demons have seen this monument. They have heard our Heavenly Father boast about His Lgbt children. Satan and his demons are angry at God and have come down to destroy God's most cherished children. Notice the scriptures say, "Satan's time is short," so he has no time to waste in his mission to hurt our Heavenly Father and His earthly children. Notice the scriptures say the "end is near." This is not an end of the world, or an end to the earth, it is an end to Satan's world dominance.

2 Peter 3:13+14
*3:13 Nevertheless we, **according to his promise, look for new heavens and a new earth, wherein dwelleth righteousness.***

*3:14 Wherefore, beloved, **seeing that ye look for such things**, be diligent that ye may be found of him in peace, without spot, and blameless.*

Isaiah 65:17-25
*65:17 For, behold, **I create new heavens and a new earth:** and the*

former shall not be remembered, nor come into mind.

65:18 **But be ye glad and rejoice for ever** *in that which I create: for, behold, I create Jerusalem a rejoicing, and her people a joy.*

65:19 *And I will rejoice in Jerusalem, and joy in my people: and the* **voice of weeping shall be no more heard in her, nor the voice of crying.**

65:20 *There* **shall be no more thence an infant of days**, *nor an old man that hath not filled his days: for the child shall die an hundred years old; but the sinner being an hundred years old shall be accursed.*

65:21 **And they shall build houses, and inhabit them; and they shall plant vineyards, and eat the fruit of them.**

65:22 *They shall* **not build, and another inhabit;** *they* **shall not plant, and another eat:** *for as the days of a tree are the days of my people, and mine elect shall long enjoy the work of their hands.*

65:23 *They shall* **not labour in vain,** *nor bring forth for trouble; for they are the seed of the blessed of the LORD, and their offspring with them.*

65:24 *And it shall come to pass, that* **before they call, I will answer;** *and while they* **are yet speaking, I will hear.**

65:25 *The* **wolf and the lamb shall feed together,** *and* **the lion shall eat straw** *like the bullock: and dust shall be the serpent's meat. They shall not hurt nor destroy in all my holy mountain,* **saith the LORD.**

What the Bible says is coming to an end is Satan and his followers and their nonsense. Satan and those he influence are coming to an end. At that time we will have a new earth and new Heaven. This new earth will be dominated by Jesus and His love and His lovers of righteousness. It will be a new Heaven on earth with no dying, no need for crying, no poverty, no food shortages and no crime.

There will be complete brotherly love among all people. No one hating others for their differences. Even the animals will live in harmony under the influence of Jesus. God's Word says a small child will play over the hole of a cobra in that day and not get bitten. The earth will be a safe and peaceful place. You and I and all of God's obedient children will be there to enjoy it for eternity. This is our Heavenly Father's promise to us. This also includes His Lgbt Children.

God's gay, lesbian, and transgender children stay sober and alert. This is not the time to seek the approval or acceptance of homophobic or other misguided children with all their evil foolishness. The end is near it could be tomorrow. God says no one knows the day or the hour that the end of Satan's dominance over the earth will come.

However, I will give you a sign to watch for: When you see the water supply being cut off from the Euphrates River in the middle east, when the Euphrates River bed starts to get low, low enough to walk across, know the end of Satan's dominance is just around the corner. You can find more details about this in the Bible just start reading.

Young brothers and sisters, I love you and God loves you. Let no man or demon take God's loving Words and promises away from you. In your time of need ask our Heavenly Father to hold you and comfort you and protect you. He is just waiting for you to call on him.

Go to our Heavenly Father;
tell Him you love Him.
Ask Him to forgive you for all of your sins,
in the name of His Son Jesus Christ.
Let your heart be light and go in peace rejoicing.

You have a lifetime of God's love,
blessings and joys ahead of you.
There is a myriad of angels
and a multitude of people
who love you out there.

Just open your eyes, look behind you
and see that myriad of angels standing there.

REVIEW

- The Bible uses the label "eunuch" when identifying gay, lesbian, and transgender people.
- Eunuchs are mentioned all throughout the scriptures.
- God loved obedient eunuchs in Biblical times.
- God loves obedient gay, lesbian, and transgender people today.
- Today's modern label for "eunuch" is gay.
- Jesus said, some gay people were born gay.
- Jesus said, some gay people were made gay by other men.
- Jesus said, some gay people choose it to live a life of honesty for the kingdom of Heavens sake.
- Jesus said, obedient Lgbt people have a name in Heaven, a name greater than Son or Daughter.
- Jesus said, obedient Lgbt people have a monument in Heaven in their honor.
- Our Heavenly Father has boasted about His obedient Lgbt children in Heaven and on earth.
- The angels in Heaven are applauding because these ancient secrets have finally been revealed.
- An angel from Heaven helped me deliver this revelation to the world.
- No demon on earth or roving about will ever take God's love and promises away from His Lgbt, children again!

A MYRIAD OF ANGELS

ARE APPAUDING

1 Peter 1:12

Unto whom it was revealed, that not unto themselves,
but unto us they did minister the things,
which are now reported unto you by them that
have preached the gospel
unto you with the Holy Ghost sent down from Heaven;
which things the angels desire to look into.

Gay, lesbian, and transgender brothers and sisters an angel came to me on Oct. 30, 1996, and changed my life forever. Due to various circumstances I could not write this revelation until now. For the past 13 years I have lived with the joys of this revelation of love from our Heavenly Father and the anguish of not being able to share it. However, God has His own timing and the time for me to share this revelation is now. Today is our Heavenly Fathers day of reckoning.

When I sat down on Sept. 5, 2009 to begin writing this book that same angel returned and he is with me now. Back in 1996, and in these last few weeks this angel has guided me through this revelation. There wasn't any earth quake, no lightning bolts, no deep voice like we heard in the movie "The Ten Commandments," just a quiet loving force directing my mind and hand.

Lgbt brothers and sisters,
I have given you God's love and promises in this revelation.
Our Heavenly Father has been missing you.

Have you been missing Him?

He has been watching for you to come over that horizon
with an aching heart anxious to embrace you again.
Our Heavenly Father's call is loud,
do you hear him calling you?

God has shown us who we are and how our lives have always fit into His plan. I want you to read this revelation over and over so you will know these scriptures off the top of your head. Our Heavenly Father has given us over two thousand scriptures in this revelation to show how He feels about gay, lesbian, and transgender children. He has covered many subjects to give us the power, wisdom, and knowledge to back us up before man and demon. These Words from our Heavenly Father are **your proof** that God does indeed love you. Let no one take these promises from our Heavenly Father away from you! I want this revelation to be written in your hearts and your minds. Demons will approach you with smiles on their faces, bumper stickers on cars, Jesus pins, and Bibles in hand, determined to steal God's blessings and promises from you again. Our Heavenly Father wants you to be fully competent and completely equipped as you stand in the face of these demons.

Don't worry about the people who do not have an ear, who do not have understanding or get the meaning of this revelation. The scriptures have made it quite clear not all will have understanding. God told mankind way back in Isaiah 40:22 that the earth was round and it took mankind over 4000 years to believe that.

Isaiah 40:22
40:22 It is he that sitteth upon the **circle of the earth,** *and the inhabitants thereof are as grasshoppers; that stretcheth out the Heavens as a curtain, and spreadeth them out as a tent to dwell in:*

Brothers and sisters I had a visit from an angel on Oct. 30, 1996 and I couldn't believe it myself at first. I couldn't help but wonder how it could be possible that no one has understood these scriptures over all these years. I couldn't help but wonder why everyone didn't know this information? I myself had read these scriptures many times over the years. Not once did I get the real meaning until I had the help from this angel. I spent the next eight months trying to prove this revelation wrong through scripture and historical information. That research only further proved this revelation did not contradict scripture and was accurate and that this revelation was from our Heavenly Father. What a loving Heavenly Father we have. He has shown all of His love for us in this revelation not only to the Lgbt Community but to all the world. This revelation is a liberation for heterosexuals as well as the Lgbt community.

This Bible knowledge has been kept secret from mankind for who knows how many hundreds or thousands of years. Knowing our Heavenly Father as I do allowing this was probably for our protection. Perhaps it would have been worse for our people prior to this time had this information been known. Perhaps He allowed it to remain secret to expose those false teachers and to bring down their financial empires as He foretold. We don't know everything God has in store for His Lgbt children or for mankind as a whole.

One thing we do know is that God did not forget about us or forsake His gay, lesbian, and transgender children. He has been watching over His precious children with a name in Heaven greater than son or daughter like a Father watching over a toddler in a park. The time has come to gather us together for the great harvest for the end is near closer than ever.

How precious is our Heavenly Father to love us so much! I am so thankful that God's secrets have been revealed in my lifetime. I am so thankful I am living at this time in history. Walk in faith and obedience to keep yourselves out of harms way and to please our Heavenly Father. Show Him how much you love Him and appreciate this revelation He has given to you and the world.

Many people are dying of AIDS, 7500 people are diagnosed with AIDS on this planet every day. Every nine seconds a person is diagnosed with AIDS in America. That statistic is on the rise and that figure goes up outside of the United States. The only safe sex is no sex.

The suicide rate among gay people in America is the highest in the world and continues to rise. Please be kind to each other and have intense love for one another. Never before since the beginning of man have our people had it so hard. Never before have we been so misunderstood and hated. The road we have traveled has been harsh and unloving for generations.

There are so many ways to show God your appreciation and your heart. Share this Bible revelation from God with others. Forty four thousand children on this planet die each DAY from starvation. In America, 1 in 3 children are hungry and living below the poverty level. Black males in America have the second highest suicide rate in the world. A university study has concluded that every time we see a black male on the news involved in a crime or violence we are watching an attempt at what they believe is an honorable suicide.

Americans have oppressed these black children of God for hundreds of years. America's media has created a false image of these black children of God not only to convince white Americans that they are poor workers, lazy, dangerous and violent, but they have come to believe that lie themselves. All these hundreds of years of oppression and false images of them has made life for them in this nation very difficult. It has created an environment of hopelessness and despair for them. Do whatever you can to help these black brothers and sisters they are God's children and victims in our nation. What a disgrace white America has been in the eyes of God. The most simple thing is required to change that: a simple change of the heart.

Countless Americans have lost their homes. Children need food, school supplies, shoes, coats, clothing, etc. Go to a homeless shelter and share this good news with our brothers and sisters there. They are not in a position to buy books and this revelation would be a blessing for them in their crises. Go to an AIDS clinic, or hospital, and share this revelation with our ill brothers and sisters so they may know how much God loves them in their hour of need. My most fervent hope is that not one more gay, lesbian, or transgender child of God will go to his or her death believing God hates them.

I could go on and on. I encourage you to show God your appreciation for the abundance of knowledge and wisdom He has blessed you with in this revelation.

Brothers and sisters did all of you get the understanding of this revelation? Let me simplify it for you one last time. I don't want one Lgbt child of God, or heterosexual child of God, to miss one word of this revelation and it's meaning.

- I listened to a world renowned preacher on the radio teach about how much our Heavenly Father hated gays.
- After listening to this preachers masterful twisting of scripture I believed it was true.
- Our Heavenly Father sent an angel to me and that angel revealed the information I have written in this book.
- God revealed the eunuchs of ancient Biblical times were Lgbt people.
- People sexually attracted to their own gender.
- God revealed that He loved Lgbt people just as He loved the heterosexual people.

- God revealed eunuchs played an important part in Biblical history.
- God revealed Lgbt people are in the Bible from Genesis to Revelation.
- God revealed that Lgbt people were a part of His past, present and future.
- God revealed the real story behind Sodom and Gomorrah.
- God revealed that Satan is out to destroy His obedient Lgbt children as well as His obedient heterosexual children.
- God revealed that Lgbt people were instructed to marry and abstain from sexual sin just as the heterosexual people were instructed to do.
- God revealed that some Lgbt people were born gay.
- God revealed that some Lgbt people were made that way by other men.
- God revealed that some people would choose a Lgbt lifestyle to live a life more authentic to their spirit.
- God revealed Lgbt people who were obedient would have a name in Heaven.
- God revealed this name was greater than son or daughter.
- God revealed there is a monument in Heaven in honor of Lgbt people.
- God revealed the acceptance and baptizing of an Ethiopian eunuch who was likely in drag.
- God revealed that He has boasted about His obedient Lgbt children on earth and among His angels in Heaven.

- God has revealed that He is calling His gay, lesbian, and transgender children together for the great and final harvest because the end is near.

Let me make sure you understood all of this revelation. Let me simplify it further. Make sure you get out and vote and get your political power back. There is no middle of the road with God. This generation has had plenty of time to muse over Lgbt issues and Lgbt rights. They have stood behind oppression against Lgbt people and have remained silent proving their hearts are dull. They have already made their stand. We will boycott these people, these companies, these churches and agencies etc. for life.
Politics and money make the world go round whether you agree with it or not. How you spend your money and who you vote for dictates the world. This is were your power lies. I advise you to start using your political and financial power immediately. Keep your power at the top of your priorities not only for yourselves but also for the generations after you.

If you continue to passively sit by waiting for Americans to have a loving change of heart you will be waiting till Jesus returns. In the meantime the suicide rate among Lgbt children continues to rise. The oppression continues to progress against us. As God is my witness after these politicians, companies, unions, churches and agencies etc. get a taste of our wrath instead of saying "We are sinners," or "We are not worthy of equal rights and decent treatment," they will be saying,

"What can I do for you?"

Lgbt brothers and sisters have intense love for one another because everyone needs a little tenderness. Remember when we first realized we were gay how we were so disappointed in ourselves how we hated ourselves. We tried everything to make it go away. We tried to deny it and were unsuccessful every time. Remember the arguments with our families and friends and watching them cut off their love over something we never chose and couldn't change. Often for many of us not one person could understand our situation.

Many of us have faced a lifetime of social rejection everywhere we turned. We have watched our children suffer rejection because of who we are and yet there was nothing we could do to change that. Our hearts were so heavy. When we looked into the eyes of another Lgbt person we saw all the same shame, pain, rejection and self loathing we have felt. It has been so hard for God's gay, lesbian, and transgender children for generations. God has heard our cries and seen our tears. The cries of God's Lgbt children have been loud, loud enough to reach the ears of God, Jesus and a myriad of angels in Heaven. You have just read God's answer to our cries.

Many of us came so close to giving up contemplating suicide. Many of our brothers and sisters were successful. No father or mother should live to see their children die from suicide. No parent should be forced to watch their child die of a slow living, breathing, social, and spiritual death, or die on the streets by violence, especially not over something that a child is born with and never had a choice about.

In the time it has taken you to read this gift, this revelation from God, another Lgbt child has been born in Chicago, in Denver, in the Appalachian mountains, in Africa, in the hills of Ireland, in the American Bible belt, in the Middle East, in China, in the most remote parts of Russia, and in downtown Tokyo. Know with confidence that God will be there with this sweet loving revelation to embrace them. What a sweet loving Heavenly Father we have. He has lifted us up to a higher ground. Our loving Heavenly Father has made everything so beautifully clear to us. When we look into each others eyes we will see so much love and happiness. Our hearts will be light in God's embrace.

God has lifted us up into His loving embrace, and we can see happiness from here.

THE ANGEL'S DEPARTURE

Brothers and sisters,
Above all things have intense love for one another.

Years ago in my early twenty's I gave up trying to help people understand my sexual orientation and the gay issue all together. I found people lacking empathy and understanding. People were far too much in love with a life of lies and deception. Not only did our ancient ancestors find the discussion of sex vulgar, but modern society finds it vulgar as well, as do I.

I have never liked talking to people about sex not even to my own family and friends. Let's face it sex has never been appropriate dinner conversation and it is never going to be. Sex between two people is a private matter and that is the way it should be.

I have never liked crowds or speaking in front of them. I have a bit of a speech impediment and have always been embarrassed about it. I have never liked traveling, hotels, airplanes, trains, buses, etc. I have always lived a very quiet, private and simple life. I have never been one to march in rallies or march in parades gay or otherwise. You wouldn't have found me holding a picket sign or rallying in political arenas for Lgbt issues or any other issues.

However, sex is what it is. We are all sexual people and we can't ignore the issue entirely. Our Heavenly Father has given me the honor, and privilege, to reveal the details of these generations of ancient Lgbt people for the benefit of all mankind. For the last days are coming to a close. Our Heavenly Father is calling all of His Lgbt children with a name in Heaven for the great harvest. He is gathering us together for safety and protection through His Word for our salvation and ever lasting life is at hand. He loves us so much and does not want to leave any one of us behind on His day of judgment.

**I stated in the beginning of this revelation
that I was not a preacher,
but I think this angel has changed that forever.**

I have always wanted to be in the life saving work of bringing people to God, heterosexual or gay, to salvation and everlasting life with our Heavenly Father. I thought maybe in my entire lifetime I might bring two or three people to God if I worked really hard. With that I would have considered my life's work well spent. Never in my wildest dreams did I imagine my service to God would be on the scale that God and this angel has made possible for me in this earth shaking, church shaking, demon shaking event that is about to take place when this revelation is published.

I am zealous to bring the world this revelation and happy to do whatever I need to do to bring all people, gay, lesbian, transgender, or heterosexual to God for salvation.

If you come to the conclusion of this book and find you are enraged or in disagreement over this revelation of Bible secrets and instruction I recommend you take it to God. Your argument is with Him not with me. My advice to you is to walk with God and go in peace rejoicing.

Romans 1:18

*1:18 For **the wrath of God is revealed** from Heaven against all ungodliness and unrighteousness of men, **who hold the truth in unrighteousness;***

*1:19 Because that which may be known of God is manifest in them; for **God hath shewed it unto them.***

*1:20 For the **invisible things of him from the creation of the world are clearly seen,** being understood by the things that are made, even his eternal power and Godhead; **so that they are without excuse:***

1:21 Because that, when they knew God, they glorified him not as God, neither were thankful; but became vain in their imaginations, and their foolish heart was darkened.

2 Corinthians 4:4

*4:4 In whom the god of this world hath blinded the minds of them which believe not, **lest the light of the glorious gospel of Christ, who is the image of God, should shine unto them.***

Hebrews 6:1-6

*6:1 Therefore leaving the principles of the doctrine of Christ, **let us go on unto perfection;** not laying again the foundation of repentance from dead works, and of faith toward God,*

*6:2 **Of the doctrine of baptisms,** and of laying on of hands, and of resurrection of the dead, and of eternal judgment.*

*6:3 **And this will we do**, if God permit.*

*6:4 For it is impossible for those who were once enlightened, and have tasted of the **Heavenly gift**, and were made partakers of the Holy Ghost,*

*6:5 **And have tasted the good word of God, and the powers of the world to come,***

*6:6 If they shall fall away, **to renew them again unto repentance;** seeing they crucify to themselves the Son of God afresh, and put him to an open shame.*

Brothers and sisters remember the things I have taught you. Keep building your faith. Change the things that you can change and forgive yourself for the things that you cannot change. What you cannot change turn over to God and patiently wait on Him to change it. God has come to claim His gay, lesbian, and transgender children. He is calling us in for the great harvest for salvation and everlasting life with Him. God has a plan for us. A plan that is more glorious than we could ever begin to imagine.

1 Corinthians 2:9+10
*2:9 But as it is written, **Eye hath not seen, nor ear heard, neither have entered into the heart of man, the things which God hath prepared for them that love him.***

*2:10 But **God hath revealed them unto us by his Spirit:** for the Spirit searcheth all things, yea, the deep things of God.*

Brothers and sisters life is a celebration. Embrace life with all it has to offer. Make the best of each moment. Stay close to our Heavenly Father and remain obedient so God can keep you out of harm's way. Although everyone on the planet should be enraged by the lack of love so many feel for our lgbt people don't let that interfere with your joys in life. Leave those lovers of Satan, those lovers of hatred and violence, to our Heavenly Father to deal with. This is a fight between God and Satan, not between gays and heterosexuals. God will change the hearts of some. Some will go to their graves in a burning rage of hatred for others, so just "Let it be so!" You are not responsible for the lack of wisdom or lack of understanding of others or their heart conditions.

1 John 5·19
And we know that we are of God,
and the whole world lieth in wickedness.

Matthew 11:25
At that time Jesus answered and said,
I thank thee, O Father, Lord of Heaven and earth,
because thou hast hid these things from the wise and prudent,

and hast revealed them unto babes.

An angel came to the disciples and instructed them to go out and preach. That same angel told Philip to go down the road to Gaza. That same angel directed the baptism of a transgender person the Ethiopian eunuch. That same angel came to my friend Sharon when we were 16 years old. That same angel came to my therapist Sandy. This same angel came to me on Oct. 30, 1996 in my time of desperation. This same angel returned to me on Sept. 5, 2009, when I sat down to write this revelation and he is with me now. Today's date is Oct. 30, 2009, and this angel's mission has again come to its completion. My guess is he will be leaving me soon as he did the last time. I will miss him and I am exhausted. Everything moves so quickly when he is here.

My emotions have been on one heck of a roller coaster ride. I feel as if I have been standing on a mountain with one of God's angels holding my hand watching 6000 years pass before my very eyes. I cannot help but notice the completion of this written revelation has come on Oct. 30, 2009, exactly 13 years to the day this information was revealed to me. I can't help but think this means something and yet I have no idea what it symbolizes. One thing I do know for sure. This is God's plan and God's timing. Everything is going according to His plan, purpose and His desire.

Brothers and sisters it has been over 2000 years since the Ethiopian eunuch was baptized. A myriad of angels are applauding in Heaven now that the completion of this revelation has been written. A myriad of angels have waited over 2000 years for this day. Our Heavenly Father, His Son Jesus Christ, and His Heavenly angels have revealed these ancient secrets, and are anxiously waiting to hear from you.

1 Peter 1:12

1:12 Unto whom it was revealed, that not unto themselves, but unto us they did minister the things, which are now reported unto you by them that have preached the gospel unto you with the Holy Ghost sent down from Heaven; which things the angels desire to look into.

Luke 15:10

15:10 Likewise, I say unto you, there is joy in the presence of the angels of God over one sinner that repenteth.

I know many heterosexual Bible teachers as well as gay Bible teachers have told you that God did not include Lgbt people in the marriage arrangement. I know many have told you God has given Lgbt people carte blanche when it comes to sexual obedience. This simply is not the truth. As I have taught you in this revelation God is holding Lgbt people to the same standards as His heterosexual people. Not one of God's children have carte blanche when it comes to sex and obedience. God has given all of His children standards to live by for our protection. Our Heavenly Father loves us so much. He is so concerned for our safety, happiness, and success in this life. He is concerned for our salvation so we will be fit for everlasting life in Heaven on earth. Not one of God's children are ever given carte blanche to run a muck as you have been told.

Many of us have forgotten our innocence,
a time when our hearts were young and light,
and full of prospects, hopes and dreams.
You have the power to return
to that place of simple innocence.
The power has been inside of you all this time.

Prior to the angel coming to me on October 30, 1996, I did not believe such things were possible. If someone would have said an angel came to them and did or said anything I would not have believed them. I would have thought they were out of touch with reality. I would have smiled and given them some council on how important it is to be realistic and totally honest when it comes to the things of God as well as all aspects of their lives. Needless to say the angel's visit made a believer out of me. I did not believe I was worthy or good enough to have such a wonderful thing happen to me and I still feel I am not worthy of this blessing. Not with all of the sins and mistakes I have made in my lifetime. Thank God our Heavenly Father is so forgiving.

One thing you must consider after reading this revelation either I did have an angel show this to me or I am a genius. I can assure you I am not a genius far from it. Many years have passed many generations, many languages, many empires, many cultures have passed and this knowledge had become lost and became secret. Why God chose me to deliver this revelation to mankind I don't think I'll ever know. What I do know is that it was written in my book of live at the time of my conception fifty two years ago. I have been prepped and molded from my birth to share this revelation with all of the world.

My time with you will be very short. I am so grateful God chose me to share the details of these generations of Lgbt people to all of you and the world. I love you all and God bless all of you.

Lgbt children of God let your hearts be light.
God loves you so much. He has a name in Heaven for you,
a name greater than son or daughter,
and a monument in Heaven in your honor.

Go in faith, obedience, and peace, rejoicing.
Above all things have intense love for one another,
for these are the last days.

Brothers and sisters, I do not want you to go forth declaring all that I have revealed to you, saying, "Rickie Bartlett said this," and "Rickie Bartlett said that," because I am only a messenger for our Heavenly Father. I want you to go forth with this revelation from God saying, "God said this," and "God said that," and "Jesus said this,' and " Jesus said that," using the over 2000 scriptures God has provided as proof for us to stand behind. I have given you God's Words and promises in this revelation through a multitude of Bible scriptures from our Heavenly Father Himself. These are God's Words to stand firm behind and to back you up so no demon in hell or on earth can ever take these loving Words and promises away from gay and lesbian people and their loved ones again. These loving Words and promises from God have made you fully competent and completely equipped for the days and years and generations ahead.

2 Timothy 3:16+17
All scripture is given by inspiration of God, and is profitable for
doctrine, for reproof, for correction, for instruction in
righteousness:

17 That the man of God may be perfect, thoroughly furnished unto
all good works.

Matthew 11:25
At that time Jesus answered and said, I thank thee, O Father, Lord
of Heaven and earth, because thou hast hid these things from the
wise and prudent,

<u>and hast revealed them unto babes.</u>

Thank You Father

Thank you Father for the loving family that you provided to raise me.

Thank you for the grandparents who loved me like one of their own children. Who practically raised me and believed I could do no wrong even when I did.

Thank you for my mother who worked herself half to death raising four children by herself.

Thank you for the kind and loving students I went to high school with. Many were kind and loving in spite of the fact that they had never laid eyes on the likes of someone like me before and didn't quite know what to make of me.

Thank you for my first love who I shall call Rocky, out of love and respect for his family. Rocky's love for me was so warm and intense, so over whelming, and I loved him back with that same intensity. That young man loved everything about me, my looks, my intelligence, my sense of humor, my shyness and my heart. Setting a standard of love and respect that I have longed for in all relationships since. Rocky's loving embrace was only comparable to the embrace from the angel on Oct. 30, 1996.

My mother saw that intense love between us and forbid us to see each other again. She could not bear the thought of two people of the same gender having such a love for each other. This action by my mother sent both of us into heartache and despair. Her decision caused both of us to run in different directions for years down a path of hard drugs and alcohol abuse in an attempt to numb our tremendous heartache and pain.

Rocky fell into crime and jail and died at a young age in a terrible motorcycle accident. I think of Rocky often and needless to say my heart still breaks tremendously when I do. Rocky and I will see each other again in the resurrection. We will both be young in body and heart at that time, and we will love each other just as we did for those few short years many years ago. It will be a wonderful experience for both of us. We will be so happy it will be so nice for us to be together again. I muse on that day often.

Thank you for all the blessings you have in store for me in the future. You are such a loving God.

Thank you for Sharon, for directing her to make an appointment with a therapist and giving her the strength to drag me over those snow banks and across that street in an attempt to preserve my life.

Thank you for my therapist Sandy, for seeing me twice a week, often Pro-Bono in her desperate attempt to teach me how to love myself. She taught me that I did deserved to live a full and productive life in spite of the fact I was gay. (who'd a thought)

Thank you for my high school football team who surrounded six of the toughest boys in our school as they surrounded me stating they were all going to "kick my ass" for being openly gay. The football team told them that anyone who throws a punch at me was going to get their "ass kicked" by them. What courage that took back in 1973. Loved them for that!

Thank you for Mrs. O. my detention hall teacher who I saw each and every morning all through high school for beating up boys, cussing out girls, and smoking cigarettes on school grounds. She would release the students in the mornings starting with "A's" one morning and starting with "Z's" the next morning. Of course that didn't effect me either way because each and every morning she called, "Rickie Bartlett" first so I had time to go out and smoke before school started. Of course the other students would start screaming that her behavior was unfair to them. Mrs. O. in her own delicate and eloquent way would scream back, "Do you want another detention?" Loved her! She encouraged me to get involved in school activities and encouraged me to take the role of mascot for the football team. She made me feel loved, understood, and accepted at a time when I felt very much the opposite.

Thank you for Mrs. Soderstien, a high school teacher, for sticking up for me when a student in the class was harassing me because I had taken on another school activity. He said, "Why do you get involved in so many things? Your just a Fag!" Mrs. Soderstien said, "Some people watch life pass them by and some people take the lead and embrace life. Rickie is the type of person who takes the lead and embraces life. You could learn a few things from him." I didn't know I was that type of person but I sure liked the sound of that. Loved her!

Thank you for Renee J., who I went to school with for many years. Renee was always very kind, loving and supportive in an environment were most were not. She stick up for me in our general business class, when the teacher was giving me a hard time for everything that I did and did not do. Loved her!

Thank you for all the companies in Illinois, California, Texas, and in Minnesota, who hired me knowing I was openly gay. Most of them always treated me with the utmost kindness, love, respect, and professionalism, and appreciated having me as a member of their staff.

Thank you for all the kind and loving neighbors you have blessed me with over the years and all the neighbors who brought me fruits and vegetables from their gardens all summer. Thank you for my neighbor Omar, for snow blowing all of my extensive sidewalks with his super, turbo, space age, snow blower, complete with wind shield and radio, saving my small son and I hours of snow shoveling in many degrees below zero weather.

Thank you for all the neighbors who did accept and respect me and had that same love and respect for my children.

Thank you for my neighbor Barb, who took my children to school each morning. Because I had to leave for work so early, refusing to take a dime for her time or gas. I appreciated that so much. My children were so small back then and it was often very cold and dark. I think of Barb often for her loving kindness towards us.

Thank you for Aurora. My landlord for many years who put me on a six month payment plan to pay back all the months of rent I was behind instead of throwing my children and I out on the streets which she could have done. Which most landlords would have done.

Thank you for the Super America cashier. Who saw that I was having a terribly stressful day and gave me a cup of coffee for free. I have never forgotten that because her generous act calmed me down immediately and it made me walk out of there with a new perspective. Please bless her Father and help her to forgive me for the dirty look I gave her as I approached the counter.

Thank you for Sue D. who spent much time and effort to help me buy my first home. She spent nine years helping me put that together. She had so much compassion for me. I noticed her compassion for me from the first day we meet. She even set up a meeting with the head of the mortgage department of a bank to ensure my success at purchasing a home. In those days there were many in that field who wouldn't have given me the time of day. Sue knew the challenges that lied ahead for an open gay single father with a small income. She took me by the hand and over saw everything to it's completion. Father please bless Sue tremendously for her loving kindness and for her loving heart.

Thank you for inspiring the entire staff at Hayden Heights Library. For assisting me in my research from 1996-1997. They rolled out the red carpet for me every time I went in. The head of the branch would often leave her desk and office in the middle of her busy day when she saw me come in to assist me personally. Breaking branch policies letting me check out many more books at a time than rules allowed. Ordering books from all over America to assist in my research. Taking all the time with me that was necessary to ensure I had every book on the topics I was researching, with much enthusiasm using their expertise and much appreciated professionalism.

Thank you for the blessing of children, and for giving me two of the most loving and wonderful children anyone could ever ask for and the greatest joy of my life.

Thank you for giving me all of the blessings you have provided for me in my life.

Thank you for all the blessings you have waiting for me in the future.

I have experienced many of God's blessings and more love than I could have ever imagined in one lifetime in this beautiful life I have had. I have been loved and adored by so many people in this life. It has felt more like a nuisance and only now do I realize what a blessing it has been. When I look back on my life from childhood to the present I have many hurtful and ugly memories that has certainly left many scares. I have experienced and seen so many things I wish I could erase from my memory for eternity. However, I must say as I look at my life in it's entirety that I am overwhelmed with the abundance of compassion, love, admiration, good times, and heart filled joy that has dominated the majority of my life.

Thank you Father for bringing me into your life.

When I reached the age of 14 I had become mature enough to piece together who I was. A person with a same gender attraction. What I quickly came to learn through verbally expressing who I was is a world of people who were very unkind and oppressive. Most of my life I have found many loved ones and society in general to be very strict, harsh, close minded and basically walking through life numb towards their own hearts as well as the hearts of others.

What I later pieced together as a spiritually mature adult is that we are living in a world that is dominated by Satan as the scriptures have taught. In this world Satan has taught mankind to ignore and suppress every basic instinct that our Heavenly Father has created within us.

When we hurt we do not show pain or cry. When we are happy we do not laugh and dance with excitement. When we are lonely or sad we show an image of a full life and confidence. When we feel love for another we deny ourselves that gift and loath ourselves for entertaining the very though or expression. This is the world we as mankind have allowed and considered orderly and appropriate.

We all share a responsibility in today's world condition and each one of us have the power to change this oppressive world. The new world order begins today with each and every one of us.

This life is too short as it is so embrace yourself, embrace others, and embrace life. God's laws and regulations are for our protection they help us to get the best out of what this life has to offer. God created us to live a full life, full of joys and happiness and freedom to make the best of what He created. It is God's joy to see us full of happiness not beaten down and oppressed.

Our Heavenly Father created love and love is a very powerful force and gift. Love can overcome hatred, judgment, prejudice and racism. It can feed and clothe a needy child and lift a heavy heart. Love can build a bridge for all of mankind all nations and all religions. Love can build a bridge to the glory of God. We all possess the power of love so use that power our Heavenly Father has given you. Remember the intense overwhelming love I described when I was with the angel.

God's love for us is so embracing, so strong, so intense, and so powerfully overwhelming. After the angel left me back in 1996, I cried my heart out because I was overwhelmed with joy. Joy for myself and for all of you. For many days after I would begin crying from out of nowhere. The overwhelming feeling stayed with me for a long time long after the angel had left. Our Heavenly Father's immense love is just one thought, just one embrace, away from all of us.

Matthew 13:16
But blessed are your eyes, for they see: and your ears, for they hear.

13:17
For verily I say unto you,
That many prophets and righteous men
have desired to see those things which ye see,
and have not seen them;
and to hear those things which ye hear,
and have not heard them.

Brothers and sisters, Adam and Eve were created approximately 6000 years ago. They were disobedient and watched with their own eyes how their descendents became so disobedient and evil that God became sorry that he had created them. He destroyed all of Adam and Eve's descendents 600 years later in a global flood. With the exception of Noah and his family.

Approximately 200 years later Noah's descendents tried to build a staircase to Heaven. As a result God gave all of them different languages causing them to walk away from the tower of Babel and relocate. Which eventually created what we call today different races of people.

Approximately 2000 years ago Jesus walked the earth giving his life as a sacrifice for mankind's disobedience. Jesus providing God's children one last opportunity to attain forgiveness and salvation and eternal life. It is now late 2009 about 2000 years since Jesus Christ was crucified. We are now only days away from tribulation, Armageddon and the millennium of Christ.

The children that are being born right now will be the last generations to make a conscious choice whether to choose good or evil. These are the last generations who will have the opportunity to choose to walk with God in obedience or walk with Satan in disobedience.

Will we teach this last generation of God's children to walk in obedience to God with love, understanding, and kindness, and respect for all people? Or will we teach these last generations of God's children to walk in disobedience with hatred, judgment, corruption, war and violence against all people? The salvation and everlasting life of these children and or their eternal destruction is in our hands.

Brothers and sisters I have spoken to you in this book with all the love, patients, understanding, and discipline that I have within me. I have taught you God's Word as if you were my own children. All the love in my heart has poured out like a flood on these 600 pages. I wish to leave you with these final words.

Live the most authentic life that you possibly can. A life of total and complete truth in every aspect of your existence. Be true to yourself and others in all things. The more you walk in truth the more successful your lives will be. Be forever cautious that you see the total and complete truth within your own lives. Because it is easy to focus on the truth in the lives of others while missing the truth in our own lives. Walk in our Heavenly Fathers Word and His truth as best as you can. Embrace everything in life with all of your heart. There is so much this life has to offer, so much love and so much beauty. I have opened your eyes, minds, and hearts to so many things in this revelation. You are now equipped to stand on solid, firm, mature ground to face the world that lies ahead of you. Above all things let no demon take these blessings that our Heavenly Father and I have revealed to you. Hold the wisdom you have obtained in this book and hold on to it tightly because your advisory awaits. You are now equipped for perfection and every good work.

2Timothy 3:16+17
All scripture is given by inspiration of God,
and is profitable for doctrine, for reproof, for correction,
for instruction in righteous:
That the man of God may be perfect,
thoroughly furnished unto all good works.

Brothers and sisters as long as there is a world where the sun shines and birds sing there will be love in the minds and hearts of all of God's creations. As long as mankind has a heart that beats and a soul that possess a shred of love God's children will continue to fall in love. I don't want to fathom a world where a person fails to look into the eyes of another and completely melt from head to toe in love and admiration. A world where a person touches the hand of another sending tingling sensations all throughout their entire bodies. A world where people have a love for each other that is so deep and so intense that the loss of it doesn't crush the heart all the way to the core. As long as our hearts beat and we breath the breath of life mankind will continue to fall madly in love with each other. Thank you Father for providing this blessing for all of us. Thank you for this rich and beautiful circle of life.

Brothers and sisters,
Lgbt/straight and heterosexual I love all of you.

May God bless you all.

Rickie Bartlett

DEDICATION

I would like to thank
the generation before me for all of their courageous efforts
on my behalf and for paving the way for this
Bible revelation.
This angel has directed me to dedicate
this loving revelation to our Heavenly Father,
for this revelation originates with Him.
I also dedicate this book to all of God's precious children
who have died in the face of, and at the hands
of lovers of the lie,
lovers of hatred, lovers of violence
and lovers of unrighteousness.
How precious the day of the resurrection will be
when these children of God are resurrected and return to us
in all their glory,
bright eyed with rosy cheeks and big smiles.
We will be there to embrace them with these
loving promises from our Heavenly Father
that He has given in this revelation.
On that day with this revelation
we will show them
the immense love our Heavenly Father
had and has for them:
a name in Heaven
a name greater than son or daughter
and a monument in their honor in Heaven.
How wonderful will that day be for all of mankind.
All of mankind will rejoice.
A myriad of angels in Heaven will stand in applause.

Show your appreciation for this revelation.
Buy as many of my books as you can
and give them to those in need.
Many hearts are heavy over this issue and this
revelation will lift the hearts of many.
Give them to brothers and sisters
who do not have the money to buy them.

Go to an AIDS clinic, AIDS ward in a hospital,
gay teen hangouts, gay bars at closing,
or just stand on a busy intersection and hand them
out to whoever will take them.

Show God your appreciation and share this loving
revelation with others.
Go to the internet and promote this revelation to others.

Help me bring these loving Words of God
to all four corners of the planet.
Take this blessing our Heavenly Father has given to you
and use it to lift the hearts of others.

Now you have proof that God does love Lgbt people

Go in peace rejoicing

E*PILOGUE 2014*

It would appear in this majestic land our Heavenly Father's desire to bless mankind with miracles is never ending. Due to another earth shaking event that has happened in my life I felt an epilogue was necessary.

I wrote this book in the fall of 2009 and published it the following year. I went on to revise the original 1611 English translation of the Bible giving it the title A Name In Heaven Bible. I revised another version of the original 1611 English translation of the Bible giving it the title A Name In Heaven Bible Revised. Both Bible's were published in early 2011. All of these accomplishments were directed under the supervision of the angel that came to me in 1996.

Late in 2011 I began a YouTube series of A Name In Heaven totally 29 videos. The purpose for the YouTube series was to bring a small taste of this information to the worldwide population. For those who cannot afford to purchase books and the multitudes of people who cannot read. Unfortunately the YouTube videos are very brief with little information. However, I did the best that I could considering the venue. It is very difficult to provide much information when you are trying to keep videos short and to the point. But I did the best that I could with what I had to work with.

All the while thousands of letters and invitations were pouring in like a flood from all over the world. Invitations to appear on talk shows for interviews and requests to make personal appearances for sermons. My heart has been overwhelmed by the enormous loving response. I thought I would be flooded by hate mail and I have received some. But the letters of tremendous love and appreciation I have received from all over the world has been a blessing that I will never forget and I will always cherish.

To this day the letters of love and appreciation continue to pour in from all nations and people of every walk of life. I have only had the time and energy to read about 25% of them. I will probably never get to all of them. I cannot count the number of letters I have received from people of all ages telling me they were thinking of committing suicide just before coming across my books and videos. Letters from children and adults who were recovering from suicide attempts and desperately seeking a kind Word from God. Letters from children who have Lgbt parents thanking me for what I have taught them. Letters from parents of Lgbt children thanking me for what I have revealed.

The last few years have been full of love from all four corners of the earth. My heart has been so overwhelmed. I have often cried over many touching heart wrenching letters. I am so grateful the Lord chose me to deliver this Bible revelation to the world.

While I was creating and uploading my YouTube videos my ministry was snow balling faster than I could handle. I was becoming overwhelmed and exhausted. I quickly came to realize I needed to rap up the YouTube series and take a long very much needed break from all work.

After creating and uploading the last video titled "Merry Christmas Lgbt Children," I went to bed feeling very exhausted and a great sense of peace and accomplishment. As I laid my head on my pillow that night I said to our Heavenly Father,

"Father, I am so completely exhausted. I have done all that I can possibly do on behalf of the angel experience that I had back in 1996. I have written and published A Name In Heaven. I have revised the Bible twice and published both of them. I have created a YouTube ministry for those who cannot read or afford to buy books.
I have done all that I can do Father and I am so pleased. I hope you are pleased as well. Together we have helped so many of your precious Lgbt children and their loved ones. Thank you so much Father for letting me share this joyful blessing with you. Thank you so much. I love you Father."

Totally exhausted I immediately went into a deep sleep. The next morning twelve hours later I awoke. The sun was shinning throughout the house and the birds were singing with joy. I was feeling a great sense of peace and happiness. Happiness knowing my days would not be so overloaded with work as the past few years had been. As I laid there I realized something was different about me. I kept thinking,

"What is different? Something is different."

As I awoke I noticed something felt odd about me. I sat up and pulled back the covers and looked at my body because something seemed strange but I couldn't figure out what it was. My body was fine. I felt very rested and at peace yet something felt very different.

When suddenly I realized what it was. I was no longer gay. I no longer had a same gender attraction. My same gender attraction was completely gone. I can't begin to tell you how I knew something was different immediately after waking up especially my sexual orientation but that's how it happened.

I have always been the type of person who doesn't want to think about anything when I first wake up. I don't like people asking me questions. I don't like talking on the phone. I don't like making decisions. I don't want to think about anything for at least the first hour. When I wake up in the morning I just want peace and solitude.

I immediately threw the covers off of me and flew out of bed in a panic. The certainty that my same gender attraction was gone was so strong and absolute. It was so positively confirming. I knew I would never be gay again. My perception of it and my feelings about it were so completely different than ever before.

The thought of ME being with a man again sexually seemed completely absurd. For the first time in my life I totally understood how a heterosexual man feels about two men being together sexually. Of course without any hatred or judgment. Not that all heterosexual men are hateful or judgmental. I just wanted to make it clear that I haven't become a hater.

I began to pace throughout the house from room to room in my underwear rubbing my forehead and the top of my head saying out loud,

"Oh my God! Oh my God! How could I have been gay for all of these years? What was I thinking?"

I kept saying those words over and over louder and louder as I continued to pace throughout the house. The more it began to sink in that I was no longer gay and that I was never going to be gay again the more I began to panic. I began to say very loudly,

"Father! What are you doing to me? What have you done? I have spent the last few years exhausting myself writing the book, revising the Bible twice, creating a YouTube ministry. I have done all of this for you, and for all of your beloved Lgbt children, and their loved ones, and now you have taken away my same gender attraction!

My ministry and all of my hard work is ruined now! No one will listen to me! No one will trust me! There's not one Lgbt person on the planet who will trust me when I tell them I am no longer gay! They will not believe me! When I tell them I am no longer gay after a lifetime of being totally gay, they will think I'm crazy! After all that I have done on behalf of my angel experience, now I am no longer gay? People will think I'm a complete liar! This just doesn't happen to people!"

All the while I was pacing throughout the house in a panic. Pacing from room to room speaking to our Heavenly Father in a loud and very upset manner. Pacing through one room filled with floral furniture, doilies, flower arrangements, statues and artificial fruit arrangements after another. Pacing back and forth past all of my Barbra Streisand movies, chick movies, movies with gay themes, Celine Dion and Disco CD's, and my cookie jar that says Kitchen Diva. All the while feeling like I no longer have any connection to any of it. Spewing profusely to the Lord with much drama,

"Oh my God! What have you done? What are you doing to me? What are you thinking? My ministry and all of my hard work is ruined now!"

I finally put some clothes on and began to calm down. I plopped down on my floral antique Queen Ann sofa and caught my breath. I just sat there stunned and silent wondering what God was up to and just thought. "Where did I go? Who am I now? What the HELL am I wearing?" I felt like I had been deprogrammed.

I sat there wondering what was to become of my ministry and all of my hard work. Wondering what was to become of my life saving ministry that had already saved so many lives, and helped so many people from all over the world. A ministry that began through an angelic visit. A ministry that the angel and I created together. A ministry that I created from all of my hard work motivated by a passion for my Lgbt brothers and sisters. My ministry that I loved so much. I just sat there for a while numb and stunned feeling absolutely devastated.

I must say for a long time I felt very out of place and very strange. I felt as if I didn't fit in anywhere. I'm not attracted to women or men now. It has been fourteen months since I had a same gender attraction. Only recently have I found a place of peace with the new me. I had been gay all of my life and my thoughts are still,

"What was I thinking? How could I have been gay for all of those years? Who was that person and where did he go?"

The fact that I was ever gay seems so absurd to me now. As I look back at the person I used to be I am pleased with that person and I do have many fond memories. I was just a guy with a same gender attraction trying to be the best person that I could be. I was living the life that was handed to me and loving our Heavenly Father with all of my heart and soul. I was trying to be the best example of a Christian that I could be. In a world that thought I was absurd to call myself a Christian and gay in the same breath.

My same gender attraction has not come back and I know that it will never return. I knew that morning when I awoke that it was gone forever. I have found a place of peace and I am now very grateful. I now realize it was a gift from our Heavenly Father. I still do not know why or what he is up to in regard to this blessing but I do consider this change with my sexual attraction a wonderful gift.

I was afraid sharing this event with my readers, and my YouTube audience, and the world, might stumble many Lgbt people. My biggest fear was that this event would detour Lgbt people and their loved ones from reading my book, my Bible's, and watching my YouTube videos. A fate that would be very heart breaking for me.

Because I believe everyone on the planet should read this book. This revelation has already saved many lives and lifted many hearts. This book, my Bible's, and my YouTube ministry, has already changed the lives of so many. This is life saving information and I don't want anyone Lgbt, straight, or heterosexual to be without this important information. Because so many are deceived in regard to the Lgbt experience and our Heavenly Father's true feelings about His precious Lgbt children.

I decided to wait a year and just see if my same gender attraction would come back. I decided at that time I would make a decision how I was going to handle my coming out. Even now I really do not want to share this coming out with the public. One reason is because any persons sexual orientation shouldn't be important and shouldn't matter.

However, I am a public figure now. There are people all over the world who know me as an openly gay man and who are familiar with my ministry. My biggest fear was that I might share this change with the wrong person and they might go to the internet and explain their own twisted version of my experience. I do realize many will have their own theories as to what happened to me and many will call me a liar. So be it.

I do understand the immense love, respect, and admiration that one has towards the person or people who taught them God's truth and brought them to God. I swell up with joy and my eyes fill with tears when I come into the presence of those who did that loving act for me. I have a deep love and respect for those people that is like no other.

I also remember the heart ache and anguish I felt when Bible teachers came to the public and announced they had prayed the gay away in attempts to save their ministries. To later learn that they straight out lied. I do remember the feelings of doubt those lies put into my heart. Those lies made me question God's love for me. Believing perhaps I could or should change my same gender attraction to please our Heavenly Father if it really was possible to do so. The feelings of doubt and disappointment in myself that their lies erupted in me. The feelings that maybe God didn't love me enough and maybe that's why I was still gay.

Let me just say as God is my witness every word in this book is pure truth. Should my sexual attraction change again you will be the first to know about it.

Furthermore, my sexual orientation has nothing to do with my ministry. I own 100% of A Name In Heaven Ministries. I do not answer to anyone and that does include the board of directors. After some thought I came to realize that my ministry is here to stay for eternity whether I am loved or hated by the majority. I do not have one reason in the world to lie about this life changing event that took place fourteen months ago. I also realize this is hard to believe. This just doesn't happen to people. But after reading this book I'm sure you have come to find many things have happened in my life that just doesn't happen to most people.

I do realize how thousands of you feel about me as you have stated in your letters of love and appreciation. Please don't let this change in me stumble you or your walk with God. God loves you every bit as much as He loves me. Our Heavenly Father is up to something. I wish I knew what it was but I do not have a clue. What I know for sure is that it is all good.

Ultimately, what it boils down to is; I have never lived a lie or lived in the closet. Not for one day in my entire life and I'm not about to start now for anyone. Furthermore not sharing this life changing event feels very dishonest and deceptive to me. I wrote this revelation in total truth and I feel this is the conclusion of my gay experience and it needs to be shared in this book with this Bible revelation.

I must say that there is a part of me that feels a little sad about this life changing event. I sometimes wonder if I will ever love again. Will I ever be loved in return? It's not logical that I will experience romantic love again considering I am not sexually attracted to men or women anymore. Which on the other hand leaves me feeling very liberated and free.

However, I do trust our Heavenly Father. I am certain that He will fill all of my needs. The needs that He feels are in my best interest to fill in this life anyway. As time passes I am becoming more and more excited about this new change in me. At this time my heart is rejoicing over it. I am confident that everything is in order as our Heavenly Father see's fit for me, for this revelation, and for my ministry.

One thing I know for certain my life has not been boring. My life in this magical land has been full of miracles. What an exciting time this life has been. My life began with a tough and harsh childhood. Later evolving into a life full of love and admiration and the blessing of having two wonderful children. Making history by writing and publishing this Bible revelation. Becoming the first person in history to independently revise and publish the Bible twice no less. Ultimately losing my same gender attraction immediately after revealing and proving to the world that God does love Lgbt people and proving with scripture that they have a name in Heaven. What a blessing that all of these miraculous things happened to one man in one lifetime. It hasn't always been easy. But, what an exciting time in history to be alive.

My life has been full of blessing and it would appear the blessings are still coming my way. I really didn't believe it was possible for me to ever have another miracle or blessing of this magnitude with all of the others that I have already experienced. One thing I know for sure our Heavenly Father is full of surprises. In this magical land of beauty and Hero's that we call earth blessings and miracles continue to happen when we least expect it. What a loving Heavenly Father we have.

My heart is rejoicing over coming out in this epilogue. My heart is free and my conscience is clear and at peace. I truly hope my coming out doesn't stumble anyone. I didn't come out to break any hearts or to stumble any of God's precious Lgbt children. I came out because of my love for truth and righteousness. I came out in hopes that all who know of me and my ministry will rejoice with me in love and acceptance. I have spent my entire life as an openly gay person. Sharing in all of the struggles and oppression. My deep love for all Lgbt people has not changed.

Considering I have received letters expressing great love and appreciation from all over the world my question to all of you is:

"Do you still love, appreciate, and accept me as much today as you did yesterday? Do you still feel the same love for me now that I am no longer gay?"

I truly hope that you do. But God knows I can handle it if you do not. My happiness and joy has never been dependent on the love and approval of others.

I am bringing this revelation to it's finale dancing, singing, and rejoicing with a song that I have written to our Heavenly Father. Lgbt brothers and sisters a day is coming when we will all sing in praise to our Heavenly Father. Just be patient. Your new day of coming out is just around the corner. When you least expect it, in the twinkling of an eye, this very same change will happen for you. This is God's promise to all of His Lgbt children whom are obedient. In the meantime live the most authentic life that you possibly can and enjoy life to the fullest embracing all of God's blessings.

Because of You

You gave me life, you give me love
Because of you, because of you
You gave me life, you give me love
Because of you, because of you

Living in the memory
Of the person I used to be
All my feelings so exposed
Revealing all of my emotions to society
It's as if your holding me
As if I hear your voice
What you've made so clear to me
Is that I never had a choice

(chorus)
Because of you, I've always loved myself
Because of you, I have never been alone or lost
Because of you, I am crying, Father
Even without you, I would have changed it if I could
If I could, if I could

You gave me life, you give me love
Because of you, because of you
You gave me life, you give me love
Because of you, because of you

My life has always been so full
Because you live inside of me
My feet have never stood still
You have always made my spirit free
Each day I feel your love
Whatever I do you are here
I can handle all the changes
As long as you are guiding with care

(chorus)
Because of you, I've always loved myself
Because of you, I have never been alone or lost
Because of you, I am crying, Father
Even without you, I would have changed it if I could
If I could, if I could

You gave me life, you give me love
Because of you, because of you
You gave me life, you give me love
Because of you, because of you

It's all been so exciting
My feet no longer touch the floor
I feel like I could just take flight
I understand it all now, it's been so grand now
I don't know what's next, blessing others I'll bet
Everyday I thank you Lord
I thank you Lord
Everyday, everyday, everyday

(chorus)
Because of you, I've always loved myself
Because of you, I have never been alone or lost
Because of you, I am crying, Father
Even without you, I would have changed it if I could
If I could, if I could

You gave me life, you give me love
Because of you, because of you
You gave me life, you give me love
Because of you, because of you

Love Rickie

Made in the USA
San Bernardino, CA
26 March 2014